RECORD PLAY PAUSE

Confessions of a Post-Punk Percussionist

Volume I

STEPHEN MORRIS

CONSTABLE

CONSTABLE

First published in Great Britain in 2019 by Constable
This paperback edition published in 2020

13 5 7 9 10 8 6 4 2

Copyright © Stephen Morris, 2019

The moral right of the author has been asserted.

A CIP catalogue record for this book
is available from the British Library.

ISBN: 978-1-47212-622-1

Typeset in Electra by Hewer Text UK Ltd, Edinburgh
Printed and bound in Great Britain by Clays Ltd, Elcograf S.p.A.

Papers used by Constable are from well-managed
forests and other responsible sources.

Constable
An imprint of
Little, Brown Book Group
Carmelite House
50 Victoria Embankment
London EC4Y 0DZ

An Hachette UK Company
www.hachette.co.uk

www.littlebrown.co.uk

To my darling wife, my beautiful daughters
and the memory of my parents

CONTENTS

PART 1:

REWIND

It must be about four in the morning by now, still dark anyway. I can't make out the red glow of the digital readout on the clock. I'm not awake by choice.

Perhaps it's jet lag. Twelve hours in the air flying east across nine time zones is enough to confuse anybody. You'd think I'd be used to

that by now. Over thirty years in the racket is surely long enough to have grasped the basics.

The sushi supper blowout can't have helped. But you can't come to Tokyo and not overindulge in raw fish and wasabi at the earliest opportunity. Sashimi in the hotel's highly elaborate wood-panelled traditional tatami dining room, starkly contrasting with the hi-tech neon glow flickering on the other side of the darkened glass. Close your eyes and you could almost forget you were on the fifty-second floor. Almost.

It could be that stopping my sleep. Vertigo. Height makes my head spin and my knees go wobbly. I can feel myself begin to plummet.

'The Park Hyatt offers beautiful views of Mount Fuji or Shinjuku', the itinerary says.

It also says we're playing at the Fuji Rock Festival in a couple of days. So not here for that long.

Maybe it's this room. It's a smart, modern hotel room in a chic expensive hotel with an extremely well-stocked minibar – three different flavours of designer crisps and two jars of sophisticated-looking nuts – three buttons to open and close the curtains and a range of fiddly 'mood lightings'. The current setting is PITCH BLACK with a bit of a dim glow from the bathroom. It took quite a bit of trial and error to get it just right.

But neither the complicated lack of lighting or the lovely crisp white sheets are doing their trick tonight. Which is very unusual: out like a light anywhere in the world is the normal course of events.

OK, best thing to do would be think of something else other than sleep, that usually works. Put your mind somewhere else and see what pops in. Dreams hopefully.

Right, here we go.

How did I get here? That's always a good question. Think of that, take your mind off it. Try and forget they have the odd earthquake here.

*   *   *

2

Best go back, all the way back, see what you can drag into the present.

'What's the first thing you can remember? Your first real memory?'

Go on, try it – it's a good game. Fun for all.

This object in the fields mystified the young me.
Was it a witch's altar or a beacon for flying saucers?

A sunny day. White, very bright white light. I think I'm lying in a pram looking up through a fine net at the sky. I've just woken up. There's a butterfly bumping into the net and fluttering about on it, maybe it's stuck, flapping about. Huge and very scary. It seems like it wants to attack me.

I'm in the garden at the back of my parents' house on Gawsworth Road in Macclesfield. A house bordered by green fields, a quiet road and a bus stop.

3

I don't like this butterfly. I want it to go away, I want to get out and get away from it. I can't, so I start crying loudly.

Later. Not sure how much later – more than a couple of years.

Waking one rainy spring morning. The dark grey clouds are low in the sky. Must have been pouring all night.

Outside there's a commotion.

A cacophony.

Peeping over the ledge of the bedroom window, I see a herd of cows right outside. Too close. I run downstairs and there are cows outside the kitchen window too.

The house is surrounded by big black-and-white bellowing cows. They've broken down a fence and escaped, they want to explore. The big back lawn is a flooded mess of mud and cow shit. I can't understand how this has happened.

Cows are supposed to be nice docile things. This lot look angry.

1

BATTERIES NOT INCLUDED

Gawsworth Road, Macclesfield.

That's the place, our back garden. That's me on the right, recumbent, sulking – always reluctant to have my picture taken, even then. It was a Sunday morning when Mum took that snap with her Kodak. That's my Sunday face.

We are on our way to church, Amanda and me. That's Amanda on the left. She's my three-years-younger sister.

We are waiting to be dragged off by our Auntie Elsie to the harvest festival at St Andrew's Church. This was where, I was told, you took things to be distributed among the poor and needy.

That's a basket of things, tins of fruit (tinned pears, at a guess) and such, that I will later very reluctantly pass on to the poor and needy. You can tell my heart's not really in it from the picture, can't you? What a slob.

I had a bit of a strop on that day. Sundays always used to put me in a bad mood. Being dragged off to church when I could be doing something much more interesting was bound to be a bit of downer, wasn't it? Well, Sundays were always like that. I remember that basket was bloody heavy even without the tin opener, which I thought would have been a useful addition to its contents.

On the bench under the basket of bounty there is a small rusty metal plaque with a few lines from D. F. Gurney on it:

> *The kiss of the sun for pardon,*
> *The song of the birds for mirth,*
> *One is nearer God's heart in a garden*
> *Than anywhere else on earth.*

I don't know why but I thought that God himself had made that wooden bench. I once tried carving my initials in it with an amber-handled screwdriver.

That'd teach God.

See that worn-down, muddy bit of grass above the step? It's at the exact spot where I realised I could ride a bike – one minute I was falling over and the next I was off pedalling furiously down the lawn. That was it. A boy on a bike spelt freedom. I was off down the road all the way to the bus stop and then the paper shop on the Weston Estate; next stop the Big City. Or at least the not-so-bright lights of Macclesfield. But first I'd have to pass the Cycling Proficiency Test. Qualifications

6

always get in the way. I didn't want to get into trouble with the two coppers who lived across the way. They'd stopped my friend Geoff from up the road and warned him about riding without lights and a bell. The reckless lives we lived on Gawsworth Road, in Macclesfield.

The area had been a rural idyll around the 1920s – just a few houses surrounded by acres of pasture.

'I remember when all this used to be just fields,' my grandma used to say on her weekly visits.

By the time I arrived on the scene the greenery was getting a little depleted, swallowed up by a new housing estate with a little row of shops: newsagent, chemist and launderette. Turn left out of our gate and you were in some kind of suburbia; turn right and you could get lost in fields and woodlands.

Sorry, I'm getting a bit ahead of myself here. We've not even been introduced, have we?

My name's Stephen – Stephen Paul David Morris to be precise. I was born on 28 October 1957 at some ungodly hour in the morning, but I do like an early start. Don't like to see a morning wasted, well, not now anyway. Back then it was another story. So much time to be wasted.

I was born blond and christened in a dress; Paul Anka topped the hit parade with 'Diana'. I was oblivious to all that back then, of course.

My parents were Hilda (b. 1923) and Clifford Morris (b. 1912). Dad was really called George Clifford but he avoided using the name George at all times. George was his father's name and he did not like his father one bit. My grandfather George was a bit of a one: a swine or a black sheep. After producing nine children, he decided enough was enough. He slung his hook and departed one Christmas night, leaving the family high and dry with no forwarding address.

It was very difficult to get any information from my father about the runaway George. He had served in the Royal Flying Corps in the First World War and came back from the front with revolutionary views. Besides that, he was a randy so-and-so and a scrounge. He was also, so my father told me, an anarchist!

My grandfather and his chums would meet in a local alehouse and drunkenly conspire to blow up Macclesfield municipal gasworks. Where he would have got the equipment to accomplish this terrorist act is anybody's guess. Ninety years later, Tesco did the job for him.

History does not with any certainty recall what became of my would-be revolutionary grandfather. He really and truly vanished off the face of the earth. Not many people have pulled that one off. There was some talk that he left to fight for the Bolsheviks in Russia, which would have been a strange move for an anarchist. There was one rumour that he may have got as far as Australia, and another that his adventure took him to glamorous Congleton, 8.7 miles away, but none of this has ever been verified. Even the internet shrugged.

Grandad George had left his wife Elizabeth Ann and a bunch of kids to fend for themselves. This would be in the early 1920s. 'Times were hard', so my father's stories of his early life went. Brothers and sisters sleeping sardine-like or hot bunking. It was a struggle for Elizabeth Ann, living off lodgers and laundry. Clifford doing his best to be a breadwinner from an early age, delivering newspapers and oatcakes. Flitting from house to house along the same terrace in Hibel Road. My father may have hated George so much that he never used his name, but I liked the idea of my grandad – a vanishing anarchist, man of mystery, black sheep.

Clifford started a trend among the Morris family: all his brothers went under aliases. Johnny was oddly christened Jack and was the musician of the clan – clarinet and saxophone were his thing. He played in local dance bands, including the Ambrose Dance Band, while Dad aka Cliff put on the dances. He was 'playing second fiddle', he said, giving me the mistaken impression that he had some hidden musical talent. My father always loved music, though. Duke Ellington was his man. He loved the Marx Brothers, too. Who doesn't like that?

The Ambrose Dance band in action.
That's Johnny on tenor sax, far left. What an ace drum kit!

Eric, the youngest brother, was also known as Spanker; whenever there was any trouble, the finger would always be pointed in young Eric's direction. Ever the scapegoat, he took his punishment manfully, hence the moniker. He reminded me of television's Sgt Ernie Bilko (Phil Silvers), always looking for an angle, a scheme or a shortcut. The other siblings were Evelyn, Nellie, Irene aka Renee, Hilda (no, not my mother), Colin aka Clonky and, strangely, another unfortunate George.

My father used to entertain Amanda and me with improbable stories of our family's history. As well as tales of my comedy-villain grandad, he told us about the Morris family's underground forced rhubarb factory and other unlikely but entertaining tales. My favourite yarn, though, was 'The Tale of Great Uncle Jack'.

Jack, so the story goes, went to serve Queen and Country fighting the Boer in Africa. The younger me presumed that these were of the hairy porcine variety. Jack contracted a mystery illness, which, for reasons that were never made clear, he couldn't see an army doctor about. Instead, he decided to seek the help of a local witch doctor. 'No Jack!' his comrades implored him. 'Not the witch doctor!' But Jack would have none of it. Off he went alone in search of the native medicine man. Just like Grandad George, he was never seen alive again. Another Morris, vanishing into the ether, just like that. I think I found the idea of soldiers fighting giant pigs more frightening than anything.

Natives, witch doctors, soldiers in pith helmets fighting possessed pigs – I had no idea my leg was being pulled.

I'd been told frequently that I had what they call a 'vivid imagination' and was 'very highly strung'.

This last phrase puzzled me greatly. I was certainly an anxious individual and a natural-born worrier but what was this reference to string? It didn't make sense – maybe a grown-up thing. Like 'How long is a piece of string?' which was the answer to most of my questions. What was this adult fixation with string?

I liked dark things (what growing boy doesn't?). Grisly murders, ghosts, vampires, werewolves – that sort of thing. Most of this was fuelled by comics.

Mum would take me and Amanda to visit our maternal grandmother, Sarah, every Saturday without fail. Grandma was a large, solemn lady, who wore bombazine and had her hair pinned tightly in a bun. I hated my grandmother's dark and dingy house. The curtains were always drawn and there was a dark presence in the house: my Desperate-Dan-bewhiskered grandfather, Fred. A veteran of Gallipoli and Mesopotamia, he got through the First World War without a scratch only to be badly injured in a motorbike accident as soon as he got home.

Fred was confined to a bed in the small front room. He'd groan when we arrived as Grandma tried to cover up the steel and leather callipers attached to his legs. He didn't like being disturbed. His threat to me was that I would be locked in the coal hole for waking him. I didn't much like the coal hole. Fred would need shaving, though, and whether he liked it or not (he didn't), come Saturday my mum or her sister Elsie would shave his whiskers.

The house was cold and dismal. The hourly chimes of the ticking clocks were the only break in the silence. The saving grace was that at the end of the ordeal we were treated to a visit to Horace Bracegirdle's newsagents to get the latest comics.

Horace was a large, florid man of Dickensian appearance. He was missing half an ear – a dog had taken the other half, my mother said. That put me off dogs for a long time. His assistant, Jill, was completely the opposite, tall and pale, with her height exaggerated by a permanent neck brace. She spoke with an odd Swedish accent; she'd had too much vinegar on her chips, my mother said. This was confusing as I liked vinegar and it never did me any harm. Horace's shop also possessed a top shelf of smut, such as *Health and Efficiency* naturist magazine – all very tame today but in the early sixties this stuff would blow a young chap's socks off. Amanda and I were shepherded away from these, obviously, to the haven of Horace's confectionery tray.

There lay the highlight of my week: A. & B. C. chewing gum. Well, not so much the chewing gum itself. That was pretty much inedible.

'It's made of dead horses,' my mother would warn in a doomed attempt to dissuade me from my addiction. Amanda got a quarter of the much safer humbugs.

My interest was more the picture cards that came with the gum. They probably tasted better, but I didn't care. I was a fevered collector of these cards, which I swapped with my friends. Some of these, such as the 'Outer Limits' series, scared me witless; and some, such as the gory Second World War battle series, were banned at school for their

THE TELEVISION TERROR

depictions of brutal death and violence. These were highly prized for their shock value. But my favourites were always the Batman series. I was desperate to collect the entire set and, despite swapping cards and chomping through a mountain of the pink gum, there was always at least one card that eluded me.

Still, there were always the comics themselves to pore over – that's what we came here for, wasn't it?

I loved Batman, the Mighty Thor, Iron Man and good old Spiderman. They lived in the USA where the colours were bright and things actually happened. Deranged mobsters, fantastic beings from other worlds and evil scientists would wreak havoc on an unsuspecting world, only to be defeated by the superpowers of our hero. I had noticed that there was a distinct lack of super-powered citizens in Macclesfield; in fact, the whole of Great Britain was an uncanny skills-free zone. There was derring-do of another form, though, as illustrated in the pages of the *Victor* and *Commando* comics. OK, they were in black and white, but the

12

(allegedly) true stories of plucky Tommies fighting off hordes of evil Jerries, whose superior firepower was no match for our tea-drinking boys' cool courage and guile, were educational and oddly fascinating. I wondered if any of my many uncles were in the elite fighting forces of the Second World War.

To a six-year-old boy, the war still seemed like a great adventure. Why didn't we still sleep in bomb shelters? Surely it was still a sensible precaution.

My absolute favourite of all of these publications was *TV Century 21*, based around the exploits and adventures of Gerry Anderson's TV wooden heroes and heroines. It presented itself as a newspaper from the future, a hi-tech world of flying cars and cities beneath the waves. The cutaway drawings of these future vehicles seemed very real and projected a world that was tantalisingly close, so long as you remained oblivious to the strings that animated this marionette metropolis.

Amanda had no interest in any of this world of the future and settled instead for a copy of *Mandy* or *Bunty*, which, of course, held no interest for me. I did have an odd fascination for the cut-out-and-colour wardrobe figurines, but most of their contents were embarrassing girl's stuff.

Growing up in Gawsworth Road in the sixties was easy. It was, if not idyllic, at least a very safe place. OK, you couldn't play football in the road – well, you could, but not for very long. The policemen who lived across the road would give you what for. But it was definitely a peaceful kind of middle-class road that led nowhere but woods, farms, churches, country pubs and the giant radio telescope at Jodrell Bank. A very cosy place to grow up in the 1960s.

Wikipedia describes Macclesfield as 'relatively affluent'; the keyword here, I suspect, is 'relatively'. Macclesfield today is surrounded by wealth: Prestbury, Alderley Edge are now home to rich and famous football and TV personalities. The town centre, though, is in even further decline than it was in my day.

Sixties Macc was a mill town that had lost the adjective 'thriving' somewhere along the way. It somehow was still making a go of it with new artificial textiles, and in 1966 ICI came to town, built a large plant and Macclesfield got into pharmaceuticals.

The town had started in the button business, then in the nineteenth century moved into silk in a big way. If you didn't work or have some connection to the weaving or textile trade, then you were just passing through. It was silk, silk, bloody silk all the way until these new-fangled synthetic textiles came along – not natural if you ask me. The static shock off a nylon shirt should have told us something. But times were changing and it was adapt and survive or enter a period of tortuously slow decline.

So although there were mills aplenty in Macc, their tall red-brick chimneys belched less and less smoke as the years wore on. They may have mostly been dark and satanic, but there was great fun to be had exploring a derelict mill.

Besides textiles, Macclesfield laid claim to being the birthplace of Hovis bread. I'll never the forget the day in 1967, aged ten, when my mother and a car full of my relatives – gleeful gloaters – picked me up at the school gates.

'Hurry up, Stephen! We're off on a trip. Hovis is on fire! It's all going up!'

Why so much excitement for a burning loaf? I thought as I squashed my way into the overloaded vehicle and we sped our way up Buxton Road.

It seemed the whole town had turned out. The road was crammed with badly parked cars. By now the pillar of grey smoke dispelled my idea that it was a faulty toaster that had excited my family to fever pitch. We joined the crowd lining the canal banks and solemnly watched as the roof of the bread mill blazed.

'Well, that's the end of that then. Town's ruined.'

'End of an era,' the ever-optimistic town folk cried. We love a good tragedy in Macclesfield. It breaks up the tedium.

I suspected my mother was either a spy herself or else head of the Macclesfield branch of Reuters news agency. Her conversations always began with 'You'll never guess what . . .'

There's no answer to that, is there?

'Fred Grainger's had an accident, fell off his ladder. They think he's broke his legs. Ooh, he is in a bad way.'

Further enquiries as to who the hell Fred Grainger might be would only produce more confusion.

'You know: Fred! Nelly's sister's husband. Used to work in the butcher's, now he's on the windows. Well, he was. Bunty rang and told me. Ooh, he is in a bad way. I'll just let our Elsie know.'

With each piece of tragic news my family grew larger and more convoluted while simultaneously teetering on the brink of extinction. I was always almost losing relatives I'd never heard of.

Then there was Parkside mental hospital. Originally called the Cheshire County Asylum, it was built in 1871, around the time the Morrises first appeared in the town, although that's probably a coincidence. There is no nice easy way of putting this: another of Macc's speciality industries was the treatment, or more likely the containment, of the mentally ill.

Parents from the surrounding areas would scare their children to sleep at night with the promise that if they did not behave they would be sent to Macclesfield.

Before you get too much of a bad idea about the place, I'd best point out that Parkside, unlike the mills, appeared quite welcoming. It didn't have the look of a prison or a sinister Victorian workhouse. It was set in parkland and was outwardly quite grand and unthreatening. It comprised the largest collection of buildings in the town, had its own fire brigade, sports club and swimming pool, and in the 1960s and 1970s the highlight of Macclesfield's year was Parkside's legendary annual Christmas Disco. Tickets were highly sought after and the night was the talk of the town for weeks before and after.

Nonetheless, the hospital was usually a self-contained world of its own, and what went on inside was shrouded in mystery and viewed with suspicion.

So throughout my childhood Macclesfield was a town with two faces: an industrial weaving town in decline and a growing centre for the pharmaceutical and mental health industries.

There was no avoiding Parkside. It was quite close to where we lived, and going to school each day meant driving past it and wondering what the hell went on in there. Like it or not, Parkside involved everyone who lived in the town. Sooner or later it would cross your path. Like the smell of the gasworks, it got everywhere. As a child, I would meet some very odd people round town, and not all of them were patients. I love odd people. I seem to attract them. Always have.

The smell of gas and the mental hospital weren't the only backdrop to my childhood. The Second World War still cast its shadow everywhere in my little world – from games of 'Japs and Commandos', to collecting those garish chewing-gum cards, and gluing my fingers together cobbling up my own plastic air force of Airfix model kits.

Spitfires, Hurricanes, Messerschmitts and Lancasters. That any of my finished creations bore any resemblance to the images on the heroic box art was for the most part down to my vivid imagination.

'Read the instructions thoroughly before assembly' was the first bit of advice I disregarded. 'Always follow the recommended sequence of construction' was the second. I just wanted to get the things built as quickly as possible. I would very rarely wait for the glue to dry before I started slapping on a coat of glossy brown, green or any other coloured paint I could find. One of the first casualties of the construction of my miniature air museum was my mum's kitchen table. I was soon told that any future model-making activity would have to take place outside the house in the cold, cobweb-curtained garage. The wearing of gloves and an overcoat for warmth didn't improve my technique but they did keep the glue and paint off my fingers – a bit.

My parents had lived through the war and experienced something that I never would. What was it like? I wanted to know. I thought that in building the kits I would find out somehow.

It was always the interior of the planes that interested me most, and the area I took the greatest care in painting. Especially the legless plastic pilot, who, glued to his seat, was mostly invisible when the kit was finished. I wanted to build a miniature world of my own. Being alone in the garage, a haven of plastic and glue, was an escape from school and my parents.

During the war my father, Clifford, had worked for Vickers and Avro in the aircraft construction game. Maybe that was where I got it from. Not that he did anything that involved the construction of aircraft itself, for if there was one thing he was not, it was being capable of constructing anything. He understood the principles, how the things worked and how they were made well enough. But the chances of him actually producing anything that could fly were zilch. He was a desk jockey, looking after technical drawings and reference books, during the war. Probably the safest thing for everyone involved. He may have inherited his interest in aviation from his father, the villainous George, or maybe he didn't fancy getting shot at. I never did get to the bottom of that one.

Before that, he was a nationwide travelling salesman in hosiery. How he got from selling stockings to his later vocation, kitchen taps, via heavy bombers is a convoluted tale shrouded in mystery.

Let's just say he enjoyed travelling. He was in Berlin with his brother Eric in 1936 to see Jesse Owens get gold. Eric told tales of abuse at the hands of the Nazis at the time but Clifford would not comment. He would not speak of such things. Eric, it must be said, was known to exaggerate at times.

My father would set off to work at 6.30 a.m. whatever the weather and would not be seen again until eight in the evening. He would have his fish supper, settle down in his armchair in front of the fire and have his four Gold Labels and two cigars. Never more, never less. Regular as clockwork.

My mother called him Cliff. He called her the Dragon – not to her face, obviously.

My mother at war.

My mother had spent the war in the Auxiliary Territorial Service (ATS). She trained at Catterick, where the men were good dancers, and served at Donnington, where they were not.

Cessation of hostilities saw my mother back in Macclesfield, working at Neckwear Ltd, one of the town's many textile mills.

My sister's arrival back in 1960 had taken me a bit by surprise. I was three and the world was still full of shocks. Mum was 'away' for a while which meant that Clifford had to take on a bit of parental responsibility as to the feeding of a three-year-old.

The Cedar Grove area of Macclesfield, my father's family home and his natural habitat, was, it turned out, not exactly noted for its haute cuisine, but Dad hadn't even grasped the fundamentals. The only thing that Clifford could cook which did not involve copious quantities of Lea & Perrin's to impart a bit of flavour was the stand-ard hard-boiled egg. Egg after egg after egg. A few days of this dietary monotony and a rather nasty red rash appeared on my skin. This was speedily diagnosed as an 'allergy', whether to eggs specifically or Dad's cooking in general was glossed over, as were the names of his previous victims.

From then on, I would dine with Mum's sister, Auntie Elsie, until the day came when I was taken to the hospital and introduced to my sister for the first time. She had a small spot on her chin. It worried me. What if it spread? What if I caught it?

Mum's return home brought back eating as normal and soon this worry passed from my mind, but Amanda's arrival meant a bit of an upheaval in the general arrangements of life at 122 Gawsworth Road.

Where was the newborn to sleep? Not with me, surely?

The layout of our house on Gawsworth Road (aka Birley; it had a name as well as a number, it was that posh) was two downstairs rooms, front and back, otherwise known as the lounge and the dining room, as well as a small kitchen and a tiny pantry. Upstairs there were two bedrooms, again front and back, a bathroom, a loo and the small 'other room'. This was what Clifford was using for his office even though 11 Cedar Grove was officially his business address. This was to fool the bailiffs presumably. They would have to deal with Uncle Johnny first, 11 Cedar Grove's sole occupant at the time.

Now you would think that the arrival of a child wouldn't present too much difficulty in a house like this: put the parents in one bedroom, kids in the other, and put a lock on the office door just to be on the safe side. Voilà, what could be simpler? No, this was too straightforward, and being straightforward was not the Morris way. There were other things to be considered, but what these were I confess I still don't know to this day. The arrangement that was finally settled upon was that Mum would have the back bedroom to herself. The office was turned into Amanda's bedroom, and for the foreseeable future I would be sharing a bedroom with my dear old Dad. I don't remember being involved in the consultation process that led to this decision.

This arrangement did not seem in the slightest bit unusual to me at first but later on I realised that everyone else thought it was a bit odd.

'You sleep with your dad? What, are you that scared of the dark or sommat?' was my friends' surprised reaction when I mentioned the inner workings of my home.

'No, course not, I like the dark,' was my tentative defence.

What I did like about this room was the gas fire. I was always on the lookout for stray matches so I could clandestinely experiment with igniting the room's sole heat source. I would turn out the lights and sit as close as I could to the hissing amber glow. It felt comfy.

'Don't do that,' my mother urged. 'You'll get chilblains.'

I wasn't sure whether I wanted chilblains or not.

By the gas fire I discovered books. I balanced Edgar Allan Poe with P. G. Wodehouse, *The Raven* versus *The Empress of Blandings*.

The thing was, Dad got up really, really early and got home really, really late, if he got home at all. His tap-selling activities meant that he had to travel great distances and was often away for days at a time. I supposed I must have been the soundest sleeper and therefore the least likely to be disturbed by his nocturnal comings and goings. My father was often troubled by night terrors. His nocturnal ravings and ramblings took a little bit of getting used to. Anyway, I slept with the light on.

While I had gained a room-mate, the business had lost an office. I think my mother was pleased by this.

Clifford Morris worked as a manufacturer's agent, having set up a company with his brothers Johnny and Eric. He sold kitchen and bathroom items on commission, and would travel around the north-west taking orders from builder's merchants. He sold taps, kitchen units, copper cylinders, sanitary ware, sink tops, galvanised tanks, baths and toilet seats.

His role was broadly that of a sales rep or middle man. The niche this job occupied has today been killed off by telesales companies, the internet or companies realising they could do the job themselves.

He would leave the house before dawn and set off with his Vauxhall estate car laden with samples, brochures and price lists of the goods on offer.

He knew a thing or two about selling. He knew that unless people remembered who you were they would be unlikely to call you when they needed you. He adopted a gimmick – everyone needs a gimmick. He would wear a bowler hat. This item of headgear may have been highly fashionable once upon a time, but in the 1960s it was becoming an anachronism. The bowler hat was my father's trademark.

He would arrange to have pens, pencils, packets of paper clips, calendars, drink mats and paperweights produced with stylised depictions of his hat and his initials GCM, and also incorporating his lucky colour, green. These he would hand out to prospective buyers. These promotional items were not masterpieces of design but they served their purpose. They said 'Call Me' and hinted at a reliable and hopefully pleasurable experience.

He was pretty successful and was widely respected throughout the building trade. His motto, pinched from the London Stock Exchange, was 'My Word, My Bond', a phrase that he drummed into me from a very early age. He did his utmost to live up to it and would do anything to avoid letting his customers down. He was thought of as an old-fashioned gentlemen and, as time went on, this became another anachronism. His was not the high-pressure sales technique. It relied more on time and effort. Sometimes visits to the furthest outpost of his empire would mean he was away from home for days at a time. Weekends he would also spend working, much to my mother's displeasure. To compensate for this lack of attention, my mother decided to become the first female motorist in Gawsworth Road.

After the arrival of my sister he moved his business into a gothic-looking building called Evington House. It was part of the former barracks of the Cheshire Militia. The building was rambling, run-down and haunted. I loved it.

On Sundays after church, I would find myself press-ganged into the family business, working at Evington House. His car would need restocking with giveaway pens and pencils (these were a great success and you still find them in builders' yards today), sales brochures and price lists, all filed in wooden trays on the back seat of his Vauxhall. For sixpence I was easily bought.

This later expanded into production of the brochures themselves. I would spend many a Sunday afternoon turning mountains of paper into hundreds of poorly stapled brochures while listening to *Two-way Family Favourites* and eventually *Pick of the Pops* on the radio.

The going rate was 100 brochures for a shilling (5p).

I didn't mind as I could never see the point of Sundays anyway. It was just dead time. There was nothing else to do on a Sunday afternoon in Macclesfield. There was cycling and playing in the fields – nothing that a visitor from the twenty-first century would recognise as 'entertainment'. The shops were shut, the pubs were shut. Once a month there was the odd parade with a band, but that was it. A ghost town would have been more fun. To make matters worse there was a semi-reprise of this situation on Wednesday afternoons when the ritual known as 'half-day closing' was enacted – you couldn't even buy a loaf. You could starve on a Wednesday lunchtime if you weren't careful.

The nadir of tedium for the casual visitor to Macc would occur around the second week of June: the Barnaby holiday. The entire town (yes everybody, every shop, every pub, every mill) would shut up shop for two weeks and descend on Blackpool for fun, frolics and warm beer. If you were unfortunate enough to find yourself stuck in Macclesfield during the Barnaby holiday, watching the traffic lights change would have been the sole leisure activity.

Luckily for my father, he lived to work. His only leisure activity was the weekend football match or athletics meeting. He helped organise the Central School Old Boys football team, which would take him away at weekends to matches, occasionally with a reluctant son in tow. Another of his soccer-related duties involved cleaning the team's dirty strips, a duty he press-ganged my mum into.

My mother, naturally, resented this and, though there were never arguments or rows, there were tense silences and a frosty atmosphere at times.

2

HOME AND ABROAD

Ah, the thirst for knowledge leads to one place and so it was with a great deal of reluctance that I was deposited each weekday at Mrs Berrington's Preparatory School for Boys and Girls. It's fair to say that me and education have never really got on. Mrs Berrington had one idea and I had another. I wanted to write with my left hand: this was not allowed. I wanted to write backwards: this apparently was madness. I would run away and hide at playtime and refuse to surrender when called. This was too much for Mrs B.

The school had what you would call a rebrand today, and became Mrs Berrington's Preparatory School for Girls. Problem solved. I was out. No way was I wearing a skirt.

Mrs Berrington did give me my first go at playing music, though. I fancied the tambourine; it had those jingly things and looked cool. But apparently it was too easily damaged and I was demoted to the sturdier triangle, which I clanged with gusto whether the tune needed it or not.

Amanda went there after me and did very well. She was a girl and didn't mind wearing a skirt, which fitted right in with Mrs B's target demographic. She was also bright. She immediately grasped that writing was what the right hand was for, and unlike me had no interest in gluing things together badly.

*　　*　　*

I started going to Christ Church Primary School in 1963. I got through Classes 1 and 2 of the infants division without too much heartache. Of course, there was the odd encounter with the slipper but there you go, that was life. No Childline for us then. Getting a hiding from the teacher's slipper or even worse, the headmaster's cane, was one of life's hazards for the boys at my school. The girls were spared and got lines instead. Probably something like 'Write out 100 times: "I must not talk to Stephen in class."'

Christ Church was, as you may have gathered, a mixed-sex school. Despite the girls showing little interest in comics and chewing-gum card collecting, we all got on with each other well. I was used to being around girls, having a sister of my own.

As Amanda was excelling and generally being good at Mrs Berrington's, she didn't join me at Christ Church. I think I had just as many female friends as boys – I wasn't shy. I would go to their houses for tea, although they were never allowed to visit mine.

If there was one thing I hated about Christ Church it was the daily compulsory milk-drinking routine. Every morning without fail the small bottles of white fluid would appear complete with tiny paper straws. I am not even sure it was proper milk. The sparrows seem to know something was up and never attacked the bottle tops. The milk certainly didn't taste like the same stuff you'd put on your Ricicles for breakfast and was more chalky water. I held a deep-seated fear that it might contain tadpoles or some other living organism, which must have come from some classroom rumour.

I would do anything to avoid the milk ration, but the only ploy that would work was to get myself appointed to the post of Milk Monitor on a regular basis. I was always first up with the arm when it was time to volunteer for the task in the morning. I am sure my enthusiasm must have seemed a bit suspicious, but once I had the job it was a simple matter of losing a bottle, either by kindly giving some poor soul an extra dose (there was the odd one who did actually like the stuff) or, more successfully, doing a bit of a switcheroo while count-ing the stuff out of the crate and making sure I ended up with an empty bottle.

If we didn't have it, though, we would all die of rickets – anyway, that was the answer I got when I asked casually, 'So, why do we have this free milk then, miss? Can they not sell it?' This was literally a school-boy error. It must have alerted the authorities to the fact that my keen-ness for milk distribution was a ploy as I was never chosen again.

I was never top of the class. My school reports usually ended with 'Must try harder.' I never did. The problem was my lack of patience. I wanted to get to the end of whatever I was doing as quickly as possible. Anything that required thinking about, like maths, bored me – it took too long and I would only get the answer wrong anyway, so why bother? I loved reading, though, comics especially. I'd read anything even if I couldn't really understand it. I'd always have a go. One book that we had to read at school that I really loved was Alan Garner's *The Weirdstone of Brisingamen*, a really scary story with a local setting. It must have done wonders for the Alderley Edge Tourist Board – this was before the footballers and toffs in Bentleys moved in.

So while I wasn't brilliant at school, I was doing all right, but I was rubbish at football. My dad could never understand that – surely anyone could play football? That aside, I made a lot of friends and avoided any really serious trouble.

It all went a bit wrong one summer morning. I was in Class 3 juniors so it'd be 1967 or 1968. Every morning we would troop into the hall for assembly. Stand there and sing the hymn with the aid of the words printed on the large flipchart-type crib sheets. Listen to a bit of a reading about how great Jesus was. Then close our eyes for a spot of praying to the Lord above. During the hymn-singing section of the performance my head started feeling a bit odd, kind of buzzy, and the letters on the board started to look a bit unusual, sort of wobblier than before and a bit more colourful. This wasn't right. I was starting to feel all clammy, there was a funny metallic noise coming from somewhere and it was a bit like the feeling I got when I overdid the gluing with the Airfix.

I got on with the praying, eyes clenched shut in the hope that divine intervention might sort it out. Mr Nichols, the headmaster, spoke the final 'Amen' and I opened my eyes, but it was still dark. I closed and opened them again. Still black. The lad on my right, eager to get to class, was nudging me to get a move on so I started shuffling to my left, hoping to follow the next in line. Bit hard when you're sightless, and somehow I managed to bump into a teacher.

'Watch where you're going, Stephen.'

'I think I've gone blind, sir,' I replied as the metallic ringing noise reached a crescendo. I fell to the floor unconscious.

When I finally came to, I was lying on the floor in the upstairs cloakroom surrounded by worried adults, still feeling very strange. Although my vision was back, there seemed to be odd blue haloes dancing around everything. Well at least I hadn't thrown up. The ultimate embarrassment. Perhaps the school milk dodging had not been such a good idea and this was a sign of the onset of rickets. I was sent off to the doctor to find out.

'Probably just a one-off occurrence, growing pains most likely, nothing to worry about.'

But it wasn't just a one-off. It kept happening, sometimes accompanied by a really strange sensation. It's hard to describe but it was as if everything was a drawing on a sheet of paper; there was no depth to anything, as though the whole world had gone two-dimensional – like a cartoon but more *Captain Pugwash* than *Tom and Jerry*. It still makes me feel weird just thinking about it.

Trying to find the upside to these losses of consciousness led me to suspect that they might in fact be some kind of superpower. A power that, if I could harness it, would give me unlimited time off school and a life of leisure. It didn't quite work. Try as I might, I could not keel over at will. Whenever I blacked out it would be always at the worst possible time or in the worst possible place. Sometimes both.

So I got sent back to the doctor, he sent me to another doctor and then another who sent me to some sort of specialist. He took blood tests, brain tests, all sorts of tests. I popped into Parkside for some of them – that was interesting. But none of this testing was getting anywhere so there would have to be more testing somewhere else.

The upshot of these investigations was that it was probably something brain-related.

'It's probably something mental, all in the mind,' was the doctor's verdict.

'Well, he has always been highly strung,' my mother replied. There was that string again.

As it turned out, I would have these occasional episodes for much of the rest of my childhood. I would eventually end up being sent to see a psychologist, then a hypnotist (honest!), then a psychologist again. This was not good. Seeing a shrink at the age of ten and I hadn't even started smoking and drinking yet.

The closest I ever came to actually flying a plane.

I looked forward to the summer holidays. Those five weeks that seemed to stretch out forever were a chance to try and escape the inexorable gravitational pull of Macclesfield and Dad's office, and to spend some time together as a family. What were we thinking? First Blackpool, naturally, then further afield to Torquay. Fawlty Towers had yet to open so we went to inspect the remains of the oil slick from the SS *Torrey Canyon* and paid a visit to Dartmoor prison. It was grim – both the prison and Dad's driving. On one excursion I recall Mum threw up on my head. We certainly knew how to have a good time.

Though it has to be said not entirely conventional, travels with my father would frequently involve being taken to inspect a town's lavatorial workmanship. He was keen on observing the local brass and sanitary ware. At the time, I could see nothing remotely dodgy in this. It was his occupation, after all, and it was a very different age. But a father and son inspecting the latest non-concussive taps and state-of-the-art urinals would in today's climate be viewed as very dodgy indeed.

For a couple of years our holiday destinations were slightly more exotic, though, before we returned to the safer bets of Paignton, Pwllheli and Llandudno.

One summer in the early sixties we set off from Gawsworth Road on a driving holiday arranged by my father. Our destination was the delightful French town of Dinard. On the roads of England and Wales, he was a reasonably accomplished driver. But once we crossed the Channel on the Brittany ferry things began to come unstuck. His grasp of the French language was about as good as his son's and my mother's navigational skills were not exactly on a par with a homing pigeon. The meaning of road signs was a constant worry.

On a typical interaction between driver and navigator, he asked, 'What's that sign say, Hilda?'

My mother, consulting the well-thumbed pages of the yellow AA guide to driving on the continent, replied, 'Chausay Deformay, Cliff.'

'What? Beware of deformed horses? Are you sure that's what it says?'

'Yes, Chausay Deformay, that's what it says here.'

Time and again we would miss the turning for Dinard as Clifford forgot which side of the road he was meant to be driving on, while me and Amanda then spent the rest of the journey looking from the back seat for evidence of the poor mutated animals. They would, we guessed, most likely have been injured by previous English motorists.

We stayed in a small hotel overlooking the bay. It felt like time had ground to a halt there around about 1921. I was fascinated by the birdcage elevator but I struggled to reach the buttons.

I shared a room with Amanda, which felt very strange. I loved opening and closing the green wooden shutters on the windows with their tiny faux balconies outside and watching the boats going to and fro across the turquoise waves to Saint-Malo.

Our delightful sojourn was short-lived. On the second night my parents returned from their nightly trip to the bar for, they said, a barrel of beer and found Amanda fast asleep and me in a distressed state. I was hysterical. The mothball-scented room, it seemed to me, had been invaded by a swarm of hallucinatory butterflies, fluttering menacingly in flashing colours. I was inconsolable and, as it turned out, running a fever.

The following day my father was dispatched with me in tow to find a doctor. I remember being dragged groggily about the town as my father asked, 'Ou est the medicine?'

We were directed through a gate into an open courtyard and there, at one end, was an illuminated green cross above an open door.

Believing his quest was at an end, my father dragged me in. I remember that along one wall there sat a row of women who were very obviously in the later stages of pregnancy. Now, in the course of our walking tour of Dinard, my skin had begun to erupt in virulent red spots. My father, more concerned with quizzing locals and thus locating the local physician, had failed to notice this fact. Unfortunately the large woman who sat behind the wooden desk had not. She took one look at me and shrieked, 'La rougeole! La rougeole! Allez, allez, allez!' as she left her seat and bustled me and Clifford back out into the street as swiftly as possible.

The now horrified mothers, understandably alarmed at the spotty, infectious child being dangerously close to them, tried to move as far away from us as possible. We were flung out onto the street and berated with what I can only guess was the French for 'Are you fucking mad?' The ante-natal receptionist's diagnosis, it turned out, was correct. I was suffering from the measles.

This was terrible! Why did I have to get ill on holiday? In the normal course of events measles was a sure-fire two weeks off school. Instead, I was shunned, isolated in the hotel bedroom for days – confined to bed as outside the sun shone. The sound of children playing and laughing on the beach outside my open window mocked me. For entertainment, I resorted to counting how many little boats crossed over to Saint-Malo and back every day. Like chalk marks on the wall marking time. No one from the hotel would enter the room – food was left on a tray outside the door – and the staff wanted me gone. The sooner the better. I was bad for business.

Eventually, and I can only assume after consuming another barrel of beer, my parents came up with a plan. My mother would take up people-smuggling. I was to be disguised, dressed from head to foot in black with my face covered with a cravat, a hat and the largest pair of sunglasses my mother could find. It was a good look, I thought, a bit like the sort of thing Ilya Kuryakin or Napoleon Solo would adopt if they were doing a spot of breaking-and-entering. My mother, Amanda and me were dropped off by Clifford after a marathon drive to Le Touquet and flown back to Lydd on a BUA Bristol Britannia – my first trip on a plane. I have to admit I still wonder how on earth Dad managed to make all the travel arrangements successfully.

Uncle Johnny was waiting at Lydd and drove Mum and her by now two sick children home. My father, meanwhile, sedately motored himself home, stopping over at Mont-Saint-Michel for a couple of days' sightseeing.

A year or two later, we took the ferry to Jersey in another attempt to have an exotic holiday.

'It's like being abroad but everyone speaks English,' Dad explained.

I liked Jersey instantly. It had been invaded by the Germans during the war and was a cornucopia of bunkers and tunnels and abandoned underground hospitals. It was my sort of place. We stayed in Bouley Bay at the Water's Edge Hotel, which was also my sort of place. The hotel apparently had no idea of the laws governing the sale of alcohol to young children. Encouraged to no small extent by my slightly giddy parents, Amanda and I would overindulge in the consumption of sickly-sweet wines – La Flora Blanche and Barsac. Now, the more educated among you will of course know that these syrupy beverages are dessert wines to be consumed at the end of a meal. We didn't care so long as it was cold and started knocking it back with the soup. We usually finished off with a Tia Maria or two. An excellent introduction to the torment of the hangover.

It was at the Water's Edge that I had my first encounter with fame, celebrity and, to be brutally honest, an evil, perverted monstrosity.

The steep winding road on the approach to Bouley Bay is frequently used in the field of motorsport that is hill climbing. The idea, I think, is that the car that gets to the top of the slope in the shortest time is declared the winner. The challenge seems to attract all sorts of vehicles (and people) and on the occasion in question it was an under-eighteens' go-karting event that was in preparation. The bay's jetty was crowded with the tiny buzzing buggies and onlookers. Not wanting to miss out, I dragged the rest of the Morrises along the quay for a closer look. The sound and smell of the tiny engines was intoxicating. This holiday was getting better and better.

Like a refugee from *Charlie and the Chocolate Factory*, I began to harass my father.

'Dad, can I have a go? Do you think they'll let me have a go? Dad! Ask if they'll give me a go. Go on Dad, pleeeeeze.'

Clifford, never backward in coming forward as they say, struck up a conversation with one of the race stewards. As luck would have it, one of the carts had broken down and needed moving. If I could steer the thing, the steward would push. I jumped in and took the wheel. Life in Jersey must be amazing – I could be a racing driver and a drunk!

As I swerved the little buggy round the corner off the quay, I spotted a small throng of young people gathered around a man with a shock of long white hair. Whatever next? For it was none other than pop celebrity and DJ Jimmy Savile himself dressed in bright turquoise paisley-patterned robes with a large silver crucifix around his neck like some poptastic monk. Now the world knows what an unspeakable bastard Savile was, but in 1967 everyone thought he was some sort of saint. I immediately lost interest in my new-found career as a racing driver and ran off after Amanda to tell her what I'd seen.

'Amanda, you won't believe who I've just seen! Jimmy Savile, he's over there.'

'Will you get me his autograph?' she pleaded.

'Oh no, Amanda, I don't think he'd like to be bothered,' I haughtily replied.

At which my sister spontaneously broke down in floods of tears. Making my sister cry was a hobby of mine. One which, to my shame, I have so far neglected to mention.

Amanda sobbed and, like a shark scenting blood, the peroxide pervert homed in on her wailing.

'Now then, now then, now then, what is going on over here then?'

He began to placate my sobbing sister with his popular banter.

Savile was very polite, and he seemed to have decided that my family were his new best friends and began asking all sorts of questions about who we were, why we were there, what did we think of the island, while signing his name on a paper napkin and puffing on a large cigar. This impressed my dad, himself a devotee of the stogie. My mother was charmed, and Savile kissed her hand. Me? I'd like to say that I knew at once I was in the presence of evil incarnate and that I felt my flesh crawl with revulsion, but the truth was he just made me feel uncomfortable, not a difficult thing to do if I'm honest, but there was something blatantly phoney about him, like he was secretly taking the piss out of us all. At the time I thought that must be how all famous people were. I thought he was never going to leave us alone, he went on and on and on. Eventually one of his acolytes dragged him off and a bright, beaming, autograph-clutching Amanda said as she waved him goodbye, 'What a lovely man.'

Not as lovely as that go-kart, I thought to myself.

Little did we know that Haute La Garenne, a children's home just ten minutes down the road from our hotel, would later become the centre of a child abuse investigation. We drove past it frequently and never knew what evil lay inside.

I really couldn't wait to grow up. Being a kid was a waste of time and nobody took me seriously. If I could have had three magical wishes they would have been to be older, to have grey hair and to wear glasses. All three would come true eventually. But by the time they did I would want none of them.

Be careful what you wish for. I should maybe have gone for wisdom instead of the specs.

3

THE SWINGING SIXTIES

The entertainment at home was by today's standards somewhat limited. There was a black-and-white TV around which we spent our evenings glued to the grey fuzzy glow. But most of the time the pleasure in our house came from the radio – a small red-and-yellow transistor, permanently tuned to the Light Programme. It was *Housewives' Choice* through the week and *Children's Favourites* with Uncle Mac (that was his DJ name) at the weekend. They were the main staples with the odd *Goon Show* or *Clitheroe Kid* for a bit of variety. I used to look forward to Uncle Mac's weekly airings of 'The Runaway Train' by Michael Holliday and 'Three Wheels on My Wagon' by the New Christy Minstrels – songs of cowboy misadventure, how they cheered me. 'Sparky's Magic Piano' was another one of good old Uncle Mac's top requests – the spooky vocoderish voice of the piano made a deep and lasting impression on me, as did the song's story with the moral 'never cheat, you will be found out'. I ignored that advice, of course. Along with the 'practise, practise, practise' message, I had no time for that. I expected to be proficient straight away. I was an extremely impatient child.

I had a request played on *Children's Favourites* once. It was for 'Carbon the Copycat' by Tex Ritter. It was the echoey delay effect on Tex's voice that got me. I didn't know what it was at the time but I liked the sound of it. However, I missed my moment of radio fame as

I was in the kitchen, elbow deep in a packet of Sugar Puffs, trying to extract that week's free gift, which I think was a tiny plastic Roman gladiator figure. Oh well.

Other than the wireless there was the record player – the oddly named Pye Black Box. Odd, because it was brown. It was definitely a box, though, standing on four spindly wooden legs. These raised the machine's inner workings so they were just out of reach of my infant fingers. I would climb on top of the settee to peer down and marvel at the black spinning platters. One day, I thought. One day.

Considering my dad was such a music lover, our record collection was a bit on the thin side. We had around six or seven discs in all. *Noël Coward in New York*, Duke Ellington's *Black and Tan Fantasy*, a Huckleberry Hound/Yogi Bear LP (think that was mine), a Jack Buchanan EP, the soundtrack to a film called *The Restless Ones* (a Christian propaganda flick featuring Billy Graham; where this came from and what it was doing in the Morrises' record cabinet was a complete mystery) and a 78 of Gene Kelly doing 'Singin' in the Rain' (a perennial favourite). Oh and Mandy Miller doing 'Nelly the Elephant'. That one was definitely mine.

Auntie Elsie Stacey, mum's elder sister and a smaller, smilier version of my mother, was a keen churchgoer and patron saint of bring-and-buy sales. Elsie's family had a musical collection that was much more engaging than ours.

The Staceys' music came from a majestic radiogram with a glowing tuner strip on which were emblazoned exotic words such as Hilversum, Luxemburg, Lille, Warsaw, Moscow. Moscow! You could actually hear what people were saying in Moscow! You couldn't understand them though, even if you did speak Russian, as it was all hiss, bleep and clatter. Despite that, this record player and radio combination was amazing. More than twice the size of our little Black Box, it was awe-inspiring. There was a door at the front that dropped down to reveal the turntable at just the right height for my prying hands to explore. Inside was a rack for storing your 45s, old 78s and 33s. There were quite a few in there too.

Auntie Elsie and Uncle John had two daughters, my older cousins Kathleen and Susan. They were 'with it' teenagers, devotees of pop music. Despite our age difference, Kath and Sue kindly shared their knowledge of what was what in pop with me. Though this did seem to involve listening to Cliff Richard and Adam Faith singles mostly, there was other stuff as well. They had singles by the Beatles, the Stones, the Zombies – Kath had the Zombies' autographs (she'd met pop stars, wow!) – the Kinks, Gene Pitney (I wasn't too impressed with him, apart from 'Twenty-four Hours from Tulsa', obviously) and, of course, Elvis. Everyone liked Elvis.

Even though I loved the sound of the records, I was indifferent to the pop malarkey generally. It seemed to me it was all a bit girlish – all screaming and chasing. Gluing and painting plastic armies were still my main passion. I spent all my free time in the company of Airfix model kits, glue and paints.

But I thought, *There's nothing wrong with listening to a few records now and then is there?* So I persuaded my mum to buy one. My first single was 'The Locomotion' by Little Eva. That was great. It appealed to me because the words were, I guessed, about a train, not some lovey-dovey romantic slush. Then Elvis's 'Return to Sender' was another. This, I assumed, was about the perils of the postal system – a much more interesting subject than rejection, of which I understood nothing, so it didn't exist. I would listen to 'Return to Sender' endlessly. I loved the sound of it. The shuffly drums of D. J. Fontana. The 'da ta da tadada dada' baritone sax bit. The song made me feel happy, made me smile. Another hit 45 was Chubby Checker's 'Let's Twist Again' – Kath and Sue were keen twisters. A sixties dance craze, the original and greatest. Me, I liked the Widow Twanky panto-style lyrics, 'Is it a bird? No. Is it a plane? No. Is it the Twister? Yeah', and the train-beat drums (I always liked a good beat). Without realising it at the time, it was the rhythm of music that interested me most. Much more than melody or lyrics.

My favourite 45 was 'Telstar' by the Tornados – the great Joe Meek's finest work. It had everything an infant space enthusiast could want in a single; that whooshing noise in the intro and the catchy organ riff. The best thing about it, I thought, was its lack of words. Groups used to go on and on about love all the time. 'Telstar' didn't have that flaw. I thought it was perfect.

That bloke Heinz, the frontman, looked cool on *Thank Your Lucky Stars*; I wondered if that was his real name? Was he related to the sauce people?

The *Fireball XL5* theme by Don Spencer was another great tune. Along with the Wild West, rockets and space were a major passion of my infancy.

The only trouble was, if I wanted to listen to any of these 45s, I had to ask an adult or a taller person to put them on for me. Growing up seemed to take forever.

It's fair to say that, by 1963, I had taken an interest in pop music.

Me and Amanda went along with Auntie Elsie to St Andrew's Church every week and, once the singing and praying was over, we would go back to her house for a cup of tea, some cake and some Elvis, frequently alternated with songs from the soundtrack of *South Pacific* or *The Sound of Music*. I began watching *Thank Your Lucky Stars* and *Juke Box Jury* on a regular basis – just to stay informed, you understand. Oh and from 1964 *Top of the Pops* as well.

Pop music seemed to be everywhere, and tales of teenagers' scandalous behaviour were always in the newspapers. Dancing and having fights mostly. I couldn't wait to be older.

It was with Kath and Sue that I queued up round the block to watch the Beatles in *A Hard Day's Night* and *Help* at the Majestic Cinema in Macclesfield.

It was around then that I became a Beatles fan and fell victim to the Beatles marketing campaign – first, it was a Beatles Easter egg and mug, then a plastic Woolworth's Beatles wig. This was a bit itchy and the dog kept running off with it. Then, one Christmas, I got a Beatles guitar from Santa.

Finally, I was 'cool and with it'. I would now be able play all the Beatles' tunes for myself. Guitars were cool-looking things and no mistake. This one was white and orange, made of plastic, and emblazoned with rather poor likenesses of the Fab Four. Ringo, in particular, looked very odd. But he was the drummer and shouldn't really have been on the guitar in the first place. He looked more like my friend Geoff from up the road than a scouse mop-top. John Lennon looked as if he was enjoying a bit of chewy treacle toffee. If they hadn't bothered to write their names underneath, I really wouldn't have guessed who they were supposed to be.

My new guitar had four plastic strings knotted to four clothes-peggy things at the sharp end. I didn't think this odd. I'd seen guitars before but I'd never bothered to count how many strings were on a guitar. It looked about right. To me this was a proper guitar.

I balanced the instrument on my knee, put my fingers where I reckoned George – or was it John? I was never certain – would have put them and began to strum.

Something was dreadfully wrong. It sounded nothing like the opening sound of 'A Hard Day's Night'. It sounded more like a bunch of rubber bands that had been badly nailed to a cigar box by a blind carpenter. Perhaps it was faulty? I adjusted the position of my digits and strummed again. Any improvement? No, worse if anything. It was definitely a dud.

What I needed was advice, so I asked Susan.

'Sue, I've got this guitar but it sounds all wrong.'

'Well, have you tried tuning it?'

Ah, tuning it, that was the problem.

'No,' I said, 'I haven't. How do I do that?'

'Well, you twiddle the things at the end until it's in tune.'

'Ooh, hadn't thought of that. Is that what they're for? Right, I'll give that a go. Thanks!'

So away I twiddled and, yes, the thing was sounding a bit more melodious. Then a bit more twiddling was accompanied by the sound of a tiny oil tanker running aground and the ping of one of the wires snapping in two. *Never mind*, I thought, *one string here or there isn't going to make much difference.* I continued with my tuning until, with a creak, a groan and a much louder crack, the instrument rent itself asunder. Its back bit had come away from the front bit. *Never mind*, I thought again, *nothing that a bit of Bostick glue won't fix.*

But in reality, I knew I was beaten. The guitar had won. I could always watch telly instead. So I did. *What a con*, I thought as I watched a western. *I'll write to that Brian Epstein and complain.* But as his address didn't feature on the guitar, I never did. My distrust of pop band merchandise began at a very early age

Another Christmas, Santa brought me a Sooty drum kit. This was more like it, no painful tuning and finger bending involved for this. Just bang, bang, bash, bash, and off you went. You could always trust a small orange bear who never spoke in public. (Sooty also played a magical xylophone and so I had one of those too. It wasn't really magical. Still, I kept the faith in my musical mentor.)

The drumming was all going well until Boxing Day. I thought my banging and crashing was sounding great, better than the guitar anyway, but it seemed I was alone in that belief.

'That Harry Corbett wants shooting!' my father announced, his attempts at a post-dinner snooze thwarted by my percussive experiments.

I was shocked.

I had never heard my father berate anyone before, certainly not a TV celebrity. What act could Sooty's chum have committed to warrant such

That bear was a marvel (seen here with his omnipresent minder). Sooty, like many would-be drummers, frequently needed protection from angry parents.

cruel and unusual punishment? I guessed this would have been some heinous crime my enraged father had just read about in his newspaper.

'Why, Dad, what's he done?' I plaintively asked.

'Ask your mother, it was her idea.'

I was baffled.

My drumsticks disappeared shortly after that and were never seen again. I tried playing the drums with my hands but it just hurt.

Sometime later that Boxing Day, we went to visit Auntie Renee in Hazel Grove, as usual. After a couple of sherries – not me and Amanda, obviously, because everyone knows children are only allowed to drink in Jersey – a *New Musical Express* Poll Winners TV special came on the telly.

'Who are this lot?' my mother asked.

'The Pretty Things,' I replied knowingly, having just heard Brian Matthew do the intro.

'Well, they don't look very pretty to me. Look at the hair on that one, looks like a bloody girl,' chipped in Renee with something close to venom. Perhaps it was the sherry but my elders seemed a bit antagonised by this particular beat combo. The Stones were on later and they received an even angrier reception from the senior Morrises.

'Ooh, turn it off, I can't stand this rubbish. Let's play Cluedo instead.'

Impressed by the reaction this music produced in my elders. I made up my mind that I would no longer like the Beatles, it would be the Stones for me from now on. They didn't make rubbish guitars and they didn't smile.

It was that simple really. You got asked 'Who do you like then, the Beatles or the Stones?' Like black and white, chalk and cheese, jam and marmalade, there were only the two choices. You had to be one or the other or you were no one.

You're absolutely sure about all this are you?

Only I don't think Brian Mathews ever introduced the NME Poll Winners show and I'm fairly sure that the Pretty Things weren't ever on it with the Rolling Stones.

Oh and while we're at it, the NME awards were shown in April, not December.

Are you sure you're not just making all this stuff up?

See the tricks that memory plays.

All right, maybe it was Easter Monday, not Boxing Day. But I'm sure the Pretty Things were on. I remember that very clearly.

I also remember the Cluedo game vividly. We argued about whether it should be Monopoly or Cluedo, and Cluedo won. It was Professor Plum in the Library with the candlestick.

I definitely remember it that way. I'm certain.

Maybe your memory is playing tricks on you. It wouldn't be the first time. When was this then exactly?

Well, 1965 or maybe it was 1964.

You can't really be certain about anything, can you?

You know what they say: if you can remember the sixties you weren't really there.

*　　*　　*

The main TV show that I and probably any boy my age was preoccupied with at that time was *Doctor Who*. It was like nothing I'd seen before. Unlike *Fireball XL5*, this had real people in it, not puppets. And it had that really eerie hypnotic yet scary theme tune. I never missed it. I remember sitting at Auntie Elsie's on Saturday evening waiting for the football results to finish. *Doctor Who* was usually preceded by *Juke Box Jury* for Kath and Sue. I was at my auntie's when I saw the episode with the first Dalek and was scared out of my wits. Yes, I literally did hide behind Elsie's settee until it had gone. 'What was that?' It was the talk of the playground come Monday.

Being a time traveller's assistant looked like a good job to have. I would add that one to my list of replies to the 'What do you want to be when you grow up?' question.

'Well, either a fighter pilot, a time traveller's assistant or a spy.'

That none of these career choices seemed widely available in the Macclesfield area was a little disappointing. But the place seemed behind the times, old-fashioned. The future was elsewhere.

Growing up, America was where we were headed. Sitting watching the Pye TV was to be indoctrinated into everything American. Gerry Anderson's fantastic puppet shows – essential viewing for any sixties schoolboy – had at their heart locations that were clearly a long way west of Macclesfield. OK, I know the later ones such as *The Secret Service* – Prof. Stanley Unwin as a puppet, anyone? – and *Joe 90* had a bit of a quirky English bent but they were a bit naff. The stuff that made those first and biggest impressions – *Four Feather Falls, Supercar, Fireball XL5, Stingray* and the unsurpassable *Thunderbirds* – were all set in some kind of mythical America. And OK, I know Lady Penelope lived in London and there was general globetrotting (in a marionette sense) in *Thunderbirds* but the Tracys were certainly of American descent. Then there were the Westerns – *Wagon Train, The Lone Ranger, Bonanza* – 'in color' the TV lied. You always knew where you were with Westerns: black hat bad, white hat good and Injuns with flaming arrows, dang varmints. The USA was where it was happening and the TV allowed you to visit and share what might one day be yours.

If I ever got to Beverly Hills, visiting the hillbilly Clampetts would be top of the agenda, and why couldn't we live in Marineville, a city that retreated underground at the threat of imminent danger? Wonder how the shopping worked – could we go one day and find out? That seemed very unlikely but watching it was as good as being there. Better, really: no jet lag or possibly funny food like the possum and grits the Clampetts ate. The language was easily mastered and if I could only learn how to smoke cigarettes it would be even more real. Then I would get a job flying some fantastic silver rocket with flashing computer-controlled whatnots, come home for tea about six-ish, and drink Scotch and smoke the night away. Oh, the dreams of youth.

It was the Pye TV that brought me the terrible news of the slaying of JFK. Yes, I know where I was on 22 November 1963. Watching the box. Same as always.

With the Cold War raging, spying was big business when I was growing up and MI5 was my first career choice. I took to reading the newspapers from cover to cover, hoping to spot a vacancy for an under-tens' spy ring. Possibly based in the north-west region. Although truth be told, I was beginning to get a little wary of the spy career. Much as I loved the guns and gadgets that were the tools of the trade, I was a bit worried by the gold-painted nudes that James Bond had to deal with.

The Avengers, though, were more my sort of spies. I could see myself driving a Bentley and Dad already had a bowler hat I could use. I used to beg and plead to stay up late on Saturdays to watch Steed and Emma Peel. I was more than a little lovestruck. Mrs Peel had legs unlike my other sweetheart, Lady Penelope Creighton-Ward. They both had cool cars, though. Maybe that was it.

It was in the course of this newspaper spy-job hunting that I began to augment my education by studying a comic strip called 'Focus On

Fact – The Fun Way to Learn'. This was a strip that ran in the *Daily Sketch*. It was here that I came across stories with titles such as 'The man who visited heaven', 'Do you believe in Life after Death?' and 'The Angels of Mons'. Fascinating, but puzzling. Some of the information it contained did seem, even to me, to be a bit far-fetched. But how could something with the word 'Fact' in the title be anything other than the gospel truth? I learned a lot from 'Focus On Fact', nothing that you might call useful in the real world, but the sort of things that would later come in handy at pub quizzes and the like. It was my introduction to the world of Charles Fort and paranormal Fortean phenomena. Not that I knew that at the time.

I received pocket money of two shillings, and sometimes two and six, a week, which was a king's ransom in those pre-decimalisation days. Where possible, I would supplement this by 'borrowing' from Amanda or any relative I came across. This hard-wheedled cash went on two things: models (still the plastic ones, unfortunately) and books. I loved to read. I was, as time went on, becoming more 'cultured'. There was a spate of family outings to the cinema or the theatre – *Something Fresh*, *Forty Years On*, which my dad picked, and a disastrous outing to see Sean O'Casey's *The Plough and the Stars*, which was one of my choices. I'd read a write-up in the *Evening News* that mentioned it was about the Clitheroe family. I naturally assumed this was the same Clitheroe family of TV and radio fame and would therefore be a rip-roaring comedy classic.

'It's a bit depressing,' was my mother's interval critique. 'Let's go home.'

'No,' I said. 'The next bit'll be really funny.'

We persevered and I learned a lot about the 1916 Easter rising. Specifically, that it wasn't funny. No wonder the play caused riots back in 1926.

The trip to see *2001: A Space Odyssey* in Cinemascope at the Theatre Royal fared only slightly better.

'I nodded off after the bit with the monkeys,' my father confessed. You'd think they would have learned not to listen to my artistic recommendations.

Mum, Renee and Dad: one Xmas or was it Easter?

It seemed that an antidote to this artistic frivolity was required, something more traditional, say. My mother decided that the best way to put me off music for life would be to introduce me to one of its mustier relatives: ballroom dancing. That I had never shown the slightest interest in the terpsichorean arts was neither here nor there. (OK, to be fair, I had been a clapping/dancing shepherd in the Nativity once and there had been a bit of maypole-ing one harvest but BLOODY HELL it wasn't by choice.)

I was forcibly enrolled in the Alex Brown School of Dancing on the second floor above three shops at the least interesting end of Chestergate. It was all butchers, barbers and grocers. Not a toy shop in sight.

Like some evil coven or secret society, these 'lessons' could only take place in the dark of winter evenings and then only on the nights that clashed with *Top of the Pops*. I wasn't a rabid fan of *TOTP*, but it was entertaining and given the choice between TV or prancing about above a barber's shop, the box would win every time. But there was no choice. So slow, slow, quick-quick, slow it was.

The good thing about Alex Brown's was it had a small bar at one end where you could have a Coke with a straw while you were hanging about. The bad thing was at the other end was a large dancefloor where you and a partner were expected to jig about in time to the music. 'Everything from the Waltz to the Paso Doble', I think the class was called. I never made it to the paso doble.

The proceedings always kicked off with 'March of the Mods' by Joe Loss – what this had to do with mods still eludes me. There were no scooters, parkas or greasers involved at all – it was just like a glorified conga line going round and round the room – but it was easy and it did make the whole thing seem even more like a comedy masonic ritual. It was all downhill from there. First, you had to get a 'partner', usually some old lady; well, definitely older than me. The pretty girls got snapped up quickly by the one or two gents who were regulars. Then came the confusing bit about who was going to be the 'man'. I thought I was the best choice for that, but things didn't work like that at the Alex Brown School of Dancing.

I then stumbled and blushed my way through what was supposed to be the waltz and then the cha-cha-cha. I couldn't tell the difference myself: they both involved getting dragged about and avoiding getting toes stood on by the lady who was supposed to be a man. It was baffling. I could not make head nor tale of the whole rigmarole.

I used to live in dread of any of my schoolfriends discovering how I spent Thursday evenings. I would have to make far-fetched excuses about broken tellies or getting sent to bed early if the subject of last night's TV ever come up at playtime on Friday.

My weekly humiliation finally came to an end when it was pointed out by one of Mr Brown's lady instructors that I had no natural sense of rhythm and no amount of teaching could overcome that hurdle. I agreed wholeheartedly – you've either got it or you haven't. It was a shame but never mind.

The ballroom dancing, embarrassing as it might have been, was not a total waste. I came away having learned (probably by osmosis) that some tunes went 'ONE-two-three, ONE-two-three'. Others went 'One and two and three and four'. I liked the last ones best.

I also learned to 'lead with your left' but I might be getting mixed up with boxing. I'm always getting those two confused.

My mother was bitterly disappointed with me. Amanda, typically, did really well at the dancing and went on Saturday afternoons too for ballet classes. She also started taking an interest in music and began having piano lessons.

The extent to which pop music could be taken seriously was brought home one Saturday when the Staceys took me with them on a church outing to Alton Towers, which in the 1960s looked almost nothing like it does today. It was all about strolling in the gardens, admiring the views or having a go in a rowing boat on the lake. There was one recent innovation though. They had installed cable cars! This was the exciting equivalent of a ride such as Nemesis today and required the now traditional bit of queuing to get on.

Somehow, during the queuing I got separated from Kath and Sue, and ended up on my own in a car with a group of three angry-looking older boys. I squashed myself into a corner and did my best to become invisible (I'm still quite good at that) when, with a loud clunk and a grinding of gears, the machinery broke down.

I was trapped high above the ground in an open-sided basket made of tin and wood with three pissed-up lads on a spree. They began shaking the car violently from side to side for a bit of a laugh.

I felt the blood drain from my face. What a way to go. I got that buzzy-head feeling that usually signalled the start of one of my turns.

'Hey you, short arse, what's the trouble?'

I'd been rumbled.

'Er, nothing,' I squeaked. 'It's a great view, isn't it?'

Each sideways lurch of the car piled on the vertigo. Oh yeah, I've got a terrible fear of heights – didn't I mention that?

'What's yer team then?'

'I don't like football much.'

'You don't like football! What's up with yer? Hey, he dint like football.' I was suddenly in dire need of a piss. 'Never heard of anyone who dint like football.'

'All right then, who's yer favourite band, eh? Beatles or Stones?'

All three turned to look me straight in the eye. I began to get the feeling this might be a more important question than the football one.

'Go on then.'

This was getting a bit intimidating. A matter of life and death.

What if these three were for the Fab Four and I said the Stones, or what if . . . Honesty, as my father was fond of saying, is this best policy. So I said, 'I like the Kinks and I want the loo.'

To my surprise, my tormentors found my reply extremely amusing and laughed like drains. They were suddenly my mates.

'Yeah, the Kinks are great. Do ya want a fag, son?'

I had no idea that liking the right or wrong kind of music could set you apart. That pop music and style were tribal.

Cliché alert: 'And so I became the class clown . . .'

I would much rather have been the class clever clogs but that meant too much work. Who actually likes clowns anyway? Fucking red-nosed, big-footed bastards. I don't trust 'em.

I discovered I could make people laugh, though. The difference from the usual cliché is that I didn't mean to. People would crack up with mirth when I thought I was saying something serious. The more serious I got, the more they would laugh. I learned to live with it. As superpowers go it was better than fainting. It could stop you getting battered in a cable car, for instance.

Meanwhile, back in green and pleasant Gawsworth Road, I decided to start a gang. I'd found a good spot for a den in one of the big fields up the road. A nice shady bit of woodland next to a fetid slime-covered pool. I was sure there were fish in there that we could catch and eat. Being in a gang would be exciting. I could live in the den, catch fish and observe people. My plan came to an end when I failed to recruit enough of my friends to join my fledgling cabal. Geoff and John from up the road were in until they found that it was stickleback for tea. They cleared off and left me in our newly built leafy hideaway to spy on evil dog walkers. I got a cold and when I realised I had no idea how to catch a stickleback or make chips, I came to my senses and abandoned my dream. Two days later I visited the den and discovered to my horror that another bunch of kids had realised its potential and started a gang of their own. They told me to piss off. Which I did.

I needed to join a proper gang. Of which there were but two: Mods and Rockers. They were on the news every time there was a bit of a scrap at the seaside.

My older male cousins all sported Brylcreemed, slicked-back hair in the traditional DA style and, though they lacked engines of their own, they did seem to know a bit about sparkplugs and stuff. I guessed they were probably Rockers. But in Macclesfield they were outnumbered by boys in green parkas, the backs of which were covered with patches – 'Tamla rules', 'Twisted Wheel' and an odd clenched fist logo with the words 'Keep the Faith'. Which to me suggested they were nice boys who went to church on Sundays. It was the RAF roundel T-shirts that grabbed me. *These guys must be into Airfix kits too*, I reasoned. *Yeah, I'd look good in a parka, especially one with a furry hood.*

'You're not having a parka,' was my mother's response. 'They're made of dead cats and all sorts.'

Only slightly deterred, I skulked off to inspect the inside of Macclesfield's Army & Navy Stores where a large quantity of green and khaki parka-like goods were haphazardly displayed in the window. Prices handwritten in felt-tip pen. The smell of damp canvas and vulcanised rubber goods. I rummaged through the fur-and-green rack and dug out the smallest-looking one I could find, pulled it on over my blazer and felt like a buffoon. The thing was nearly down to my ankles and my arms only reached the elbows. *Well, I might grow into it.* Who was I kidding? Until they did parkas for pygmies I was stymied. It did smell a bit like dead cats though. Red-faced, I exited the shop to find my Mum and buy a cornet from Granelli's.

I became fascinated with Jodrell Bank Observatory. A short bike ride up the road to Holmes Chapel and there was this looming great dish that scanned the stars like something out of *Doctor Who*. What was a radio telescope for exactly? I assumed it was some Top Secret military base. The front line of defence against any impending flying-saucer-type invasion. It fed my imagination, my science-fiction dreams of tomorrow's world.

Any chance I got, I would ride my bike in its direction, watching it growing larger and larger above the trees as I pedalled. I didn't want to get too close in case it spotted me or something. How did they make something so big? More importantly, why was it just up the road from Macclesfield, where anyone with a pushbike could find it?

I would lie awake at night, listening for sounds that might suggest the beginning of some alien onslaught. There was only ever the wailing and moaning of my slumbering father, as he began one of his nightly soliloquies, making phantom sales pitches or violently arguing with his brothers. This was most likely a side effect of his habitual four-Gold-Label nightcap. And most likely the reason my mother would not share a room with him.

4

EDUCATION

In 1969, two American men landed on the moon. Who'd have thought it? The furthest any man had actually boldly gone, ever. This was the future. I scrounged a tape recorder from my dad's office and made a tape of all the news bulletins of the entire Apollo 11 mission's progress. I even included a few bits of my own commentary.

In Macclesfield an equally unlikely event took place: I passed my eleven-plus exam. I'd always fared badly in school tests. Every time I did some swotting, which wasn't very often, learning my times tables off by heart until I could do them in my sleep, something would go wrong. Instead of being asked what is 12 x 10, the examiner would want to know how long it would take to fill a bath of a certain size.

You want a plumber, not an ten-year-old lad, I thought.

Previous warm-up exams hadn't gone well but they were of no consequence other than me getting a bit annoyed with whoever it was for asking such stupid questions. The eleven-plus though, this was the big one. The result would determine my educational future. The teachers made many attempts to put us at ease, reassuring us that this was not an exam that you passed or failed: it was just to ensure that we went to the right secondary school for our needs. Passing was not a sign of cleverness or failure a mark of ignorance, they told us. They didn't fool anyone. This was what the whole of my time at Christ Church had been building up to.

The outcome of this examination determined whether my next place of learning would be King's School Grammar or Broken Cross Secondary Modern. I surprised myself and everyone else by getting into the all-boys' King's. All I knew for certain about either of these schools was that at Broken Cross you played football, which I knew how to do badly, while at King's there was compulsory rugby – about which I knew nothing other than it looked dangerous. It seemed to involve running about with a funny-shaped ball, then rolling around in the mud and getting injured a lot. I wasn't looked forward to any of it.

Christ Church had been a mixed school, although there was a sort of gradual segregation that increased from the age of about nine. You didn't willingly play with girls, but a few of them were my friends. It was going to be weird going to a place where there was no female company at all.

So, after the long summer holiday of 1969, it was off to grammar school for me. My first day did not go well. I arrived at my allotted classroom only to discover I was the only one from Christ Church: my mates either ended up at Broken Cross or had been put somewhere else. Probably to stop us forming an escape committee or something. I was shocked and disappointed. I was in a different school with different rules and different manners, and I knew nobody. So there was a lot of 'Hi, who are you? Where are you from?' early on. I didn't much like being called by my surname either. It was as if I was a dog. There was also the jolly old tuck shop where you could buy unhealthy confections of all kinds. I didn't mind that bit.

My first couple of years at King's followed the average-must-try-harder standard I had set for myself earlier. The only thing other than the tuck shop that I really liked was the school library. I loved browsing through encyclopaedias looking for bits on Voodoo and Black Magic.

My classroom was in the music block and the form teacher was head of the music department. At King's, you were taught music whether you wanted it or not, and it was more serious than the triangle bashing back at Mrs Berrington's. Here it started more delicately with the mastering of the recorder. I wasn't sure about that either. The class's tuneless ensemble renditions sounded like a flock of angry pigeons arguing over crusts.

I think my dad liked the idea of this music tuition more than me. He was a firm believer that knowing how to play an instrument was a benefit. The next thing I knew I was signed up for clarinet lessons. I felt a little bit railroaded. Given the choice, I would've had another go at the guitar, but that class was heavily oversubscribed. Everyone always wants to be the next Hendrix or Clapton, and so did I. You could look cool strumming a guitar. The clarinet is a lovely-sounding instrument but it would not make me look cool. It would make me look like a dick.

I approached the thing with a bit of a reluctant sulk from the word go. I thought the clarinet was a crap instrument to be learning. Name one top record that's got a clarinet on it apart from 'Stranger on the Shore' by Acker Bilk, or one group that features a clarinettist in any kind of semi-permanent capacity. See what I mean.

'It'll be OK. Uncle Johnny'll give you some tips. He's a bit of a virtuoso on the old liquorice stick.' That was Dad's response to my sullen demeanour and grumbling.

Over the years I had got to know Johnny quite well from my visits to Dad's office. He was the brother who stayed in answering the phone doing officey things while Dad and Eric went off travelling, chasing orders and selling their chromium and nickel-plated wares. He was all right but he wasn't what you would call a bundle of laughs. Like most of the male Morris family, he had a bit of a Slavic appearance. He reminded me of Bela Lugosi, which made him seem slightly unapproachable, but I gave it a go.

'The thing about the clarinet,' he said, 'is once you can play it, then you can play anything.'

55

Anything? I thought. *These fools learning to play the guitar are wasting their time. Little do they know that the clarinet was the gateway to virtuosity on all musical instruments.*

'So I'd be able to play the guitar as well?' I asked, seeking clarification of this instrument's miraculous capabilities.

'Eventually,' he replied. My hopes were a bit dashed. 'But wind instruments are all the same, like the sax. Play a clarinet and you can play a sax no problem,' he concluded, well and truly crushing into oblivion whatever hopes I had of discovering a hitherto unknown route to axe-hero status. 'Come upstairs. I'll show you.'

I'd never been up the stairs at 11 Cedar Grove before. It was gloomy enough downstairs in the living room. Perhaps the upstairs didn't smell as much of boiled cabbage. A little nervously I followed Johnny up the stairs to a small, musty-smelling and even dingier room full of all sorts of junk and old books. In short, my sort of room.

Johnny reached up to a shelf that held several battered black cases as I blew the dust off some old books: *Aero Engineering Principles and Construction*, volumes one to nine. How to build a plane – wow! I started to browse. Meanwhile, my uncle's nicotine-stained fingers had produced a clarinet from one of the boxes on the shelf. He blew a few notes and it sounded good. It sounded like a tune anyway.

'Now,' he said, opening another of the boxes, 'take a look at this.'

He produced a number of golden tubes from the dusty box. In no time at all he had combined the pipes to produce a lovely-looking alto saxophone. He blew again – it sounded great. Maybe playing the sax wouldn't be that bad after all. There were lots of records with sax on them – the sax was kind of rock and roll, wasn't it?

'That's a good book you've found there. Would you like it?' he asked after finishing his sax solo.

'Yes, please,' I replied.

'It's one of your dad's, so you might as well have it. Actually, I've got something else you can have that might help with your music lessons.' He opened another of the boxes. This one contained another gleaming sax. *No! He's not going to give me that, is he?* By now, I thought that would be fantastic. *It will make me look really cool! Good old Johnny, not as tight as folk made out.* He rummaged about in the bottom of the case and finally pulled out a folded brown envelope. *Cash as well,* I thought, *perhaps an early Christmas gift.*

'There you go,' he said, handing me the envelope as he slammed the case shut. 'These softer reeds should make it easy going at first.'

He snapped the case shut as I tried to smile and look grateful. It wasn't easy.

My tastes in literature were beginning to get a bit avant garde for a twelve- or thirteen-year-old. As well as the sci-fi of Philip K. Dick and Michael Moorcock, I had been fascinated by the coverage of the *Oz* 'obscenity trial': Richard Neville, Felix Dennis and Jim Anderson had become my heroes. Anything described as having a tendency to deprave got my attention. To me, it was the most interesting thing since NASA put a man on the moon. I loved Tony Palmer's book on the trial and Richard Neville's *Play Power* was a mine of information on counterculture. I read whatever underground books I could find – Timothy Leary's *The Politics of Ecstasy* was a good one (I had to buy two copies as one got confiscated in English class), though I think I only understood a quarter of it. I shared my interest with one of my new schoolfriends, Phil Sturgess. We became co-conspirators and underage drinkers.

Meanwhile, I took to the playing fields of King's with an unusual enthusiasm and gusto only to discover I was crap at rugby too. It made no sense. How were you expected to get to the other end when you could only pass the ball backwards? I was not alone in my failure to be sporty and soon new friendships were formed among my fellow aesthetes. We were looked upon as malingerers, conscientious objectors or boys who were lacking in moral fibre, and attracted disdain from the many tracksuited, be-whistled games masters.

This was a grammar school, after all, as its carefully trimmed cricket pitch at the front and its not quite as carefully trimmed muddy rugby fields at the back gave testament. The teachers were always called 'Sir' – even the token woman was called Mrs 'Sir' Schofield. They swanned around in those long black robes that are usually topped off with the daft mortar-board headgear, like something out of 'The Bash Street Kids'. My school world consisted of underground toilets and changing rooms, used mostly for illicit smoking; long corridors with worn wooden floors that gave off a mingled smell of sweat and floor polish, and signs forbidding running in the corridor. This was an institution of learning and its rules and timetables, marked out by the ringing of an electric bell, had to be obeyed at all times.

There was a sixth-form common room with a record player and Pop Art posters on the walls. But that was out of bounds to the likes of me. The older boys strolled around in their ex-RAF greatcoats with copies of Cream's *Disraeli Gears*, *Led Zeppelin III* or *Deep Purple in Rock* under their arms. The album sleeves, concealing their homework, were boldly displayed like tribal markings; hair daringly strayed over their collars. Parkas were so last year, and I had never even got to have one. I took an instant dislike to these older boys with their show-off ways. I decided there and then that I would never ever like Cream or Deep Purple – I was undecided about Led Zeppelin. I felt it was a matter of principle. The greatcoat-wearers were posers, fakers – the enemy.

Another of my new friends, Kim Macintyre, had an older brother, Bert. In the course of going round to Kim's house for tea, I visited Bert in his room. It was a revelation. He had decorated his walls with pages from wallpaper sample books and on the floor were neat stacks of *NME*s from the last three years, all carefully placed in chronological order. Bert was trying to perfect the 'schizophrenic hair style', short on one side, long on the other, with a matching wispy half-beard and moustache. I liked Bert. He had a proper stereo set up there too, and stacked against the wall was his album collection. After a bit of album flicking, he placed his selection on the turntable and we were treated to a bit of Zappa's *We're Only in it for the Money*. Some Captain Beefheart and a bit of the Velvet Underground and Nico followed. It was not the weird unlistenable, impenetrable noise that I was expecting – this was all right. The sleeves were brilliant. I resolved there and then to get a proper stereo. There was no way you could appreciate such fine recordings on the old black box that wasn't even stereo. I put my mithering hat on and set to work.

My family were easily persuaded, surprisingly, and one Saturday afternoon we visited Hodgson's in Chestergate and returned home with an ITT Hi-Fidelity Stereo. It was like so much of the 1970s generally: brown and orange in colour. The siting of this new source of musical wonderment was controversial. That it was to be placed in my (and Dad's) bedroom was not what my mother had envisaged but that was where it was going. I put the speakers as far apart as they would go. One balanced on the wardrobe, the other hanging on the windowsill, brown wires trailing everywhere. 'The Locomotion' and 'Return to Sender' had never sounded better.

I needed to expand my collection, though, which meant that I started doing more jobs in Dad's office at the weekends. This mostly involved stapling the brochures together and then arranging them into categories. I was not exactly fastidious in my work but got paid anyway. As soon as I had amassed enough cash, I was back at Hodgson's.

The cellar was done out like some hippie dungeon and this was where the vinyl of interest was. With northern soul blaring from the speakers, I commenced to browse the sleeves.

The flicking through a stack of 12-inch cardboard and plastic, the searching for one title only to let another catch your eye, the perusing of the sleevenotes, the filing for future reference or the spontaneous purchase – this was what most of my teenage years were made of. You can do all that online now at yer iTunes and Amazon or whatnot now, but honestly – and I know I sound like an old twat here – it doesn't come close to the physicality of holding something real and somehow alive in your grubby mitts, getting it neatly put in a logo-emblazoned paper bag and then stalking off home to see if what you'd spent your last pennies on was pure gold or diabolical garbage. Sometimes it's hard to tell the difference.

Here I was then, making my first trawl through the stock. So much to choose from. I must have gone through everything three or four times, much to the annoyance of Barry the proprietor and his regular paying customers. Finally I made my selection: Hawkwind, *In Search of Space*. How could such an amazing sleeve fail to contain spectacular music? I took it to the counter only to discover to my embarrassment that I had underestimated the extent of my funds; I was ten new pence short. Blaming decimalisation and the poor standard of teaching for the eleven-plus, I returned Hawkwind to the correct alphabetical location. I was determined not to leave empty-handed. I felt everyone was looking at me and I grabbed the first thing my eye fell on that was within my price range.

This was how I ended up with Melanie Safka's *Gather Me* in my nascent record collection. History credits this as Melanie's magnum opus, but it wasn't really what I was after at the time. I pretended it was for my sister and left annoyed with myself. That 'Brand New Key' track was catchy though. It was the inspiration for the Wurzels' 'Combine Harvester'.

I resolved to increase my brochure-stapling productivity and a few weeks later, with increased confidence and finance, I sauntered down into Barry's dingy vault of 12-inch vinyl and coolly made my exit, Hawkwind firmly under my arm. I was in business.

You get a lot of talk such as 'Oh I heard this record/that band and it/they changed my life.' I suppose *In Search of Space* did that for me.

Not straight away, in a blinding, flashing 'now I am different' moment, but subtly in a drip-drip-drip way. I loved everything about that record. The sleeve was fantastic – the way it opened up like a puzzle box adorned with weird spacey graphics and a picture of what was clearly a naked girl on the inside. It came complete with a book, more a pamphlet really or a manifesto of sorts. 'The Hawkwind Log' was full of more freaky pictures and a lot of words. I had no idea what half of it was about but I was intrigued. What could it all mean? The music, though, that got me pretty quickly – swirly, swooping, spacey synthesisers and a driving rhythm. I had no idea what instruments were making the sound. I just knew I liked it. And I wanted more of it. I think I had decided that I wanted to be a hippie. I was thirteen.

Rock replaced plastic and glue as my principal obsession. I absorbed as much as I could. No rock-based fact, however far fetched, was too small to waste. I soaked up every drop of its minutiae. This was something worth learning about.

Albums by Zappa, the Faces, the Velvet Underground, the MC5, Neu! and Faust followed in a regular routine of stapling then off to the record shop to spend the cash. I had become a reader of *Sounds*, a weekly music paper. I preferred *Sounds* to the *NME* because it smelt better. A new copy of *Sounds* had an aroma all its own, some sort of nutmeggy smell, and every Thursday morning started with a good sniff of a fresh copy of *Sounds*. I wasn't alone in this. A few of my classmates were picking up on the same sort of stuff at the same time, and album lending and music criticism became the main topic of conversation, that and Monty Python. My friend Phil took to wearing black Chelsea boots and the widest flared trousers you could get without being pulled up by King's thought police. Very snazzy. With his hair daringly over the collar length prescribed by the school's strict dress code and his black-framed specs, Phil already looked like a card-carrying member of the Beat Generation. We both aspired to be older and cooler.

I desperately wanted a black polo-neck shirt but such things were not available in Macclesfield, or anywhere else in my size according to my mother (my stylist at the time). Never much of an existentialist, my mum.

I would go round to Phil's house, where we would try our best to look bohemian while trying to understand what people saw in jazz. We'd listen to Sonny Stitt and Rahsaan Roland Kirk and wonder was it any good. I'd heard enough jazz to know, mind you, and nothing had impressed me. That was the downside to having a record player in a bedroom shared with your dad. My father's record collection suddenly bloomed in parallel with my own. Where did he get it all from? I think he'd had most of it stashed with Uncle Johnny at Cedar Grove, just waiting for an opportunity to smuggle it into the house unnoticed by my mother. Well, that opportunity had arrived. When cancer claimed Johnny, the contents of Cedar Grove were decanted into the office and then, in dribs and drabs, smuggled into our bedroom.

There was more Duke Ellington than you could shake a stick at, Count Basie, Ella Fitzgerald, Art Tatum, Stéphane Grappelli, Jack Teagarden, Johnny Hodges . . . you get the idea. The biggest problem for me was the only time Dad could realistically listen to this was first thing in the morning before he departed on his travels. It became a kind of diabolical alarm clock. Bessie Smith may well be the best female blues singer ever but I doubt that she ever sang that early. Six in the morning without fail (well, eight at weekends), he would crank up the volume and all possibility of sleep was gone.

To me, my dad's music was all noise and not in a good way. I could have kept quiet about it, but I didn't. It was the old 'you call that music, it's rubbish!' argument that has raged since time immemorial. It could be quite ferocious.

Now, in the twenty-first century, I can listen to one of my daughters' latest musical obsessions and recognise where its inspirations lie. In the same way, she somewhat reluctantly listens to one of my songs from the good old days and admits that it does sound very much like ********'s latest (band name deleted to avoid embarrassment). There was no such common ground between my father's and my musical inclinations. At the time it was a fact of life: whatever your parents liked, you hated; whatever your parents wore, you hated. There was a sonic Berlin Wall between us. My side faced the future, his the pre-war past.

Listening to LPs was one thing, the whole experience of actually seeing a band live was another. Bert told tales of seeing Frank Zappa and Pink Floyd at the Free Trade Hall in Manchester. These, combined with the gig reviews in *Sounds*, convinced me I was missing out on something. I desperately needed to find out what it was.

'Can I go and see a band? On my own?'

'No you can't!'

I tried to explain all the plus points of allowing me to swan off on my own to Manchester for a night of musical entertainment but I was having a hard time being convincing. So I settled for repetition.

'Please can I go and see a band?'

It became a war of attrition. 'Something's Gotta Give', as Ella Fitzgerald was often heard singing at sunrise in our house, was my inspiration and my torment.

Finally an accommodation was reached. It was to be trial by gig. My father would take me to see one of his bands and I'd take him to see one of mine. How this contest was to be judged or what the prize might be were two of the finer points we never ironed out. Before he had a chance to change his mind or introduce other terms and conditions, I dug out the latest copy of *Sounds* and turned to the concert listings. Truthfully it wouldn't have mattered who it was. I just wanted to see a live rock band, any band would have done, Van der Graaf Generator, Wishbone Ash, Pink Floyd or Jethro Tull. Well, no, not just any band. What I wanted was something with a bit of depth. Some honest to goodness hip credentials. Some counterculture resonance, heroes from the pages of *It* and *Oz.* They had to be hip.

That Mel Bush has a lot to answer for.

On the evening of the 17 March 1972, the entire Morris household prepared itself for a night out. Mum and Dad were done up as if they were off to a gala dinner at the town hall while me and Amanda felt the casual look more appropriate. We set off in the Austin Maxi for the Free Trade Hall in Manchester, for that was the venue for tonight's entertainment, and providing that entertainment were Hawkwind with Status Quo as the support.

I think Mum and Dad started getting a bit nervy when they got a look at the rest of the paying customers in the bar.

'Look at the state of him, Cliff. My God.'

'What's that smell, is that marryjewarana?'

'I think that's patchouli oil, Dad.' I tried to sound reassuring as we took our seats on the balcony, a safe distance away from the stage.

Status Quo back then were not the national treasures they are today, though to be honest they didn't sound that much different. Back then they were thought of as a bit of a greaser band, not that this would have made the slightest difference to my parents' opinion of them.

'Are the next lot going to be that loud?' enquired my mother during the interval, searching her handbag for more cotton wool to stuff in her ears. She could have had a mountain of this stuff and it still wouldn't have deadened the aural assault that was to follow.

Hawkwind were fantastic – I don't know what I was expecting but they were everything I thought a rock band would be. Pounding drums, thrashing guitars and a couple of elves hunched over synthesisers that resembled the supermarket tills of tomorrow. There was even a sax. The light show was hypnotic with strobes and projectors flashing cosmic colours. The speaker cabinets and bass drums were painted with fluorescent, futuristic glyphs like the controls of some trippy UFO. I was transfixed, engulfed as the music just flowed from one barrage of sound to another without stopping. There was no 'and now here's one from our new album' like there had been with Quo. No, this was a million times better than the album. It was relentless. What respite there was came in the form of doomy, echoey, sci-fi poetry about spaceships and such.

My mother's attention was by now more focused on the audience's response to the sonic onslaught. A couple of guys commenced head-banging in time-honoured fashion with hair flaying wildly. Mother feared some sort of seizure was in progress. This really was brilliant.

Things reached a peak when Stacia, Hawkwind's scantily clad dancer, took to the stage. After a bit of wild gyrating accompanied by a frantic beat and some echoey sax honkings, the statuesque Stacia, bathed in strobe light, commenced to strip off what little she had on. This shock was too much for Mum and Amanda. They exited the hall faster than you could say 'Bad Trip Man'. Clifford lingered for a few minutes more before he too felt it necessary to beat a hasty retreat. The killjoys! Eventually it became clear to me that unless I fancied a long walk back to Macc, I had better join them.

My 'Well, that was good, wasn't it?' went down even worse than Hawkwind and we drove home in silence, if you discount the ringing in our ears. My first proper gig; my parents' last. It made a big impression on me.

The sound of Hawkwind could also be heard at the dead of night in the normally tranquil pastures in the vicinity of my house. I had discovered music on the move. On a battered Sanyo recorder, Bert and I would take cassettes of Can, Terry Riley, Stockhausen – the weirdest noises we could think of – and would venture out into the fields at twilight (we always forgot to take a torch). We would play these sounds as loud as possible to the bovine audience as some sort of experiment. Maybe we were trying to attract passing UFOs? What happened mostly was we got cold and lost in the dark, and had to hitch a lift home.

One time, though, we were ambushed from the self-same glade where, years earlier, I had tried to build a den. Like the troll in 'Three Billy Goats Gruff', a couple of young farmers decided we were trespassing and were ripe for a good kicking. You read about these things, but never think they'll happen to you. Not in a field in the middle of nowhere. Obviously, they were not late-night music lovers.

It is curious that the seeming idyll of rural pasture at dusk should attract so many young people indulging in bizarre pastimes such as bovine DJing, flying-saucer spotting, stickleback fishing, ghost hunting or just general trouble hunting. The seemingly empty fields were filled with possibilities conjured up by the dwindling light.

As neither of the combating parties had any form of illumination apart from the stars and the cloud-covered moon, it was soon obvious that the trading of blows was not going to solve anything. Bert and I were incompetent pugilists and our attackers seemed unaccustomed to the art of the moonlit punch-up. We did a bit of confused wrestling and futile punch throwing, accompanied by the traditional shouting of insults.

Then we legged it into the gloom, stumbling over hedges and barbed-wire fences, becoming completely lost in the process.

I replaced the batteries that had fallen out of the cassette player in our battle. And accompanied by the strains of Can's 'Augmn' and 'You Doo Rite' and, appropriately enough, Riley's 'Poppy Nogood and the Phantom Band', we picked our way through a minefield of cowpats until we reached a road. It was very late and there was not a car to be seen. On a country B-road at the dead of night in the seventies, this was only to be expected.

Unlikely as it sounds, we were eventually rescued by a minibus full of semi-pissed cleaning ladies on their way home from a cleaning-ladies convention.

'Where y'off to, lads? Hop in.'

The ladies were giggly and confused by our hastily concocted explanation that we were out doing a spot of night fishing.

'Where's your rods then?' one shouted from the back.

'Ooh, get your tackle out, lads.'

'Put yer radio on and let's have a sing-song.'

Hitching in the 1970s was the most common method of getting from A to B for the skint and wheel-less. It was also a great way to meet weird fuckers – grey, sleazy geezers mostly. Getting picked up by the ladies in the minibus was the first time I'd ever been given a lift in a vehicle containing members of the opposite sex. Hitching was risky and asking for trouble, particularly if I was on my own, which I usually was, but I was young, so of course I thought I was immortal and knew better than everyone else.

What I wanted more than anything was to get away from Macclesfield and go somewhere where things happened. Manchester – things happened there. Or even London – things definitely happened there all right. I'd read the books.

5

LITTLE DRUMMER BOY

Whatever next?

Three weeks after the Hawkwind debacle I was back at the Free Trade
Hall again to see David Bowie. This time I played it safe and went
with Phil for company.

I'd first heard of David Bowie back in 1969 at the height of my
space-travel frenzy. Like Telstar, 'Space Oddity' seemed to me the best
record ever made. I remember feeling very disappointed when, despite
appearing on *Crackerjack*, the song failed to get to number one. I began
to suspect that the pop charts might be rigged in some way.

The bits of Bowie that I'd heard were either from the *Space Oddity* LP or tracks off *Hunky Dory* that were getting played on late-night radio, mostly by John Peel. He'd play 'Queen Bitch' on *Sounds of the Seventies*. The singles 'Oh You Pretty Things' and 'Changes' both got regular plays on the way to school on the Tony Blackburn breakfast show of all things. Bowie must be good, I reasoned, because he went on about the Velvet Underground and Andy Warhol in interviews in the music papers. He was weird (he'd worn a dress on one of his album covers and that qualified him as weird in the eyes of most folk) and I liked weird. I wasn't sure if he was folky weird, poppy weird or rocky weird. He was, of course, a bit glam but everybody was in 1972. If you didn't wear glitter, eyeliner and stack-heeled boots you were nobody.

The gig was a bit different from Hawkwind; there was a space connection but not a full-on sonic and visual onslaught. He made a strobe-lit entry accompanied by 'Ode to Joy' from *A Clockwork Orange*. Bowie, with his flame-red hair and glittery turquoise jumpsuit, was exciting in a completely different way to the stoned sonic attack of Hawkwind.

I'd never watched a proper rock axeman (that's what they called guitarists in those days) in action before and Mick Ronson had all the moves down pat as he played at trying to steal the limelight from Bowie. Apart from the Jacques Brel solo acoustic bit in the middle, this definitely felt like a band, not a singer with a bunch of backing musicians.

Which got me thinking. What was a band exactly? What were these people actually like when they weren't on stage. What did they do? Did Mick Ronson playfully run off with David's cup of tea? Did they all live together in a tower block, like in *A Clockwork Orange*? Was Trevor Bolder the bass player's two-pronged beard real or was it stuck on with glue, only to be removed in the quiet of a dressing room after the performance? After the show were they whisked off to sophisticated parties where they would be plied with champagne and courted by hot and cold running groupies? Bowie's much confessed bisexuality made this all the more fascinating. They all looked as if they'd come from the future and as it was a look that didn't involve having hair down to your armpits, I thought I could get away with looking a bit like that at home/school. OK, maybe not the red dye and the make-up and the jumpsuit and that, but . . .

Hawkwind, I thought, must live on some sort of a cosmic farm somewhere in the depths of the country where they made their own amps and brewed their own acid, jamming the day away in a Day-Glo strobe-filled barn until they got busted by the pigs or someone, Stacia probably, told them that tea was ready and they'd better knock off the drugs for a bit, they'd been cosmic enough for one day. How this music stuff actually got turned into a record intrigued me.

I would lie on my bed listening to the German band Faust's beautiful, totally transparent first album and wonder where had this music come from and how had it actually been created and by whom? There were snippets of the Beatles' 'All You Need Is Love' and the Stones' 'Satisfaction' – how did they end up in there?

Did those songs happen to be on the radio when Faust were recording something else and they got accidentally mixed in? Or did they have the ability to mimic the sound of any band at will, like a musical Mike Yarwood? Maybe the Beatles and the Stones actually popped into Faust's studio one day for a cup of tea and got roped into proceedings.

Was this actually the work of a band at all or was it some Teutonic supercomputer program that churned the stuff out?

I bought the single 'Starman' from the stall in the bar at Bowie's gig and played it to death for the rest of the weekend, especially the B-side 'Suffragette City'. I decided that I was going to buy everything that David Bowie had ever done as soon as I could get enough cash. Oh, and I started smoking so as to appear sophisticated. But I think that was Phil's idea.

Ziggy Stardust came out in June 1972. It had only been two months since the Free Trade Hall gig but it felt like an eternity of waiting for Bowie's newest record. I could now re-experience the gig over and over again. I saw Bowie every time he played Manchester after that. Every time the crowd got bigger, until the one in June 1973, just after *Aladdin Sane* came out, which was full of screaming girls who were probably about to become Bay City Rollers fans. I'd seen Faust the night before and suspected Bowie might be 'selling out', the ultimate rock crime. He'd gone from cool rock star to teen idol in just over a year. Whether this was a crime or not was usually pronounced by the *NME*.

Ziggy, though was one of *those* records. An instant classic. From the drum intro of 'Five Years' to last chord of 'Rock and Roll Suicide', it was (and still is) perfection. He was singing about the same things I was feeling. By the end of 1972, Lou Reed's *Transformer* had been released. That Bowie-Ronson production, along with *Ziggy*, convinced me that David and Mick were total geniuses.

As well as welcoming nicotine addiction, Phil and I had a few other ideas. Number one, obviously, was that we should start a band. Who in their right mind wanted a boring job sat in an office or a factory? The life of an underground counterculture noise merchant – that was where it was at. We could make a disturbing racket that people might mistake for art just as well as the next bunch of freaks. So why not join the revolution? We were hip cats. We knew the score.

Phil was saving up for a guitar. He'd already got a sax from some-where, on which he would produce convincing, honking, Zappa-type sounds. I'd given up on the clarinet. It really was bobbins – I, of course, blamed the instrument for this.

My main problem, I thought, was that most of the lessons were taken up by trying to teach me how to read music and count time. It was like learning to read before you could talk. I just wanted to be able to play a tune and quick! None of this C sharp F lark. I wanted to play avant-garde rock, not be constrained by outmoded musical conventions like the 'proper' notes and that shit.

I'd had a go on Phil's sax and I couldn't even get it to squawk. (I think Uncle Johnny may have been pulling my leg.) Maybe I should get a guitar as well, Phil suggested. *Absolutely*, I thought, forgetting my earlier disappointment, *I'd be good at that. Anyone could play a guitar. Just look at the vast number of guitarists there are. It's got to be easy.*

Our other idea was: 'Let's buy some pot and get stoned.'

There was this guy, Hobbo, a sort of friendly neighbourhood freak who hung around the school gates at going-home time, dressed in full freak get-up. A mangey brown fur coat, loon pants, long, lank greasy hair and the reek of patchouli about him. Phil had been sounding him out on the quiet and he reckoned that there was some good stuff turning up in the next couple of weeks, and that if we played our cards right, Hobbo could see us right.

Phil had said, 'Yes please, I'll have a fiver's worth of that,' and was now looking for someone to go halves on the deal.

Everyone knew that all the bands were stoned most of the time. This would be a way of finding out if a bit of pot smoking could give us some insight into how their collective minds worked. *Worth a try*, I thought, *got to try everything once, haven't you?* We acquired Rizla papers and Old Holborn tobacco, and set to learning the art of fag rolling. After a lot of burnt fingers and tobacco swallowing, Phil managed to get his roll-up qualifications first. My early attempts looked like badly made Christmas crackers. They burnt like a fuse of cartoon dynamite and my God they tasted awful.

One of the downsides, and there were many, to sharing a room with my father was the lack of any privacy. There was nowhere I could safely conceal anything illicit from my parents and, since the Hawkwind incident, I had the definite feeling that I was being eyed with suspicion. Funny looks over the marmalade at breakfast, that sort of thing. So Phil was going to have to handle the stashing of the goods. And as Phil's mum worked evenings at the Belgrade Hotel, his home was also the ideal venue for our drug-crazed experimentation.

Hobbo was almost as good as his word (a rare hippie characteristic) and we ended up with half of what was expected.

'There's been a big bust in Manchester, man. Don't tell anyone where you got this from, right,' he said as he palmed a lump of black stuff into Phil's eager clutches. We had scored!

'Don't worry about that,' I said, 'mum's the word,' and legged it in case the pigs were watching.

As soon as his mum's next shift rolled round, I was off to Phil's for 'tea'. As well as the hash, Phil had managed to get a quarter-bottle of Pernod from somewhere (we were sophisticated drinkers by now). After a couple of bath mugs of Pernod and water, we were off. Phil got out the £2.50 black lump and we studied it. What were you supposed to do with it? How much do you put in and, more to the point, how do you break the stuff up? We tried cutting off small chunks with a butter knife and rolling them up but they just fell out as soon as we went to light up.

Phil then remembered some of Hobbo's pre-sales mumblings. 'He said something about having to sweat it.'

'That's just hippie speak for don't worry,' I reasoned as Phil got out a Ronson lighter and applied a flame to the intransigent lump. 'Don't set fire to it, man! It won't work after it's been burnt. Stands to reason, it'll just be ash!'

To my amazement the stuff succumbed and in its heated state took on a crumblier texture. We soon had a prototype joint ready for lighting up.

'Best do a couple in case you get so you can't remember how to do another,' I suggested, which he did. Then, with a great sense of ceremony, he lit one up.

Quickly passing it to and fro like a frantic game of pass-the-parcel, our first number was soon burning our fingers. We tried fixing it on to a paper clip so as to extract the very last dregs from the thing. The roll-up disintegrated in the process.

We put on some Beefheart and waited.

'Can you feel anything yet?'

'Not really. I think my eyes have gone a bit fuzzy though.'

'Let's have the other one then.'

So we fired up number two and took this one at a slightly more relaxed pace.

'Christ, this stuff tastes a bit rough. It's like smoking carpet slippers. You don't think Hobbo's ripped us off, do you?'

This sounded like the most hilarious thing I'd ever heard in my life and I began laughing uncontrollably. Before long, the pair of us were collapsing in laughter. Another slug of the Pernod and Rahsaan Kirk was blasting out.

'Bloody hell, this track's good, man. I've never noticed them like little tinkly bits before. It's like . . .'

'Metal jelly?' I suggested.

'Yeah, metal jelly.' We fell about once more.

All the random parping and tootling that had seemed chaotic before was now the most natural thing in the world. It all made perfect sense – there was even a sort of melody to it.

'Quick, let's have another one before your mum gets back.'

I'd never imagined getting stoned would be like this. I'd thought that you would slip into a mild state of catatonia and experience visions of an otherworldly realm, possibly inhabited by pixies and fairies, like in 'Focus on Fact'. I had never thought it would be so bloody funny. For £2.50, or half of £2.50 to be pedantic, it was certainly value for money.

'No, let's save some for next week. We'd better get the windows open and let the smell out.'

So, still in the grip of hysterical laughter, we fiddled with the suddenly complex mechanism that controlled the opening of Phil's windows.

The chill night air brought with it the onset of mild paranoia.

'Your mum'll know we're stoned.'

'No, it'll be all right, she'll go straight to bed. S'long as we act normal we'll be fine.'

'What's normal?'

'Shit, I don't know. Do you?'

'How do you *act* normal?'

After some confused debate, we felt that normal ought to involve the making of some supper and we made our way cautiously into the kitchen. We were still there some time later, marvelling at the vivid blueness of the gas burning in the grill, when Phil's mum returned.

I tried not to look shifty wolfing down the most delicious cheese on toast I'd ever tasted, and I was off on the last bus back to Macc, wondering how the hell we'd managed to get away with that one. His mum never even raised an eyebrow.

I could now see why Hawkwind were probably smoking mountains of dope. It certainly made you think differently about things and music sounded ten times better than when you were straight. I even thought I finally understood what jazz was about, so I went and bought a Charlie Parker record. It sounded terrible.

So that was idea number two out of the way, and I think you could say it was an unbridled success. Now for idea number one . . .

The band scheme.

I'd mithered and cajoled my way into getting a guitar. I was hoping for a nice Strat or a Flying V but settled for an Arbiter six-string acoustic and a book by Bert Weedon called *Play in a Day*. That sounded promising so I got an Alan Lomax book of American folk songs so I would have something to play the following day. I had learned a valuable lesson from my experience with the Beatles' instrument and insisted that the bloke in the shop tuned the guitar before I left. He even chucked in something he called pitch pipes. I thought these were for playing along with, like a harmonica or something.

A day came and went and my knowledge of guitarmanship had not gone up in the slightest. *That book must be crap. It couldn't be me, could it?*

So I went to a guitar teacher on Saturday mornings. Perhaps he had a better book or some way of cheating. The first lesson consisted of learning the nursery rhyme/folk tune 'Bobby Shafto' and one chord. Still, once I'd got the hang of it I'd be on to something by the Who next. But no, it was just 'Bobby bloody Shafto' over and over again. This couldn't be right. It made my fingers hurt. I persevered.

But not for long. At school, I had discovered the dulcimer, a stringed instrument that was dead easy to play. It had three strings and made a lovely sound. It was acoustic and great for folky ballads – Joni Mitchell played one a lot – but not really rock and roll. I planned to put a pickup on it and, with an amp and distortion pedal, invent the world's first electric dulcimer. It turned out that using a hammer and nails on such a delicate instrument was not a great idea. I put its splintered remains away in a cupboard and never mentioned it to anyone at school.

The band idea, though, had got a bit of interest at school. Bert and his brother Kim (by now better known as Snot) were in and a couple of other lads, Mark Bolshaw and Mike Marshall, were very interested. Phil reckoned 'Axiom Kinetic Truths' would be a good name for our band, but when I pointed out it was a bit of a mouthful he was slightly miffed.

'Fine. I was thinking of using that for my first solo album anyway.'

Thinking up band names and song titles was something I did all the time. All of them were terrible but that didn't put me off – it made double chemistry go quicker.

Bert, I think it was, came up with the name 'The Sunshine Valley Dance Band' with the reasoning that such a harmless and whole-some-sounding name would enable us to get lots of bookings in totally unsuspecting straight places. It was subversive, he said.

'That sounds cool,' I said, but I didn't know what subversive meant. So 'The Sunshine Valley Dance Band' it was.

Taking advantage of Phil's mum and her night work once again, we settled on his residence as the venue for our first rehearsal/audition. One Saturday night, we set to work making a racket, and a fairly tuneless racket at that. To cut a long, boozy, tortuous story short, it was obvious that not only Phil but everyone present was a better guitarist than me, so I reverted to type and started banging things. His mum's pots and pans mostly.

'You can be the drummer,' was Phil's verdict, 'and you can apologise to my mum about the broken crockery.'

We got one song done and called it 'The Worm Song'. To call it a song may be going a bit far. A loud noise accompanied with shouting the word 'worms' is probably about right.

God bless Mrs Sturgess. There's weren't many people in those days who'd leave their house in the care of a bunch of lads with a collection of scrounged microphones, amps, guitars and beer. We did our best to tidy up but there was a degree of collateral damage. It was pretty obvious we'd have to find an alternative venue for any future rehearsals. And I'd have to figure out how you played the drums.

It was around this time that I first heard Van Der Graaf Generator. I'd seen the name about a lot in the *Manchester Evening News* gig ads. They always seemed to be on at the University or UMIST. That gave me the idea that they were a local band.

Van der Graaf Generator was an intriguing name for a band, and it made me wonder what the hell they sounded like. So I borrowed their second album off Bert and became a fan for life.

It was the drama in Van der Graaf's music that got me. That slightly insane melodrama. I loved their magnum opus, the twenty-three minute 'A Plague of Lighthouse Keepers'. It was the tale of a solitary lighthouse keeper losing his mind. Heavy stuff, in prog terms. They made a very raw and intense sound. Nothing as whimsical as Genesis or as trickily complicated as King Crimson, but still something quintessentially English. Their singer Peter Hammill had done a few solo records and these were even rawer and more minimal. I played his *Chameleon in the Shadow of the Night* daily – it was a very affecting record. (Yes, I'm well aware of how naff some prog titles sound today.) 'Music to accompany a nervous breakdown' was how one music paper described Van der Graaf. The darkness and depth of their sound is what drew me to them.

Van der Graaf also had an interesting drummer. I listened to Guy Evans's drumming on the records to see if I could figure out what he was playing, but just got confused. It was tricky and complicated. I'd never be able to do that.

Keith Moon was a more obvious inspiration – who wouldn't want to be Keith Moon? He was the world's most (in)famous rock drummer. But listening to Who records was no help either. I couldn't make head nor tail out of what was going in the Drum Dept.

I went to see the Who at the Belle Vue in Manchester and did my best to watch what Keith Moon did in person. It seemed mostly to involve acting as a human drumstick dispenser and juggler. Apart from that, it was a classic rock gig. Townshend's windmill guitar, Daltry lassooing the microphone, and an almost stationary John Entwistle. Keith Moon was exciting and entertaining to watch, an amazing drummer, but I was never going to be Keith Moon was I? There was only ever going to be one Keith Moon.

So instead I settled on Moe Tucker of the Velvet Underground as a musical inspiration. Then, if I ever got to be any good, maybe Jaki from Can or Guy from Van der Graaf. Hey, even Ringo had a couple of good riffs – just a couple.

Watching the Who did give me one idea, though: get plenty of drums and people will think you know what you're doing.

This was a common theory in the early seventies. All the top drummers had two bass drums. Added to that, I thought that the more drums you had the more likely it was that sooner or later you'd succeed in hitting one.

I began carefully studying the drummers that appeared on *TOTP* every week. The camera never seemed to linger on them for long, though, and it seemed to me that all they were doing was going 'boom-crack-boom, boom-crack' most of the time. I could do that – who couldn't? In fact, if you didn't overthink it, this drummer lark looked simple. Most of them seemed to play more or less the same beat whatever the tune. I tried banging out 'boom-crack-boom, boom-crack' on a table top – easy. There was none of that nonsense with six strings but only five fingers to put on them. None of the blowing and finger waggling and none of that play-a-C rubbish. Why did it always start with a C? Surely it should be an A. I knew my alphabet and the way it related to music made no sense to me at all. Not to mention all that sharp and flat codswallop. It seemed to me there was none of that convolution. Plus I'd never heard of a drummer going out of tune. Why had I never realised this before? It seemed perfect.

Instant gratification was what I was after and the way of the drummer seemed to promise that. However, there was the small matter of the equipment. I dug about in the old toy box looking for the Sooty kit. I knew it was tiny but it could be a good gimmick and you've got to have a gimmick (one of the first rules of showbiz, I'd been told). The bits of it that could be found were useless, completely wrecked. If I hadn't know, better I would have said it had been blasted by a shotgun at very close range, perhaps by a close relative, so that was a nonstarter.

It was going to be difficult to persuade my parents that I had finally found my musical calling after binning the clarinet and pestering them incessantly for a guitar, which now lay neglected and gathering dust in the corner of the bedroom. I would have to work like a demon, and be really nice and pleasant to everyone. Both things near impossible for a teenage boy in the 1970s.

My first attempts at putting the case for a percussion-based career met with a resounding 'No!' but that did not deter me. This was only to be expected. It would have to be another war of attrition.

I read interviews with famous stickmen (the 1970s percussive equivalent of an axeman) and picked up a couple of things. Mainly that drumming required dexterity or coordination – specifically ambidexterity at the very least. I got the impression that this was a skill easily mastered. Can you pat your head and rub your tummy at the same time? You can? Wallop, you're a drummer! I took to head patting/tummy rubbing at every opportunity. This then moved on to head patting/tummy rubbing while simultaneously tapping my feet. A little bit like dancing, but a more stationary kind that didn't involve women pretending to be men. The other thing that drumming required was the ability to count reliably.

'Don't worry, most of the time it's only up to four,' a pro drummer said in one of the interviews – hey, I could do that in French and German at a pinch.

Given that all you needed was a flat surface to hit, you could both practise drumming and annoy friends and relatives anytime, anywhere. Another win-win! Being a corner-cutting lazy bastard, I had found my musical medium.

6

ISOLATION

Hobbo, who we now referred to as 'the dealer' or more commonly 'the man', had gone missing from his usual school-gate skulking spots.

'Probably been busted,' we reckoned and this was hampering our quest for more mind-altering substances a little, but only a little. For Phil (again) somehow got hold of something called *MIMS – Monthly Index of Medical Specialities*. It was a medical guide for prescription medicines with colour pictures and descriptions of effects, side effects, dosage, etc. It was like an I-spy guide to DIY drug abuse. I would surreptitiously go through the bathroom cabinets at home searching for old pill bottles and then refer to this handy guide to see if there was anything worth nicking. Usually there wasn't, but *MIMS* made no mention of what could happen if they were combined with Pernod and sherry in large quantities, so there was the odd bit of blind testing. But nothing that came close to two quids' worth of hash.

There was another hipster type, called Adam, in our class, and he was a sort of off-and-on friend. His parents, so he told us, were fab-and-groovy types – his dad was an actual artist. Adam's problem, as far as I was concerned, was his fondness for Yes and the early works of Marc Bolan. Now, T. Rex were all right – 'Ride a White Swan', 'Jeepster', 'Get It On' were all great singles – but Bolan's first album,

My People Were Fair etc., was just airy-fairy nonsense. Adam wouldn't have it: Bolan was God as far as he was concerned and he wouldn't let me forget it. His other boast was that he had an actual real live girlfriend, who he claimed hung out with a bunch of 'really far-out guys'.

One morning he rolled into class, copy of *Prophet, Seers and Sages*, T. Rex's crap second album, under his arm, and starts up with this confession.

'You'll never guess what happened last night . . .'

Expecting some sort of sordid and highly improbable sexual revelations, I tried to appear disinterested. 'Not sure if I want to know actually.'

'I took a trip.'

'Oh yes, where to?'

'Outer space, man. Outer space!'

'Oh bullshit. Fuck off.'

'No, I went round to one of my bird's mates and he laid a trip on me. It was like cosmic, man.'

'No really, *fuck off.*'

'No it's true, man, I've still not come down.'

'Hey Phil, have you heard this? Adam's tripping.'

At which point Mr Newbold entered the room and we pretended to be interested in the conjugation of French verbs.

Break time came and Adam was at it again.

'It was really cosmic, this lamp turned into a planet and we flew into it. Totally cosmic.' Cosmic was Adam's favourite adjective. Not at all tiresome. 'It was full of these weird creatures that could talk just by thinking. All green-and-purple-coloured they were.'

'You got any more of it then?'

'No . . . but Charlie's going up to Manchester next week to score. He'll get some for you.'

'Could he get us some pot as well?' I asked hopefully.

Even if he couldn't, just the acid on its own would be great.

I did think it a little odd that Adam's psychedelic adventure didn't sound much like the ones described in the books of Tim Leary. Perhaps it was some really strong stuff and, anyway, he did say he was still out of it. I found it a little suspicious and didn't expect much to come of it.

My plans to become a drummer hadn't exactly set the world on fire either. I'd borrowed a pair of sticks (which allegedly used to belong to Woody Woodmansey from the Spiders from Mars), bought the Gene Krupa *Drum Method* book – which almost made sense – and was tapping away on the settee in the hope I would get taken seriously. I trawled through the *Manchester Evening News* classifieds and the small ads in *Melody Maker* and *Sounds*, hoping to find some drums in my price range – free to ridiculously cheap – but they all seemed a bit on the expensive side.

I'd started paying even more attention to the drumming on records and at gigs. I'd seen Buddy Rich on TV – the greatest drummer in the world, they said. I thought he was just an arrogant show-off. He sounded like an angry man urgently rolling a barrel full of marbles down a never-ending flight of stairs. There was no way I was going to be doing any of that stuff. Besides, it looked too much like hard work. No, to me the most interesting drummers were the ones who kept it simple like Jaki Liebezeit or Moe Tucker. I didn't like the showing-off thing. Even back then, I figured the drummer's job was to hold the band together, not to stand out. It's a thankless task but someone's got to do it.

My mother was still laughing sceptically at my plans for a career in 'music'.

'You? In a band? You couldn't say boo to a goose! You'd be home in no time. You never wear that nice check shirt I bought you . . .'

My father wasn't impressed with my new choice of instrument either.

'Drummers, Stephen, I've never met a sane one yet. They all end up taking morphine and drinking absinthe, rotting their brains. You don't want to end up like that, do you?'

'No,' I lied, 'but it's all different nowadays,' hoping he had forgotten the Hawkwind gig, which he hadn't. I wheedled and I cajoled, I wouldn't give it a rest. I told him I was saving up and I'd even started selling off some naffish records to raise a bit of cash. (These naff records were a result of me misunderstanding the terms of the Britannia Music Club. I had been lured into membership by the opening offer of free albums, and expected our relationship to remain on those terms for the rest of time. But they started sending me shit ones that I was expected to pay for every month. Always read the small print.)

As part of the deal to accomplish my percussion purchase, I found it best that I keep my end of the gig deal and show an interest in my father's musical heritage. I had still not been forgiven for Hawkwind.

Keeping my end of the bargain, I was taken by my father, twice, to the Southport Floral Hall (quite a journey from Macclesfield; well, it was with my Dad driving). First it was to see Count Basie and His Orchestra, and then a few weeks later Marlene Dietrich. Count Basie was all right, a lot better than I expected, to be honest, but I really thought Marlene Dietrich was fantastic. She was getting on a bit but she still had that charisma. A pre-war Berlin decadent chanteuse vibe, all in gold lamé and top hat and tails. A kind of Nico for the old folks. She was undeniably a star that refused to fade, transcending the showbiz cliché shit.

I had to admit to Clifford that I had enjoyed both gigs more than I expected, but especially Marlene's.

I love that quote of hers: 'Do you think this is glamorous? That it's a great life and that I do it for my health? Well it isn't. Maybe once, but not now.'

I only wish I'd read it sooner.

*   *   *

Meeting girls was a large incentive in considering rock music as a possible career path. The problem was that I had noticed that most of my fellow gig-goers back in the seventies were men.

Unsurprisingly, females didn't seem to like the music of Frank Zappa. They certainly didn't like Captain Beefheart and, so my friends told me, they didn't like Emerson, Lake and Palmer or Yes much either. You can't really blame them for that though, can you?

'Girls buy singles, boys buy triple concept albums,' some record exec once said (probably). He was a man (definitely).

OK, maybe I am stereotyping a bit here. In fact, 'glam rock' had its fair share of female devotees, especially in the Roxy/Ferry genre (the roots of part of punk and new romanticism, I reckon). I once threw myself into the carriage of the last train back to Macc and found it proudly occupied by a troop of beguiling sirens heading home from the Roxy night at Pips, looking for the most part like they had just escaped from a mild 1940s air-raid drinks party (if there was such a thing) with the odd pink-satin-tie-wearing spiv in tow. Having just legged it from a Van der Graaf Generator gig, I was shunned. Even lighting up the old black and gold Sobranie (usually a guaranteed conversation starter) failed to impress.

The ladies love a uniform and I was in the wrong one.

Earlier that evening at the Van der Graaf gig, I had been in the Manchester Uni bar and been struck by how everybody – absolutely everybody – was dressed identically. Long hair, flared denim, Afghan coats and a reek of patchouli. These were not exclusively fans of Van der Graaf, but run-of-the-mill student types. No one had anything remotely original about their appearance.

Now, owing to my being an underachiever in the education department, the bars of universities were foreign to me, so this nonconformist conformity was a bit of a surprise. Mind you so was the price of the drinks. If I had known that study was the route to cheap booze for a few years, I would have tried harder.

It was no surprise that my visit to this haven of cheap booze and patchouli was short-lived. I was kicked out for not being studenty enough. I had that effect on places of learning. Maybe my face just didn't fit in this identikit crowd.

My fellow late-night smoky train travellers, on the other hand, were at least making an effort at sophistication and that was beguiling. Why hadn't I noticed that before?

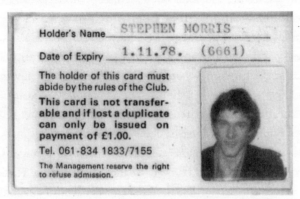

I was very proud of the 6661 membership number.
What were the rules again?

Back at home around 1973 there was a bit of an upheaval brewing. Clifford's tap peddling had been going great guns and it was decided that we were moving to somewhere closer to his office. No. 52 Ivy Lane, a large detached Georgian house with a big back garden complete with an ornamental pond full of fish and frogs, was a mansion compared to Gawsworth Road. Although it didn't have the same proximity to the countryside and wayward cattle, it did have a good number of bedrooms. A room of my own!

Well, it was more like a large cupboard than a room, and was stuck under the eaves of the house. I installed the hi-fi and my record collection, and set to decorating what wall space there was with a couple of Dalí prints and a Peter Hammill poster.

Privacy at last. What could possibly go wrong?

Well, maybe the acid. Oh yeah. That.

Unsurprisingly, Adam's mate Charlie was a dead loss in the supply-ing of drugs, his wheels let him down, he was waiting for a shipment from St Ives, there'd been a big bust in Manchester . . . I wondered if this Charlie wasn't Adam's imaginary friend.

The coffee shops of Soho were notoriously lively places for young people to hang out, everyone knew that, and Macclesfield had a few similar establishments. Well, they sold coffee. There was the Cavendish Café on Queen Victoria Street, the Chicken Spit in the Market Place and the Wimpy Bar in the Grosvenor Centre. The Wimpy had the advantage of large windows on two sides that gave a good view of any approaching prefects, teachers or parents, giving the illicit smoker ample time to stub out their fag, hide the ashtray, waft away any linger-ing smoke and start furiously sucking a Polo mint.

We would sit there, despondent and bored, pouring sugar into our frothy coffee (don't think they were called cappuccinos then, not in Macc), seeing whose would sink the fastest. We'd not seen hide nor hair of Hobbo for weeks and were beginning to fear the worst. To keep ourselves chemically entertained, we'd been indulging in the drinking of cough medicine in a big way: you had to drink a lot of it and it wasn't that much fun really. But you've got to make an effort, haven't you? We spent our time trying to figure out the optimum dose of Phensedyl and settled on two bottles of the stuff as a minimum for any sort of buzz. This would mean going in to Boots and asking for four bottles at a time.

'It's for me gran, she suffers terribly with a cough, especially in this weather.'

This implausible yarn unsurprisingly worked only once. After that we had to branch out to other chemists to score our linctus.

One day the clouds parted, the sun came out and an unmistakable rancid-fur-coat wearing, lank-greasy-haired individual was sighted by the Post Office and heading our way. Hobbo was back in business with some fresh stuff.

We got two microdots off Hobbo. Unlike Adam's illusive 'Charlie', Hobbo was the man. So at last we had the stuff, but it was a bit like owning a very tiny bomb. What if we had it and turned into raving lunatics and tried peeling our faces off with a cheese grater? This could happen, apparently, so we decided to wait until we were presented with a nice calm, relaxed environment, with no possibility of bad vibes of any kind.

We gave it a week, then thought, *Fuck it, let's go to the rugby club disco and have it there.*

It was the best Saturday night I'd ever had. The DJ's three flashing lights were as spectacularly vivid as anything I'd ever seen (how did he get those colours?). And some of those present did occasionally appear to have heads like dogs' (I'd been looking at the cover of Genesis's *Foxtrot* before I came out, so that may have had something to do with it). I found this extremely interesting, as was the inevitable brawl when it started up. It was like a piece of performance art. I stood mesmerised by the fighting, grinning like a fool, skipping out of the way of the bits of glass that came flying in my direction leaving vibrant vapour trails in their wake.

When the police arrived, their blue light gave an extra stroboscopic dimension to the light show, but as most of the other punters were being dragged off in the direction of their van, I felt it best to make an exit. I spent the rest of the night trying to light a cig off a Belisha beacon. Brilliant, and I'd only had half a tab. When I finally made it to my new bedroom, glad that Dad's nightly display of snoring prowess now took place elsewhere, I still found sleep elusive so I let myself be entertained by the flashing colours that were now being projected on the inside of my eyelids. The only downside to the trippy experience seemed to be that it did go on for a very long time, and by the time sleep and I renewed our acquaintance, I was getting a bit bored of it all.

Still, excellent value for money (25p). I would be getting some more of this. You needed plenty of time for tripping so weekends were best, but it didn't stop me having a quarter of a tab at school to see if it livened up English and Geography classes. It didn't. Nothing would.

I think my problem was, and probably still is, that I don't like being told what to do. Even if I know that what I'm being told is right, I will take against it instinctively because it has come as an instruction. Christ Church had been fun because it had been education through play most of the time. Things were different at King's. I did my best to try and learn their way but it was not for me. I'm not trying to say I was a great rebel or anything – perish the thought. I just hated the authority that said, 'This is the way it is and you will obey or be classed a fool.' I didn't mind being a fool in their eyes. To me, their days were numbered anyway.

Finally the great day arrived in our new house and I became the proud owner of a brand new Olympic drum kit. I set it up in the front room and set to bashing it. I didn't know if it sounded any good or not, but it was really good fun hitting it. Well, it was for me. The rest of the Morris household were less amused.

'Stop that racket will you' and 'If you think you're leaving it there you've got another think coming' was my mother's initial reaction. 'Put it in your bedroom and out of the way.'

The bedroom was already a bit claustrophobic, and once the drum kit got shoehorned in, there was no room to swing a cat. Eventually a compromise was reached: during the day the drums could be installed in Dad's room. He wasn't there most of the time so couldn't grumble. What was there was the physical embodiment of one of my father's eccentricities. He had long been interested in keeping fit but now the extra space in the new house had given him the opportunity to acquire various gizmos: a jogging machine, an exercise bike and a chin-up bar. He performed his morning exercise routine to the sound of Ellingtonia or big band stuff blasting out of his own music system and rousing the rest of us.

He also developed an odd obsession with time. His bedroom was home to at least three alarm clocks and he took to wearing two watches – maybe he found the ticking restful or reassuring in some way.

As soon as the Duke's dawn chorus was over, I would carefully squeeze out of my bed and begin to clear clatteringly the forest of cymbals and drums that blocked my way to the bathroom. It was a fire hazard, a health-and-safety nightmare. The process would be reversed every night, with a crash-bang-wallop as I moved the kit back into my tiny room. I would then climb over it to get to sleep. If nothing else, it was good practice for roadie-ing, but I got the feeling that I was still sharing too much of my life with my dad.

The drum lessons I had (there's always a catch) were actually fun. A lovely bloke called David Greenwood came round once a week. For his day job, he played with the Hallé Orchestra and did percussion teaching on the side. He spent half the time trying to teach me stuff called rudiments and, for the other half, things would just degener-ate into a rambling drum jam session. The pair of us bashing away would sometimes attract an audience of passing dog walkers who would shout up at the window such praise as, 'For God's sake, give it a rest!' or 'Where's the Indians?'

These were my sort of lessons – not much learning and a lot of messing about. I think Mr Greenwood enjoyed them as much as I did, but he did tend to leave a trail of fag ash on the carpet, which didn't go down too well with my mother.

Still, I felt I was getting the hang of the drumming lark. I could hold down a pretty steady beat and chuck a few rolls in here and there. That seemed about as much as most drummers did, so I felt quite pleased with myself. By now, I was paying very close attention to Jaki

Liebezeit's drumming. It seemed really simple but complicated at the same time, and I would try to work out the riff to Can's 'Yoo Do Rite' or 'Oh Yeah' whenever I got a chance. I was also taken by the drums on Captain Beefheart's stuff, especially *Trout Mask Replica*. This was essential listening for the serious teenage male music fan. On first listen, most people dismiss this album as unlistenable shit, but to the Beefheart scholar/true believer it is a work of primitive genius. I had no idea at the time who the drummer on this record was as there was no credit on the album sleeve. At the time I supposed this was just one of Beefheart's wackyisms – perhaps the drumming was done by a passing child? Years later, I found out that the drummer was John French aka Drumbo, and his name had been removed from the sleeve due to some disagreement with the Captain – how showbiz, how trite. Anyway, I thought whoever he or she was doing the drumming was bonkers, and I did my best to play something that sounded a bit like 'Moonlight on Vermont' or 'The Blimp'. (In fact, Sunshine Valley Dance Band rehearsals sounded chaotically similar to *Trout Mask*.)

I decided that I liked German drummers best and, as well as Jaki, I listened to Klaus Dinger from Neu! for bits I could copy. The more repetitive and insistent the better. Bands from Germany – Can, Neu!, Amon Düül II, Tangerine Dream, Kraftwerk – were the most interesting. I liked their politics, their approach to the business of music, and that most of them were trying to create something entirely new that didn't rely on England or America for its inspiration. The bands seemed very enigmatic and their line-ups seemed to change frequently. There was very little chance I would ever get to see one play live. What interviews and articles that made it into the music papers I found confusing. Maybe it was the language? The music seemed very active and experimental, very direct; anti-marketing and anti-virtuoso in much the same way that punk would be a few years later.

*   *   *

At school I was getting a bit of reputation. Phil had 'accidentally' let slip that I was still seeing a psychologist and, before I knew it, I acquired a new nickname: 'Psycho'.

I enjoyed my visits to the head doctor. It was a half-day off school and all I had to do was talk about stuff. I was good at that. I hadn't keeled over for a bit, but I kept seeing the doc every couple of months or so.

One of the questions I got asked was, 'What do you see yourself doing in the future?'

I could have gone for the facetious answer like 'undertaker' but for once I took the question seriously and thought about it.

'Probably join a band, play the drums and mess around with synthesisers' was my oddly prophetic reply. I was listening to Roxy Music a lot and Brian Eno had become another role model. *(No Pussyfooting)* by Eno and Robert Fripp was a perfect soundtrack after a bottle or two of Phensedyl – it captured the sleepy syrupy cough-linctus vibe perfectly.

'You'd probably be good at that . . .' was the doc's reply. I think this was the first time that anyone had said I might be good at anything. I took it as encouragement. I ignored her punchline, '. . . messing around.'

I had never advertised the purpose of these visits to the teachers or anybody else at school. I just said, 'Got a doctor's appointment, sir,' and that was it. No questions asked. My mistake had been telling Phil, who in turn told everyone, and now I had to put up with the mocking.

'Hey you, Morris! You mad or what?'

Or 'Oi you, nutter!'

I tried to laugh it off but didn't do a very good job. I got a bit paranoid. Parents and teachers began giving me funny looks.

'Weirdo!' became a popular nickname. I quite liked that one, better than 'Psycho'. I liked the weird and unwanted in life.

A badge of honour then.

*   *   *

I took solace from the thought that being a drummer in a band was a good idea. The rest of the Sunshine Valley Dance Band, though, weren't feeling quite so optimistic about having a potentially deranged drummer. One slightly less shambolic practice ended abruptly. Just as the drum pounding and screaming, wailing feedback were reaching a crescendo that almost sounded like a tune, the police arrived, we were busted. And that was that.

'It was never going to get anywhere anyway,' were the attempted words of commiseration from the parents, which just riled me.

'HOW DO YOU FUCKING KNOW THAT THEN? YOU FUCKING PSYCHIC OR SOMETHING?' That didn't go down well.

I ranted, and the thing about ranting is that most of the time it gets you nowhere and doesn't really make you feel any better, unless you really want a badge with the word 'Twat!' on it.

So, I was once again not very popular at home but at least nothing got broken, well, apart from the band. I consoled myself with the thought that I was better off solo. I mean, the world was crying out for the solo drummer wasn't it? Only a matter of time.

While I stuck to drumming on my own, my parents reassured themselves with thoughts of 'He'll grow out of it,' 'It's just a phase, they all go through it,' and 'Well, it keeps him out of trouble.' And the less likely 'He'll meet a nice girl and settle down.'

Which was fine except . . .

One day in the new year, I was back at school, happily avoiding learning anything in a Physics lesson that might one day be useful, when who should make an unexpected visit? None other than Mr A. H. Cooper, the headmaster himself. A man rarely seen apart from his daily motivational speech that the timetable called 'Assembly'.

'Morris,' he barked, 'come with me.'

The class fell silent and everyone seemed to be looking at me, as if to say 'He's over there, sir. Now he's for it.'

'Yes sir,' I said meekly and followed him out. *Perhaps this is about me coming top in classical studies and he wants to congratulate me or give me a prize or something*, I thought, but something about his manner seemed to suggest that the giving of prizes was the last thing on his mind. He ushered me into the headmaster's study, pointed at a chair and said, 'Wait here.' So I sat and waited.

He reappeared about fifteen minutes later and led me into an office where two short-haired chaps in blue blazers with brass buttons sat.

'Morris, these two gentlemen are from Macclesfield Police and they would like to have a word with you.'

Oh shit.

'Stephen – it is Stephen, isn't it? – we've had a report that you've been taking drugs,' said the nice cop.

Oh big shit.

'Where are you getting them from?' shouted the nasty cop.

'Now, I'm sure you don't want to get into any trouble, do you?' said Constable Nice.

'Are you taking horse?' shouted Officer Nasty.

'And we don't want you to get in any trouble, really. It's the dealers we're after, not casual users like yourself.'

'Are you on opium? Why is your desk full of empty cough medicine bottles?'

I had to hold my hand up to that one because it was full of Phensedyl bottles and Boots the Chemist bags. No books at all.

I felt tiny and scared and I wanted to go home, but the nice/nasty copper business went on for an eternity. If they just wanted to frighten me, they succeeded.

Eventually Mr Cooper interrupted them and began a bit of a long-winded explanation as to why we were there.

It transpired that what had happened was that Adam, who had been buying the odd tab off Phil, had for some reason felt the need to unburden his guilt and tell his oh-so-cool parents what he had been up to. I

94

didn't have a problem with that, but why had he felt the need to tell them about what Philip and myself were getting up to? I felt a bit, well, grassed up – there is no other word for it. Grassed up and angry.

Adam's parents, it turned out, were not quite as cool and right-on as he believed, and they had phoned the Law and the school in that order. The three of us were busted.

I was kicked out of King's (well, actually I was only suspended but they've never asked me back – perhaps they will one day), and I was told to expect further visits from the drugs squad. Mind you, Phil and Adam got the boot as well so at least I wasn't on my own.

My parents were, naturally and quite rightly, not pleased by this turn of events.

I'd fucked up. Yet I didn't think it was any fault of my own and I wasn't remorseful in the slightest. It's amazing how our own misfortune is always the work of others, isn't it? That's exactly how I felt: it was them, it was everybody else. I sunk into depression. An ominous big black cloud began to descend on my life.

The thing was, I was supposed to be taking my O levels in a year, and where would that be happening then? First port of call for resuming my education was Macclesfield College. Unfortunately, my co-exiles Phil and Adam had got there first and the powers that be felt that two was a nice round number of drug fiends, thank you.

Next stop, Wilmslow County Grammar School. A resounding no from them. They had a zero-tolerance policy on drugs and stupidity.

I was all for just getting a job, any kind of job, but preferably one where there was no work at all involved, that kind of job. Oh, and one where you didn't need any qualifications. Mum and Dad were having none of it. They would get me into a place of learning if it was the last thing they did.

So one day I was taken for a bit of a drive by my dad. Like an unwitting dog being rehoused, I was taken off on a trip to Audenshaw. I had no idea where the hell Audenshaw was, but it seemed to take ages to get there. Our destination turned out to be Audenshaw Grammar School, a seat of learning located on the other side of Stockport, towards Ashton-under-Lyne. There was the usual neatly trimmed playing field at the front, and the mingled smell of the sweat of youthful males and floor polish pervaded the interior. Up a flight of well-trodden stairs, along a hushed corridor to a door with three chairs outside. We sat.

'Not again! Why the fuck are we here?' I hissed.

Clifford went in first to see the man in charge and explained my situation. I was then summoned and asked by the head bloke, 'Do you want to come to this school?'

To which I replied, 'No I don't! It's miles from where I live and I can't see the point anyway.' Which was not the answer he was looking for.

'Well, I'm afraid I have some rather bad news for you: you start on Monday,' replied the head twat. I'd taken an instant dislike to him and his place of learning. He thought me feckless and lazy, and he was probably right. We parted on bad terms.

To get to Audenshaw I had to first catch a train to Stockport, then another to Guide Bridge, then walk across a lot of marshy wasteground and there it was ... looming. I was usually late. Going to Audenshaw felt like banishment to Siberia. I would board the train full of commuters reading paperbacks and by the time I got to Guide Bridge, I was alone in the carriage, ready for my trek across the muddy wasteground to the gulag.

One thing I enjoyed about Audenshaw was its Religious Education classes. These were great, completely ignoring the Bible and going straight in there with demonic possession and stigmata, and I'm sure there was even mention of a poltergeist. It was as if the course had been written by the blokes who did 'Focus on Fact' or someone who'd read a lot of Charles Fort. There was a bit of Buddhism and witchcraft – the life of the apostles didn't feature.

A bad thing about the place was the cadet corps. They would dress up in military drag and march up and down with pretend rifles, doing drill and stuff like some warped teenage Dad's Army.

A few years earlier this would have been right up my street, playing at soldiers with toy rifles. But since I felt I was now a fully paid-up member of the counterculture, all this establishment shit was not for me. Unless they needed a drummer, of course, then maybe I would have considered it.

One morning, late again, the bloke who ran the cadets caught me skulking in the cloakroom. His eyes lit up when I explained the trouble I had getting to school each morning.

'I think I have a solution for you, young man. I live in Hazel Grove and if you could manage to get there at six-thirty I'd gladly give you a lift in my car. I haven't seen you at cadets yet. Would you like me to show you round? We have a jolly old time.'

I had no idea what sort of a jolly time a young man could have with a pretend rifle, and I didn't much want to find out.

After that encounter, I decided that I would be leaving Audenshaw at the earliest opportunity. There was no way I was going to be indoctrinated into some Mancunian version of the Hitler Youth. I might be being a bit unfair to Audenshaw here, but I felt isolated and banished – I hated pretty much everything and everybody at that time. There were some good lads at the school (a couple of them later ended up in a band called V2) and I did become a member of the Syd Barrett Appreciation Society thanks to one.

I began to stay on the train until it got to Manchester, and phone up the school pretending to be my dad. I would explain that I was ill and wouldn't be in for some time. I'd spend the rest of the day wandering around record stores and bookshops, trying to make five cigs last all day. I felt like I was being stalked by that big black cloud. Home was one screaming row after another. I felt better outside in Manchester, mooching in the rain and stewing in my thoughts. This truly felt like banishment.

My roundabout self-education away from school was ongoing. I was beginning to read more non-fiction books and would grab anything that seemed to have the scent of Zen, some kind of esoteric philosophy or a hint of the occult about it. I guess it started with *Zen and the Art of Motorcycle Maintenance*, a bestseller at the time, but I think I found the repeated use of the term 'a priori' off-putting. I really liked Alan Watts's *The Way of Zen* though. All this was mixed up with some books I'd pick up from the House on the Borderland, a little alternative bookshop on Tibb Street, where I would usually start my Manchester skiving sessions.

The bookshop was named after a supernatural horror novel by William Hope Hodgson and run by a guy called Dave Britton. His main income came from the sale of hardcore porn and it was quite funny to watch these guys coming in, trying to look casual as they nervously browsed the filth section, just a shelf along from the sci-fi stuff. I think Burroughs and Ballard was the dividing line between the two.

I'd spend all morning in there but, perhaps surprisingly for a teenage boy, I wasn't there for the porn. I was angling for a job in the shop or maybe could pick up some drugs-related info as I whiled away the time browsing through the shunned *Necronomicon* and books about Magick, the Hermetic Order of the Golden Dawn and Aleister Crowley. Anyone who got billed as the wickedest man who ever lived was bound to have something interesting to say. It was fascinating gobbledygook.

Then I'd go and hang about in Piccadilly Plaza for a bit, reading the latest *ZigZag* (Pete Frame's 'Rock Family Trees' were always a favourite), have a coffee in the Wimpy. Then I'd spend the rest of the day visiting record shops – Virgin, HMV, Rare Records and Black Sedan.

I loved Black Sedan. It had a huge stock of bootlegs – multicoloured vinyl treasures in homemade Xeroxed sleeves. The rock-and-roll equivalent of home-brewed ale, their reputation and rarity promised so much and usually delivered so little. It didn't stop me wanting them badly. I never had enough cash though.

If I did have any money (and if I did, I'd probably nicked it), I'd go and see a band in the evening just to avoid going home (any band would do). I saw Jeff Beck that way. He was good and Gentle Giant weren't as bad as I thought they'd be, while Humble Pie were ace. Or I'd go and sit through the double feature of *Easy Rider* and *Woodstock* again, or the movie of Moorcock's *The Final Programme*. It was nowhere near as good as the book, of course.

As soon as I turned fifteen I made it official. I announced to my parents that I wasn't going to school any more. Thanks to some quirk of the law at that time, I could just jack it in and leave with no come-backs from the police or social services. So I left. Not a single O level to my name. Nothing. Nada. That'd teach 'em to try and educate me. (I did nick a load of poetry books from the library though – I still have them.)

Needless to say, this didn't go down well at home. How my parents refrained from killing me I'll never know.

My masterplan was that I would hitch down to London and get into a band. There were always loads of drummer-wanted ads in the music papers, but there was a problem: they all came with the caveat 'must have own transport'. Somehow I didn't think having a bicycle with a puncture would count.

Newly liberated from scholastic drudge, I took to hanging around in pubs full time. Most landlords were either very tolerant of the fact that I was only fifteen or they were nearly blind. As is only natural, I made some new friends – drug fiends to a man. Chief among these was Dizzy. He had what you might call an open house/commune/ squat and when the pubs shut a few of us would go round there for a spliff or whatever was on offer. There was one guy, Dobbo (not to be confused with Hobbo – this one had much shorter hair and was unpredictably violent), who specialised in burglary and vandalism, and liked to combine the two when breaking into chemist's or doctor's surgeries. He always seemed to have a pocketful of pills, usually assorted, but with no real idea of what they were save for the knowledge that they came from an alarmed cabinet marked 'Dangerous Drugs'. They helped make the time pass quicker.

The problem as always was money, or the lack of it.

I had thought that Dad might take me on doing odd jobs at his office, at least I had some experience of that, but he wouldn't entertain the idea. I was always scrounging bits here and nicking bits there and generally making myself unpopular at the best of times, so it wasn't really surprising that he didn't want to know me.

Eventually Uncle John (Elsie's husband) took pity and said he'd give me a trial working at Atwell and Jenner's mill where he was a manager. It was bloody hard work. Well, when you've never done a proper day's work in your life, any work seems hard. I was shifting huge rolls of fabric on to massive cutting tables, then slicing it into sheets to get it loaded onto the looms. The machines made a great noise when they all got going, a really powerful, insistent, industrial rhythm. It was a proper northern job, 'working int' mill'. I got myself a cloth cap – I did really – but I thought the clogs might have been pushing it a bit. The pay wasn't great but it were better than nowt, as they say.

What cash I managed to save after drug and alcohol deductions went mostly on the acquisition of more drums, records, gigs and my new favourite thing, festivals.

7

THE GREAT VINYL ROBBERY

Fancy a game of Where's Wally? I'm actually
in this snap somewhere.

I had already played with addiction, but now I became a genuine vinyl junkie. I would tour record shops doing the vinyl flip-flip thing, pausing to restore dislocated items to their correct alphabetic position. I would have a shopping list in my head, built from reviews of the latest releases by new bands I thought might be interesting, bands that John Peel had being playing that month, names of groups that I'd spotted in *ZigZag* or *Creem*. Sometimes I would be attracted to LPs just because I liked the look of the sleeves, and I was drawn to stuff on labels I liked: United Artists, Harvest or Zappa's Straight. Finally, I would be looking for the two most important categories of all: US imports and long-deleted or scarce records that the shop's previous clientele had missed. American imports were highly prized. US record companies would often put out LPs before they were available in the UK, and the American breed usually came in sturdier sleeves than their British cousins. They came at a premium but I'll swear a lot of them actually sounded better too.

You could find black gold in the most unlikely places. A paper shop in Macclesfield had a first edition of *The Velvet Underground & Nico* with the peel-off banana intact – until a young child tore half of it off. Sacrilege! In Manchester, the record sections of the Kendal Milne department store were a good place to trawl. Lurking among *The World of Mantovani* and Tom Jones's *Greatest Hits*, I found the first Stooges album, *Permanent Damage* by the GTOs and *Farewell to Aldebaran* by Judy Henske and Jerry Yester. Rare Records – where Ian Curtis used to work but I didn't remember him – occasionally had gems but you had to be quick. Procrastination cost me the first Jobriath album and, more annoyingly, *International Heroes* by Kim Fowley. I spent years after that trying to find a decent copy of *International Heroes* that did not cost an arm and a leg. I only found it a few years ago courtesy of the internet and, honestly, it felt like cheating. For me it was the searching and hunting down – refusing anything other than a mint first pressing with gatefold sleeve and lyric sheet – that was the best part of record buying. Today I can find all my coveted teenage 33s on Discogs or some other website in a couple of clicks. The thrill of the vinyl chase is no more.

I would leave the shop with my latest acquisition in its paper bag (if I hadn't nicked the record), before getting it home to the hi-fi, gently peeling off the piece of Sellotape securing the bag, sliding out the sleeve and thoroughly inspecting the contents. I would slip Side A on to the turntable, drop the needle and sit back, bathed in a warm glow of the run-in crackle then, wham, the heat of satisfaction or disappointment. From the first one-two-three-four of the Modern Lovers 'Roadrunner' I knew I'd struck gold. Same with the MC5's *Back in the USA*. Other times, though, just a hot and deflating feeling that I might have been conned. Oddly, it was often the records that initially seemed a dead loss that would eventually become the most enduring.

After leaving Audenshaw I continued going to gigs on my own. Keeping out of the house for as long as possible seemed like a good idea.

Mainly it was at venues in Manchester city centre – the Free Trade Hall, of course, but occasionally bands would opt for the plusher theatres such as the Opera House (Genesis) or the Palace Theatre (Pink Floyd, the Kinks), or the not-so-posh such as the tiny Houldsworth Hall on Deansgate (Peter Hammill).

Slightly further afield were shows at Manchester University or UMIST and the Apollo at Ardwick, which is probably the only venue from those days that remains to this day. Bigger bands such as the Who or the Stones seemed to prefer the King's Hall at Belle Vue.

The smaller venues were always the most interesting and, typically, the most difficult for me to get to. This necessitated scrounging a lift off someone and/or a long walk/hitch home. The Stoneground in Gorton was housed in an old fleapit of a cinema (it was renamed the Mayflower, scene of a couple of early Joy Division gigs). The price of drinks seemed to change by the hour. The audience would either sit crosslegged and appreciative at the front of the stage, or take part in some wide-eyed freaky dancing at the back, under the blacklight. The clientele was nearly as fascinating as the bands. I saw Magma but missed out on Can and Amon Düül – to my everlasting shame.

The newest and allegedly purpose-built venue was the Hardrock near Old Trafford cricket ground. You could smell the newness. The Hardrock, despite its location, was a great place to see a band. It didn't have that stale-beer-stained carpet fragrance that was the hall-mark of a venue steeped in history. I saw Bowie there a couple of times, Genesis (again) and Hawkwind (of course) on the Space Ritual tour in November 1972. Now that was a fantastic show. The oddest bill, possibly of all time, was at the Hardrock: Lou Reed and the Tots supported by Fairport Convention and Phillip Goodhand-Tait. A very peculiar line-up, mixing the extremes of the English village and the American city. But there wasn't the same rigid categorisation of music back then. It was all one thing under the broad heading of 'Rock'.

The journey home from gigs in Manchester was broken by a spot of supper at Manchester legendary all-night Plaza Café. The Plaza only served one dish: the Biryani. It was usually served as a half – to ask for a full biryani was the height of gluttony. The standard meal was advertised as chicken, although having witnessed a crate of scraggy, greyish birds being delivered late one night, pigeon may have been a better description. (There was also an undefined 'meat' option, but I never met anyone who tried it.) The bright sunshine-yellow rice and 'chicken' was served on a plastic plate with a bowl of sauce, available in varying levels of mouth-melting intensity: Mild, Medium, Red Hot, Suicide or Killer. Later, they added Atomic to the list for the hardened connoisseur. Half a Suicide, my usual, cost under 25p, about all I'd have left after a night out. I seem to remember that Charlie the owner and the Somali staff wore industrial-grade wellington boots for some reason, perhaps to protect their feet if they accidentally stepped in the corrosive sauce.

Eventually I broadened my horizons from the indoor late-night event to become a solo all-day damp festival-goer.

Buxton 1973 was one of the first ones. It was only 11 miles up the road from Macclesfield, so it was easy to cadge a lift.

I'd gone mainly to see the Edgar Broughton band and the Sensational Alex Harvey Band. I was also quite looking forward to seeing the Groundhogs. Unfortunately, fearing for their safety in the teeming rain, they didn't bother playing. Roy Wood didn't fancy the rain either and beat a hasty retreat along with the rest of Wizzard.

To put it mildly, it was grim. The site was bleak enough and the pissing rain and cold topped it off a treat. It was like a Derbyshire Altamont with more rain. Following what had become a seventies tradition at these sort of gigs, the Hells Angels decided to take over the festival security. They'd done it the year before and it was now an annual day out for them.

I knew some bikers in Macc and though they were an unpredictable bunch, I'd never had any trouble with them. The Devil's Disciples, as the Macc chapter called themselves, only had a moped between the four of them. They were surprisingly easy-going, unlike Macc's skinheads, whom I always managed to offend in ways that I failed to understand – usually earning me a good kicking.

The Buxton Angels tried to extort money from the punters who wanted to use the toilets, but somehow this was more sad than scary. They did attempt a bit of drunken rampaging, but with the cold and damp, I don't think their collective heart was really in it.

Headliner Chuck Berry soon cleared off after an en masse Angels duckwalk invasion ended his short set. You could see his tail-lights bouncing across the moor as the audience bayed.

Buxton the year after, 1974, was better. Thanks to windowpane acid, ginger wine, dry ice and Mott the Hoople, it was brilliant! Even the Angels smiled! We certainly knew how to have fun in those days.

Going to festivals alone could have been a recipe for disaster when my only way of getting about was either by pushbike or hitchhike, but surprisingly considering the huge number of coppers that would turn up without fail at these events, plus the fact I was mostly either very drunk or tripping, I never got stopped once.

I began hanging about in the Hare Krishna tent where the disciples of Lord Krishna would dish out free chapatis as long as you joined in with the chanting and bell dinging. There was never any question of having to become a fully paid-up member to qualify. The closest I got into anything resembling trouble of the bonkers cult kind at these solitary outings was at the Great Western Express.

This took place at White City, darn London way in 1973. It rained again. Funny how a UK festival in July is pretty much guaranteed a downpour. There was something very sad about watching Sly and the Family Stone doing 'I Wanna Take You Higher' and 'Dance to the Music' against a backdrop of cold grey drizzle.

Canned Heat came on, and a week later I would see them doing exactly the same set and break a guitar string in exactly the same song. I wondered if this was what Woodstock had really been like.

As White City was at an athletics/greyhound stadium, you could at least find some shelter in the stands. It was while I was doing this that a cheery bunch of folk spotted me – three lads and a couple of girls who looked like pretty normal festival-goers: denim loon pants and sewn on patches of the peace-and-love variety. They struck up a conversation.

'Hi, you look a bit lost. Are you looking for someone?' Always a good conversation starter in any situation.

'No, have you got any drugs?' would have been my normal stock reply but maybe these were undercover filth or something, so it was a nervous squeak. 'Er no, I'm not. Ta.' I hoped they'd go away.

One of the girls then piped up with 'Would you like one of our magazines?' and started digging about in her orange-and-blue crocheted shoulder bag. She produced something that looked a bit like this . . .

That got me interested.

I had seen this sort of publication before, not in Dave's hardcore section at the House on the Borderland, but at the slightly more genteel but very trendy Percival's bookshop near the Library Theatre in Manchester. I did a lot of browsing there on my daily tour of Manchester record shops as it was on the way from Rare Records to Black Sedan. I recognised that the magazine was the work of Moses David, that much I knew from my idle magazine browsing. As for what it was all about, I had no idea. It just sort of rambled on and on about Jesus and screwing. The pictures, plus the close proximity of words such as 'Devil' and 'Sex' were bound to appeal to a lad of my age.

'Oh yeah, Moses David, I've read a lot of his stuff.' Trying to impress. 'Have you got any drugs?' They obviously weren't under-cover feds so I thought I was safe.

Almost as one, their eyes lit up.

'Are you here on your own?' one of the lads asked curiously.

'No, we haven't got any on us but I know where you can get some. Have you got any friends with you?' said one of the girls.

'Whereabouts are you from then?' As a group they kept getting closer and closer. *Just being friendly*, I thought.

'I'm from Macclesfield,' I said, just being friendly back, 'near Manchester.'

'Oh,' said the other girl, 'that's a long way home, isn't it?'

'I know,' said the first girl, 'why don't you come home with us? We've got loads of room.'

I have to admit that initially this did seem a tempting prospect: running away from home and living in a London hippie squat had crossed my mind with increasing frequency in those days.

'Yes, we can get some drugs and then you can come with us. You don't want to go back to Manchester, do you?'

Appealing as this scheme was, it didn't sound quite right. I'd read the *News of the World* and I was getting a funny feeling about all this. Time for our reporter to make his excuses and leave.

'Just a mo, I'm off to the loo,' the old Morris escape line. No sooner had one of them said, 'I'll come too,' than I headed for the nearest exit as fast as my legs would carry me. I legged it out of the stadium and got straight on the tube.

It was very weird, a bit surreal. It dawned on me later, after I got over missing Ray Davies throw a wobbler at the gig, that they were members of the Children of God, an ever-so-slightly dodgy cult. Jeremy Spencer of Fleetwood Mac had not been so lucky – he'd gone home with them in LA a year or two earlier. It did not go well.

You should never talk to strangers. I always do though – they're very interesting.

The beginning of 1974 saw me slogging the week out at the mill, daydreaming of which album I'd get at the weekend, doing lists of potential buys in my lunch hour, usually after a trawl of the local record shops. Then back up the hill to the shifting of rolls of material from storeroom to cutting bench to loom. This was the way things went every day except for Wednesdays.

Wednesdays were half-day closing so there was not much music browsing to be done. Like a bloody ghost town it was. It was one of those Wednesdays when, having some time to kill, I thought why not pay Dizz a visit. I'd not been round for a week or two. Maybe he'd have bit of dope to sell. But I wondered if anyone at his house even got up before twelve. It seemed unlikely but it would kill a bit of time.

When I got to White Street, the curtains were all drawn and the place looked empty. But what the hell, might as well give a knock. I could always leave a note or something, just to let him know I'd called.

No answer. I was all set to shove a note through the door when it opened a crack and a mop of corkscrew hair and a pair of bleary eyes peered round.

'Hi, what the fuck do you want?'

'All right, Dizz, got any pot?'

'Not so loud. Come in.' The eyes darted left then right before the door opened wider.

So in I went. Dizz vanished in the direction of the kitchen and reappeared with a big brown bottle full of pills.

'No dope, man, the town's dry, nothing nowhere. There's been a big bust. Fuckin' DS. Got these, though. Here, have a few.'

'What are they?'

'All sorts man, all sorts, bit of this, bit of that, triple mandies some of 'em, I think, or they might be . . .'

'No, it's all right. I'd best be getting back to t'mill.'

'Oh fuck that – try a couple of these! What are you, man or mouse?'

There was a bit of a Pinocchio vibe going on here, wasn't there?

I should have just put the pills in my pocket and buggered off, saved them for later or something. But no, I had to swallow them there and then. What harm could they do?

At this point someone changed the film from Disney to something more Philip Marlowe. You know, the bit where 'the broad slipped me a micky'.

I fell down a rabbit hole to oblivion.

I don't know what the pills were but they didn't agree with me. I blacked out sharpish and kept drifting in and out of consciousness. Maybe it was one of my turns. The only memory I have is of the Derek and the Dominoes album side one getting played over and over and over and over. To this day I can't hear 'Bell Bottom Blues' without feeling queasy. They used to say 'Clapton is God'. Not in my book he isn't.

I eventually came round sprawled on the floor between Dizz's sofa and the fireplace. Someone had thoughtfully covered me with a rancid rug. It was night. The trouble was it was Thursday night. I'd been out for a day. Oh well, I was fucked, so I went back to sleep and decided I'd stay in this two-up two-down commune for a bit. Try living the bohemian life on the left bank of the River Bollin. The house was a basic old-fashioned terrace with a proper outside lavvy, no mod cons at all. Most of the other houses in the row were empty and it wasn't hard to guess why. But beggars can't be choosers. It took a few days' before the rest of the house's hippie occupants noticed I was still there.

I really couldn't face the row that awaited me at home. I'd done it again. Properly fucked up. But as long as I avoided facing the consequences, I could just pretend they wouldn't happen. Put it off for another day and then another. Dizz played the congas in bands and I thought if I hung around with him long enough then maybe I'd get a job in a band too. I thought it'd be a bit like running away to join the circus but with amps instead of animals.

I imagined that living in a commune would be a glamorous life fuelled by drugs and rock and roll. Much like the tales of life in Ladbroke Grove in Richard Neville's *Play Power* and the underground press. I kind of expected warmth, water, food and drink too.

If I wanted any of that I would have had to skulk off home and hope nobody noticed I was a part-time sellout.

I never got a job in a band and I didn't wash much either – I'd forgotten to pack any toiletries – but I did take up crime. I tried my hand at house breaking, milk-bottle theft, meat theft. Not easy, that, I can tell you: the theft of a joint of meat from a butcher's was a three-man job needing guile and cunning. The usual train-fare dodging, cigarette theft and then record theft; living at Dizz's was non-stop crime. The vinyl heist though – that was to be my undoing.

A bunch of five or six of us set off from White Street to Manchester. Looking like a psychedelic version of the *Beano*'s Bash Street Kids, we fare-dodged our way to Piccadilly, and set about relieving Lewis's record department of a large portion of its stock.

Most record shops would just have the record sleeves on display and keep the vinyl out of sight behind the counter, but Lewis's for some reason didn't take this simple precaution.

We were a motley-looking collection so, if we had entered en masse, our intentions would have been obvious. One by one, we would go in, lift a couple, then come out and let someone else have a turn until we'd got as much as we could carry between us. All that was needed was a large enough coat to secrete the goods in. You had to be quick and not too choosy – if I'm honest, 90 per cent of the stuff we lifted was total shit. There was one album by Man (*Winos, Rhinos and Lunatics*) that I quite fancied but that was about it. It was the Bay City Rollers, Showaddywaddy and David Essex mostly. Shit chart stuff. I liked bands who never troubled the top twenty and once they charted more than once I went off them. Alice Cooper, I thought, was the bee's knees until he started having hits. Then I had to trot out the old line, 'Yeah, he's OK. Not as good as he used to be, mind.' I was a bit of a music snob.

Quality didn't really matter, anyway. The plan was to flog this vinyl haul to the second-hand shop in Macclesfield Indoor Market once we got home. Criminal masterminds that we were, first of all we went into the café next door to the record store to have a cuppa, still carrying the trove of stolen albums. Somehow we had failed to notice that the caff was still part of Lewis's. Predictably, the law turned up. We got arrested, bundled into a van and taken down to Bootle Street nick for grilling. I tried the old 'A big boy did it and ran way and left me holding these records officer' defence but the Manchester police were having none of it. I got locked up in Bootle Street with a stranger who claimed to have been beaten up as part of his interrogation. That really cheered me up.

Eventually Dad turned up. God knows how the police managed to get hold of him and drag him away from his tap peddling. He wasn't pleased to see me. Apoplectic is the word I'm looking for.

'Where the hell have you been?' and 'What've you got yourself mixed up with now?' were among his first words along with 'bloody' and 'idiot'.

I'd gone too far, yet again. Would I never learn?

'I've a good mind to just leave you here and let the police sort you out. Your mother's had enough of you.'

Mind you, I did get in the papers when I had my court appearance. I got off with a fine and a suspended sentence. That was the end of my life of (largely) drug-induced hippie crime.

It all could have been worse. For more than one awful moment, I thought I was going to end up in a cell for a long time. But how was I going to keep out of trouble while being bored in Macclesfield?

Macclesfield of the late seventies did not have the best of reputa-tions (it's gone downhill since). Firstly, there was the aforementioned Parkside Hospital, the inmates of which were occasionally found wandering around the town, much to the alarm and distress of the unwary visitor. Then there was the youth subculture: a healthy contingent of mods or proto-skinheads, mostly without scooters, and an equally healthy contingent of greasers/bikers, again mostly without motorbikes. Between these two strata was a floating mob of 'young farmers' who could go either way and were best approached with caution. These apprentice agrarians rarely had any useful drugs.

Heroin had a broad appeal in the town, and I came across a number of guys – most of them called Bob or Dave – who were devotees. The majority were pretty straight-looking, and they were either working in garages or hospitals. You would not have guessed they were users. They seemed honest and trustworthy and level-headed. They weren't, but that's how you'd peg them on first meeting. Over the years that I spent drinking and drugging in the town, these superficially normal smackheads all either OD'ed or met other junk-related ends. Everyone was always 'surprised'. I tried most things but I was always very wary of smack. My limited experience of it wasn't something that I particularly enjoyed. But the cliché is that it takes all sorts . . .

To sum up what sort of person I had become:

- I stole money and booze from my parents and my sister;
- cigarettes from my father's car;
- records from just about anywhere;
- milk from doorsteps while simultaneously stopping cars at 4.30 on a Sunday morning just to get a light for a soggy dimp.
- I broke into the odd house;
- was an inveterate smasher of windows;
- was a compulsive liar;
- and was a compulsive crier.

I wanted to break out.

8

LIFE IS A CABARET

Unsurprisingly, I was no longer welcome at Uncle John's mill. Very reluctantly, my father finally suggested that I could have a job working for him. As if that would keep me out of trouble. I think the job description was 'dogsbody', which I took to mean skiver.

Clifford's tap-peddling business had been booming and he'd expanded the offices at Evington House. It was now home to a staff of six – soon to be seven. There was Bert Lee, who had taken over Johnny's job of running the office, and five girls, Susan, Big Liz, not so big Liz, Hilary and Ann, who either answered the telephone or typed out dictaphone-taped letters and memos from my dad. The memo became my father's favoured method of communication with me. I think he found it less infuriating than trying to talk to me.

My dad would drag me into work at 7 a.m. and set me to filing stacks of invoices and dockets. As a fervent LP organiser, I found this surprisingly easy and almost relaxing. Once my father left on his daily travels, I could settle down to doing as little as possible. This mostly consisted of arguments with the girls about their choice of office music. I always lost these musical disputes and the ambience of fluorescent strip light and cigarette smoke was augmented by a soundtrack of poptastic chartbound sounds. This was immediately silenced at 5.30 when my father returned from making his calls. He would then deposit more invoices and dockets in the filing tray before going to his attic desk to dictate more letters and memos until returning to Ivy Lane.

Practise, practise, practise. That's what I did twice a day, usually at lunchtime (home was only five minutes up the road from work) and evening, drug-induced benders permitting. It didn't make me any friends, but it made me feel better – there's a lot to be said for percussion therapy. I began to get pretty good at drumming too, not good in a way that you could class as being technically perfect but good in a way that I enjoyed. The only trouble was there still wasn't much call for a solo drummer, except maybe in the Boy Scouts, and I was getting a little bit too old for them.

The ever-expanding drum kit that I carted in and out of my father's room every morning and evening now comprised two bass drums, two snare drums, seven tom-toms (I was saving up for number eight), four or five cymbals and a hi-hat. They were a random mix of Premier, Hayman, Ludwig and Olympic, black, red, silver and mahogany in colour. Oddly, I never considered buying a proper drum stool and just perched on whatever rickety chair or stool I could find lying about. (Drummer tip: always get yourself a nice comfy stool to avoid spinal problems later in life.)

I did my best to appear responsible despite still being in disgrace after the great vinyl robbery. The job at the office was not going badly. Even so, I thought it would be a good idea to avoid my previous employer, Uncle John, for a bit. I wouldn't be visiting Elsie's for a while.

I settled into a life of clerical work. From filing, I was promoted to answering the phone, then taking orders, chasing orders, dealing with complaints and, best of all, working the telex machine. It was a cushy job, to be honest, and apart from having to unload a furniture van full of kitchen units every week, not exactly physically taxing.

My father, feeling that I was a natural at the office-dogsbody malar-key, decided that he would indoctrinate me further in the noble art of tap peddling.

I would receive an introduction to life on the road and get to accompany him on his sales calls. My joy was unconfined. The prospect of these trips out in themselves was not too bad. It was more the way they were to be conducted that bothered me. Clifford, as everyone always referred to him, always thinking of potential sales gimmicks, had dreamt up the idea that on these excursions I should dress myself exactly like him. A mini-me, complete with nice suit and bowler hat. I thought, not unnaturally, this was the worst thing I'd ever heard. Clifford's mind was made up, though, and no amount of whingeing and moaning would convince him otherwise. I sold out my scruples for a packet of fags and I reluctantly hit the road.

It was the most embarrassing thing I had ever done. Clifford could pull off the whole bowler hat/suit ensemble, being an old-fashioned dapper gent was his natural look, but me? I was hoping I might look a bit like Alex from *A Clockwork Orange*. I didn't. I looked like TV comic Freddie Davies.

I'd got to know some of the guys in the builder's yards on the phone. My appearance in person, along with my father's introductory spiel of 'And this is Mr Morris junior,' cracked them up. They pissed themselves. Despite feeling mortified and wishing for the earth to swallow me, I did my best to laugh along and appear interested in the minutiae of the plumbing and building trade. After the fifth or sixth call, my father realised I was not going to be the sales asset he had imagined, admitted defeat and told me to stay in the car for the rest of our day out.

My 'I told you it was a bad idea' wasn't exactly tactful and for the duration of our silent drive home, I thought I was about to find myself jobless yet again. I returned the chapeau with a shudder and we agreed never to speak of it ever again.

*   *   *

I was put back to work in the office. With no qualifications to my name and a criminal record, who else was going to give me a job anyway?

The money was less than I got at the mill but I did get a day a week off to do an OND in Business Studies at Macc College as well as evening classes in shorthand and typing. At the latter, I was the only lad in a class of thirty giggly girls.

Most hot-blooded young men would have realised that there was a lot of potential in this situation. Not me. I felt intimidated – like a gatecrasher at a hen party. I was easily singled out. The whole thing was cringy and embarrassing. So, after two weeks, I fled yet another place of learning and never returned.

I must have been paying some attention as I managed to pick up the basics of touch typing – it's still useful today – and also something called Pitman shorthand script, which involved scribbling things that looked like hieroglyphics. I didn't stay long enough to discover what the point of that was.

No, I'd made my mind up: I was educated enough, thank you.

I'd passed my driving test on the second attempt. I could ditch the pushbike and move on to four wheels. Road legal at last. That was enough learning for me. The only qualification I really needed was a full licence. I could now take up car scrounging until I'd saved up enough to get a motor of my own. An unexpected side effect of becoming a driver was that I became far more popular with the young ladies at work. They needed lifts to nights out at Genevieve's, Pips and other Manchester nightclubs. I would drop them off on my way to gigs and round them up on the way home. They chipped in a few quid for petrol and bought me drinks.

Towards the end of 1974, around my seventeenth birthday, I met a fellow percussionist named Phil Swindells (not to be confused with the other Phil). He was a year or two older than me and a really good drummer. He played in local banjo bands, jazz groups, all sorts of stuff – he was an in-demand drummer.

'You'd like Phil. He plays the drums too,' they would say down the pub. Why do people always think like that? I thought it was opposites that attracted.

He was nothing like me anyway. He drank only lemonade, drove a car safely, thought the drummer Carl Palmer was cool ... and Phil could play the drums 'properly'. Try as I might, I could never play like him, but on the other hand he couldn't play like me either. He could play swing convincingly, something I never could. To compensate, I had developed a way of playing that I thought looked and sounded like I knew what I was doing. I was not technically proficient at all. What I lacked in finesse I compensated for with energy and stamina. I had developed what they call a 'unique style'.

Phil was always gigging and he always knew of someone who had odd bits of kit to sell cheapish.

One Saturday lunchtime, he rang up in a bit of a panic. He'd got himself double booked and wanted to know if I could I stand in for him at a pub gig in Leek – 'Just light pop stuff,' he said, 'nothing complicated.' I was flattered that he offered me the gig. I jumped at the chance, anything to get to play with a band. Phil told me to turn up at six and meet Doug and Dave in the pub car park. How on earth I thought I could just turn up and play with someone without rehearsing with them first, I do not know. (On reflection, the more likely explanation lies in the fact that 1974 was a bumper year for LSD, pre Operation Julie, which just about destroyed the acid business in the late seventies. Most weekends, I was away with the space cadets.)

Doug and Dave turned out to be a couple of elderly gents – a pianist and an upright bass player. It went downhill from the moment they asked if I'd brought my own dickie bow. The most recent number in their set was 'Tie a Yellow Ribbon'. It was 'mood' music for couples having their Sunday night chicken in a basket. There were complaints. Not all from the audience.

'Can you play a bit quieter?' was Doug and Dave's frosty catchphrase.

As first gigs go, I suppose it could have been worse, but I am not sure how.

'Try everything once' has long been a motto of mine, and now I could strike cut-price cabaret off the list. I didn't ask if I'd see them next week. I already knew the answer.

It wasn't Phil's fault, though he was very apologetic, explaining how he didn't think it would be that bad. A few weeks later he was on to me again. Another band he was standing in with were after a permanent drummer. Not really his cup of tea, and he thought it would be more up my street.

'It's more rock and heavy stuff,' he went on.

That sounded promising. This outfit were younger than Doug and Dave and had much longer hair. Well, they had hair. Two guitars and bass, the traditional line-up. They did covers of 'All Right Now', 'Honky Tonk Women' and 'Black Night'. Unfortunately, my unconscious attempts to steer these 'standards' in a more Krautrocky direction did not find favour with the rest of the group. The lead guitarist and bass player were soon exchanging wincing looks with each other. Undeterred, I soldiered on. I was enjoying myself – surely that would be infectious.

By the second, 'Can you play a bit quieter?' I had a pretty good idea where this would end up.

'You're not that bad really, but I think you need a few more lessons. Tell Phil we'll see him next week.'

I took the hint.

That's the way my musical career went for the next few months: a chain of unsuccessful auditions and one-off gigs. I enjoyed the playing with other people bit. It was just that other people didn't enjoy playing with me. I think the problem was that my 'unique style' was a bit too unique for most.

My record collection was expanding even faster than the drum kit. I was still trying to buy at least one new record a week and I listened to as many different bands as I could. There really wasn't much that I didn't like. I'm not counting music that was in the charts – that was music that I hated with a passion. I would still watch *Top of the Pops* on the TV every week just so I could vent my spleen and laugh at every act's shit attempts at miming, while at the same time fantasising about what I would do when I was on the show. *TOTP*, the show I loved to hate to love. I still remember the time in 1972 that both Hawkwind and Bowie were on. 'This is more like it!' I shouted at the TV, but the TV wasn't listening. 'It'll be Amon Düül next!' It wasn't.

Looking back now, I can see what my problem was with *TOTP*. I thought that I was watching a show about contemporary popular music (and, to be fair, *TOTP* did little to dissuade me from this assumption). *TOTP* actually had more in common with the showbiz traditions of variety than anything rock and roll. The regular sexy dance routines from Pan's People and crap pop acts like the Rubettes and Paper Lace would appear alongside novelty acts such as the Wombles (featuring, as Wellington, Chris Spedding, who would shortly go on to produce the Sex Pistols' demos), and then you'd get something great such as Bowie, Golden Earring or Mott the Hoople, all presented in the same cheery sausage-writing style. Nowadays nostalgia allows *TOTP*'s naffness to be overlooked as part of its charm. I watch compilations of the old shows and sigh, 'Ah those were the days. Pilot – I wonder what happened to them?'

Of all the musical styles in the world, the one for which I reserved a special hatred was disco. Particularly the kind peddled by the Bee

Gees in *Saturday Night Fever*. I liked Nik Cohn, on whose *New York Magazine* article the film was based, but how the fuck did he end up with a movie like that? It was the work of the musical Antichrist. I was not alone in having that view. *Saturday Night Fever* was generally reviled by serious young male music fans of the day, and Abba too were scorned for doing the Devil's work. What a dour lot we were.

Now, of course, it's a different story. 'Jive Talkin'', which came out in 1975 (two years before the film), brings back memories of a particular time and place in a way that Patti Smith's 'Horses' doesn't. I never ever owned a Bee Gees record, much less went to a funky disco (well, maybe once or twice, but Krumbles in Macc wasn't like the one in *Saturday Night Fever*), but the perseveration of that track always evokes long-forgotten feelings of 1975. It's an idealised seventies, one that never actually happened to me, but a kind of collective memory of the time. That music, particularly popular music, can work as an emotional time capsule, a link to memory, is something extraordinary. That we have no control over what stays with us and what fades (why don't I remember Nils Lofgren more clearly than I do? I listened to him enough), that the mechanism is apparently purely subconscious, is fascinating. Am I remembering the actual past or the mythologised past of the 'good old days'?

Back then, in the real mid-seventies when disco was just starting to enter the mainstream, I would curse every second of *TOTP*'s tinsel-prismatic sheen, except, of course, when someone I liked came on. Then I would cheer them on for taking the piss out of the whole charade.

I hated 99.9 per cent of its spangly content with venom. 'How dare the BBC put this disco shit on my TV at 7.30 on Thursday evenings when there's some proper music in the world that never gets a chance ...' went the pompous letter I never sent to *Points Of View*. Honestly, at the time I just did not see the point of disco: it got filed away under 'Vilified' along with anything my dad liked.

It was *The Old Grey Whistle Test* that catered for the likes of me and my friends – serious bands presented by serious people in a serious manner. That was more like it. Like John Peel's radio show, it was scheduled as late as possible to deter the accidental, more easily musically offended viewer. It had all the greats – Roxy Music, Captain Beefheart, Mott the Hoople, Can, Alex Harvey, Dr Feelgood, Alice Cooper and the New York Dolls, who presenter Whispering Bob Harris had taken some sort of instant dislike to and made no secret of it. He would later have no truck with punk either, giving rise to the perennial thorny question: was it possible to simultaneously like Little Feat *and* the Sex Pistols? I loved it all. The Felix the Cat/twenties flapper videos the show's producers put on to accompany some of the album tracks were a little bit naff, and they never had Amon Düül on, but nothing's ever perfect.

'Pop tripe' aside, I listened to every other kind of music: country, folk, funk, etc. This is probably why later in 1975 I ended up in a kind of folk-rock group whose name is lost in the mists of time. A good thing, no doubt. I think it was something to do with flowers of some kind, but I can't be certain. Perhaps it was birds? Maybe it was such an awful name I am ashamed to remember it.

They were a group put together by an acquaintance of Phil Swindells called Will Edwards. I used to see Will in the pub and we'd talk about music, what records we were listening to, and weren't the charts full of shit? That kind of thing.

A big night out in Macclesfield was usually a Friday, end of the working week. A gang of us would meet up at someone's house (never mine – living with my parents ruled that out). We'd put on some dubplates and have a few spliffs. Then play a bit of Johnny Guitar Watson or the Meters and roll a couple more joints, before commencing our grand tour of the public houses of Macclesfield – or at least those from which none of us were barred. A pint or two in each and then move on to the next. We'd try and end up in the Bear's Head for closing time in the hope of a lock-in. Failing that we could always try getting into Images or 'going on' Krumbles. I don't know why but it was always referred to as 'going on' the respective nightclub like it was some kind of horse.

Most of the time my face didn't fit and I'd get knocked back at the door. But if I timed it correctly before the pub closing-time rush when the place was pretty deserted and the door staff less attentive, I could get into Images. It served only lager on draught and a sparse selection of spirits, and there was usually an old bloke with slicked-back grey hair and a pink cravat at one end of the bar, leerily eyeing up any new female customers. The girls would give him a wide berth and, loaded up with rum and black, head for the small room at the back with the dancefloor. There was also a small balcony, reached by means of a wrought-iron spiral staircase down which many a pissed punter would tumble come closing time. The DJ was usually Barry White – no, not that Barry White. Barry was the guy who sold me the Hawkwind LP and now had a record shop of his own and moonlighted on the decks. He was pretty good – for Macc on a Friday night, he was perfect. He played a selection of soul classics and Parliament-Funkadelic's. 'Give Up the Funk (Tear the Roof Off the Sucker)' was always a hit with the late-night revellers. The mixing of hash, bitter and draught Holsten Pils, though, was a risky business. I found the trick was to stagger out into the cold and homewards before the room started to turn a full 360 degrees. The chill air would take the edge off long enough for my legs to gain adequate momentum to propel me back up Park Lane and home to bed without throwing up in a bin.

Then Will decided he'd start a band. We'd all decided we'd start a band at some time or other, and usually nothing came of it once we'd sobered up. But Will stuck at it. He played bass and soon he'd found a guitarist/singer and a keyboard player, and scrounged/bought some gear. He asked me if I'd like to do the drumming. Of course I said yes, and we started spending Saturday afternoons together rehearsing at the MADS Little Theatre in Macc. I should point out that Will was like Phil Swindells, another wholesome lad. He was a Christian youth-club goer and the rest of the group were of similarly healthy persuasions. I just about got away with smoking cigs but skinning up would have been a big no-no. Not that anyone was hardcore God Squad or anything – but (unfortunately) they were 'really nice'.

The first problem, and I suppose it's any band's first problem, is what music do you play? Sue, the keyboard player, wanted to do some songs that the guitarist hadn't heard of; Will wanted to do songs that the guitarist and Sue hadn't heard of; and I wanted to do a John Cale song ('Fear Is a Man's Best Friend') that none of them had heard of. Eventually we decided to start doing a Bob Dylan song. It was 'You Ain't Goin Nowhere', which embarrassingly I wasn't that familiar with, but the dithering had gone on for long enough. All Dylan songs sound a bit similar, I thought, so I just pretended I knew how it went and bluffed the rest. Anything just to get playing.

And so I learnt to drum and smoke while sitting in front of a fireplace.

It was a bit hesitant, stop-start, but eventually we got the hang of it and it didn't sound too bad. It even sounded a little like Bob Dylan. At least the day didn't end with the don't-call-us-we'll-call-you not-so-cheery goodbye.

The next week, after we'd remembered how to play the Dylan song again, things went a bit better, but there was still something awkward about it all. We all got on OK, but we were all shy and introverted with each other.

I'm ashamed to admit I can't recall the name of the guitarist, so let's call him Nick until I receive his official letter of complaint. His long, straight, blondish hair, Lennon specs and denim jacket with the big, rounded lapels gave him the look of either a shaggy John Denver or a trendy history teacher. He was a bit of a folk-club veteran and had written a song or two. 'Perhaps we should do one them?'

Original songs ... just like a proper group. So Nick played us a song in a folky singer/songwriter sort of vein and it sounded OK, but as it was just guitar and vocals I couldn't imagine what the drums were supposed to do on it and when.

The stuff I'd done with bands before – cabaret stuff and rock classics – I knew how they all went after a fashion: first bit, second bit, first bit again, second bit again, another bit until it stopped. But I just couldn't grasp this song of Nick's – it was like learning a foreign language. We made a cassette of us all playing the song but all you could hear were the drums, and no matter how quiet and gently I attempted to play it just got worse. So we relied on the tried-and-tested method of nodding to each other at the point where the changes were going to occur, and one in three times we got it right, almost, and that was good enough for Will. For if this was anyone's band, then it was his. Will, along with his friend George, who ferried us about in his orange Beetle, was the manager of sorts and he had faith and a bit of money.

We would go and record a demo of Nick's song in a proper record-ing studio, enter it in a songwriting competition run by Piccadilly Radio, play some gigs and get a record deal – easy.

The first bit was a breeze. Will booked Strawberry Studios in Stockport for half a day. The studio was owned by 'local legends' and 'professors of pop' 10cc.

10cc made very clever records. The production on them was always state-of-the-art and the lyrical subject matter was usually quirky. I like quirky. That 10cc were still based in the north-west/rainy Stockport and were investing their pop gold in the furtherance of other local bands, rather than flying off to the sun and swimming pools of LA, also struck me as something to admire.

Tucked behind the wedding-cake shape of Stockport Town Hall, Strawberry, with its gold discs, mirrored walls and aroma of fresh brewing Cona coffee, was awe-inspiring, fascinating and educational. I had a pretty good idea of what a recording studio was and what it did. But seeing a proper mixing desk and a twenty-four-track tape machine up close left me slightly awestruck. I mean, how did it all work? What did those lights mean? What was the buzzing noise in the headphones you had to wear? Should I mention that buzzing or not? These and many more questions were left unanswered but I learned a couple of things about the recording of drums. One was that it is not easy, especially if the drummer is virtually clueless – like myself. The second was the solution to the difficulty in the recording of drums lay in covering the heads first with toilet paper and gaffer tape and then, if that didn't work, draping them with tea towels and stuffing cushions into the bass drum. This seemed to me to make them sound worse, but what did I know? I had to play with head-phones on, but they kept falling off. I was going to fuck the song up, I knew I was. *How does it go again?*

We were supposed to do two or three songs but ended up only doing one. ('Being in a Band: Lesson 1': recording will always take longer than you think it will, no matter what the song is.) Nick's song was recorded, overdubbed and mixed by teatime. Not bad. My first day in a recording studio and, I have to admit, I thought it would be my last. Will duly entered the song into the Piccadilly Radio song contest.

We then managed to land a gig at Poynton Folk Club supporting Horslips – Ireland's premier folk-rock band. Horslips themselves were pretty sure that was the case as they turned up in their own customised Transit with 'Horslips – Ireland's Premier Folk-Rock Band' emblazoned on the side. I was impressed. *Wow, professionals*, I thought. *The romance of sleeping in the Transit as you make your way to the next gig.*

Our set was terrible. Luckily most of the audience had yet to arrive by the time we floundered onto the stage and floundered off again to deafening silence. 'Could have been worse,' I said, for it's part of the drummer's job to be eternally optimistic even in the face of unspeakable adversity. It's also part of the drummer's job to be universally ignored at times. This was one of those times.

Nick's song didn't win the Piccadilly Radio song contest, but it didn't come last either. It was in the runner-up category (is there anything sadder?), for which we received an invite to a 'do' at the Poco a Poco nightery, a Stockport club/casino that seemed to burst into flames quite frequently.

Here, the winners and runners-up would be presented with prizes by the judges, including sometime Womble Chris Spedding. I liked Chris Spedding, who was already a fabled session guitarist, so I went. Using the full range of my conversational skills, I said 'Hello, Chris' to him. I wonder if he remembers.

Not long after, the band drifted apart/went back to college/ rejoined the folk circuit/got a better job elsewhere. Any or all of those things.

The Poco was a class venue. I threw up there many times.
I particularly liked the Bitter Suite.

Faith, I had discovered, is not enough to get a band anywhere; neither is the combination of faith and money. I felt bad because Will must have spent quite a bit of it – half-days at Strawberry didn't come cheap. What we lacked more than anything was motivation. I remembered what a struggle it had been trying to get the Sunshine Valley Dance Band to make a proper racket. If there's no unshakeable conviction that what you're doing is fantastic, that it's you against the world, then you should be doing something else.

There is a very fine line that separates self-belief from ego-gratifying self-delusion, but passion can be infectious and unstoppable. In Macclesfield it was in very short supply. It still is.

On the plus side, the day in Strawberry did get me interested in how drums actually sounded. Tuning and all that nonsense was something that I didn't really understand (and I still don't fully); the only way to find out about that kind of thing was in the rare interviews with drummers usually tucked away in the back pages of *Melody Maker*, and they were frequently contradictory in the tips-and-advice department. My advice here, if you're interested, is to practise. Do it enough times and you'll work out what to do instinctively. Try explaining it to someone, and it sounds like mush.

The nights out at the pub and the late-night, dope-smoking, album-listening parties were a way of having a laugh. It was a way of forgetting the fact that, realistically, I was going to be stuck working in an office, answering the phone or going on the occasional embarrassing sales excursion with my dad for the rest of my life.

If I dwelt on my situation long enough, things would turn black, like they had when I was not going to Audenshaw. I could get maudlin. That would then turn into depression, then something worse. Self-medicating with dope and booze while listening to and reading about as much music as I could was my attempt at a cure.

An extended trip out to a drink-and-drugs-fuelled music orgy might be the answer. Once again the lure of half-cooked burgers, Hare Krishna chanting and the never-ending queue for the shit cabin called. Where did I put that sleeping bag?

Reading Festival 1975 would be my last festival for a while. I went with Phil Sturgess from school (not the drummer Phil), and the whole thing seemed a little bit of a 'for old times' sake' kind of deal – not so much my friendship with Phil, but the whole music scene felt like it needed to change somehow. Maybe it was just me, but it all felt a little bit stale.

Since my last festival outing, the audience had discovered a new form of 'self-expression'. This consisted of hurling cans and the odd empty, half-empty or full beer bottle – occasionally containing piss – in the general direction of the stage to express disapproval with the act currently performing, or maybe just life. Most of these fell short of their intended target and landed on the innocent bystanders nearest to the stage. Those left uninjured by this rain of metal, glass, beer and piss expressed their anger by returning fire to the rear. And so the Reading Festival beer-can artillery duel was born. It was both scary and dangerous. Proof, if any were needed, that there's never a Hells Angel or a policemen around when you need one.

I was looking forward to seeing Hawkwind again but, despite getting suitably stoned, I found that they were boring beyond belief. The excitement of 1972 had gone – maybe it left when Lemmy got fired a couple of months before Reading. It was, coincidentally, also Stacia's last gig with the band.

On the plus side, Dr Feelgood were razor-sharp and stupendous. No frills, just raw rock-and-roll energy. Chirpy cockney Gary Holton's Heavy Metal Kids had something exciting about them too.

With hindsight you could see what would be coming in the next year or so. Even the Ozark Mountain Daredevils were surprisingly not bad and the Kursaal Flyers were fantastic but Supertramp and Yes *again*? Why had I come here? Yes to me symbolised everything that was wrong with music. Concept albums that went on and on – *Tales from Topographic Oceans* – do me a favour! Even the most elevated of consciousnesses would have struggled to see anything but old farts blabbering on and on and on. That Lou Reed couldn't be arsed turning up said something. (He was probably sick of people asking him whether *Metal Machine Music* was a joke or not.) If I remember correctly, and my mind by the third night was ever so slightly addled, the comedy rock band the Albertos stood in for him in spirit by kicking off with the Velvet's pastiche, 'Anadin'. It was very apt, as was their Yes send-up 'Close to the Bar', the Albertos' legendary Manchester drummer Bruce Mitchell sharp as ever. I did my best to love the Mahavishnu Orchestra featuring John McLaughlin but just got headache. Bruce Mitchell versus Billy Cobham? Mm – no contest.

If you were pretentious enough, you could say, 'I could almost feel the contractions of punk waiting to be born.'

PART 2:

FROM WARSAW TO JOY DIVISION

I could almost feel the contractions of punk waiting to be born.

Stick a bunch of blokes of a certain age together and give them enough booze, and they will get all misty-eyed about some year in the late 1970s, generally 1976. For this, gentle reader, was what is widely accepted to be the Year Zero of punk.

A quality periodical unsuitable for adults.

The debate will then descend into where-did-it-all-actually-start? territory. Was it the first Stooges record? Or the MC5's *Kick Out the Jams*? Maybe the first New York Dolls album, the first Velvets or maybe it was the Deviants or something by the Pink Fairies? Unlikely as it sounds now, maybe it was the first Roxy album for, without glam, punk and new wave would have looked very different. Oh, and while we're at it, what about northern soul? Though that is perhaps stretching it a bit. Perhaps it was the Modern Lovers' first LP. What about Alice Cooper – surely Alice had been a punk at some time?

Alice Cooper was the first band that I can remember people really getting upset and shocked about.

'A man with a girl's name?'

'He performs with a live snake?'

'Mock executions?'

OK, this wasn't entirely a new idea. Screamin' Jay Hawkins and the anglicised version, Screaming Lord Sutch, had been doing a similar act for years, and I'll bet they weren't the first.

All the same, the guardians of the nation's morals said such behaviour was too much for the young people of Great Britain. That most of Alice's act was purely theatrics was by the by. It went to show that if you upset the right people you could go far, you could make a name for yourself.

You could make a pretty good case for any of the above-mentioned bands as punk progenitors. It's a bit like trying to pin the tail on an unwilling donkey, but it's a lively after-dinner conversation pretty much guaranteed. The weird thing is that, back in the mid-1970s, all the teenage kids who went on to love punk would have been listening to much the same records – heavy rock, bits of Bowie, Iggy and Lou Reed, and of course a fair bit of prog – but that was all swept under the carpet after 1976 for fear of mockery or persecution by the musical cognoscenti. These days, it's nearly OK to admit to owning *The Snow Goose* by Camel, but in 1976 it was a real no-no, a musical faux pas.

I don't think there is any real answer to the question 'When did it all start?' Punk wasn't one big bang but a slower coming-together of a number of things, musical and social, from 1975 onwards, eventually gaining critical mass at the end of the 1970s, and collapsing and fragmenting into the 1980s.

The first bands that I thought of as playing punk rock were the Stooges and the MC5; bands that were about anger and energy. In the very early days of punk, it was the American bands that I went for first: the Ramones and the Modern Lovers' classic first album.

If the 1960s were all about peace and love, then by the end of the 1970s that was replaced by boredom and frustration.

In music, there was a lot to be bored by: bored by bands putting out triple-length concept albums of airy-fairy nonsense, bored by guitar solos that went on and on, definitely bored by drummers performing endless, self-indulgent drum solos that were the aural equivalent of Mogadon. That more of them weren't guillotined is a wonder.

The music press was full of news of punk bands and tales of the goings-on at the Roxy and the 100 Club in London, and at CBGBs in New York. Full of talk of things that were being done, that were new and fresh and vital, driven by youth, not by the out-of-touch old farts who ran the record business (the most boring of them all).

I remember staggering home from the pub one Saturday night to see the Sex Pistols do 'Anarchy in the UK' on Tony Wilson's show *So It Goes*. It looks a bit tame when you see it now but in 1976 it was electrifying: they were shocking the old folks. That was exactly what I wanted to do and had been wanting to do for ages. Now it was happening and someone else was doing it.

'New Rose' by the Damned was the first UK punk single, just beating 'Anarchy' by the Pistols by a couple of weeks. I bought it and virtually wore it out. It was jam-packed full of energy, an incandescent three minutes that managed to reference the Shangri-Las in the process. The Pistols and the Damned were soon joined by Buzzcocks and the Clash in getting heavy rotation on the Morrises' stereo. *Never Mind the Bollocks* came out on my birthday. I didn't get given it as a present.

The appealing thing about the Sex Pistols particularly and punk generally was the way it really did upset people. The self-appointed guardians of public morals, aka the acolytes of Mary Whitehouse, would turn up with placards bearing slogans such as 'Ban this Filth' at the first hint of anything that threatened their conservative Christian viewpoint. This included homosexuality (obviously), virtually the entire output of the BBC, Alice Cooper (of course), Chuck Berry, violent films, unchristian films (they loved picketing cinemas) and even a play about the Romans in Britain. To Mrs Whitehouse, punk was like a red rag to a bull. The Pistols swearing on Bill Grundy's *Today* show, by today's standards pretty hard to spot, caused an outrage of biblical proportions. It might seem comical today, but to some, punks were seen as the disciples of Beelzebub: the sky was falling in. The share price of EMI (for a short while the Pistols' label) plummeted. It was front-page news. The old folks were scared. Three fucks, two shits and one bastard on teatime TV was all it took. Bring on the revolution.

This was exciting!

I'd been to see old favourite Frank Zappa at Stafford a couple of weeks before 'Anarchy' came out and, much as I liked Frank's stuff, it seemed to be veering straight into that long-winded-virtuoso-self-indulgence territory. What might have been interesting or amusing once upon a time was now getting fucking tedious. I still bought Zappa's records, just in case it was an off night, but there was definitely something written on the wall. I left the gig feeling disappointed and a bit let down.

Punk was turning everything on its head. Most importantly for me, it had that DIY ethic: you could make your own record, fuck the majors, you could do anything you wanted, be anyone you wanted.

I wanted to get involved. Anyone could, it was all inclusive.

One record that, for me, really added to this overall wind-of-change feeling about music was the release in January 1977 of David Bowie's *Low*. If there was one single LP that would influence me, this was it. *Low* sounded to me like music from another dimension.

The high energy of punk rock was nothing new. High-energy rock had been around since at least 1969 with the Detroit sound of MC5 and the Stooges. What was new was the attitude and DIY rebellious spirit that it represented. But in 1977 what Bowie did with *Low* was different: experimental in an almost Krautrock kind of way. It's two sides fitted my life perfectly. Side one as pre night-out mood lifter and side two as come home, chill out.

9

WARSAW

On 26 May 1977, the band Warsaw first entered my life. I'd gone to the Free Trade Hall to see Television and Blondie. I loved Television. Their first album is a classic and this was a great bill, showcasing the diversity of what punk/new wave was about. Blondie and Television were from opposite poles: Blondie did the three-minute classic dancey pop songs and Television played the longer, evolving art-schooly kind of tunes that were a bit more cerebral. The music papers had raved about Tom Verlaine and Richard Lloyd's 'sizzling twin lead guitar interplay' ever since 'Little Johnny Jewel' in 1975. The way the two worked together on *Marquee Moon* sounded more abstract and jazzy than most of the other NY bands.

Television, unfortunately, were to be one of the first new-wave bands to fall victim to the dreaded old-school showbiz blight of musical differences. Their original bassist Richard Hell (cited by Malcolm McLaren as the inspiration for the safety-pin punk look) was, it seemed, a bit too rowdy and not new wave enough, a little too wild and maverick for Verlaine, whose real name is Thomas Miller. If you take your name from a French symbolist poet there is always the distinct possibility you may be taking it all a tad too seriously. Hell left or was pushed, and went and formed the Heartbreakers (no, not Tom Petty's band) with ex-New York Dolls Johnny Thunders and

Jerry Nolan. He then parted company with them and went on to form the Voidoids. Hell certainly got about.

Blondie would later become pivotal – the band that crossed disco's uncool and indie's cool with 'Heart of Glass', a musical landmark. Tonight, though, it was just cool pop supporting cool art rock.

In the bar at the intermission after Blondie's set, I queued and fought for half a shandy (drinking and driving responsibly), and being on my own ended up buying a copy of a fanzine off a bloke. I was hoping it would make me look a bit less of a lonely loser. I retired to a corner for a browse. The mag was called *Shy Talk* and it was the work of a guy called Steve Shy. Its homemade pages were filled with items about the Manchester punk scene, Buzzcocks, the Drones and I think the Worst were in there too. It was both an informative and educational read. Near the back there was a section that, for obvious reasons, caught my eye: 'DRUMMER WANTED'.

Three newly formed bands were looking for drummers: the Fall, V2 and Warsaw. I'd never heard of any of them. Possibly a look of mild interest passed across my face, but most likely not, as I stuffed the rag in the old bulging right inside pocket, polished off the shandy and got back to my seat pronto to beat the usual last-minute rush. This was the standard drill at the Free Trade Hall and had been for years, along with shouting 'Wally' and throwing paper planes off the balcony – there were some hippie traditions that would not die quickly.

Television impressed. They did most of *Marquee Moon* and finished with a couple of covers – 'Knockin' on Heaven's Door' and 'Satisfaction'. They also did an unreleased track, 'Foxhole', which I thought sounded pretty good. It boded well for their next record. I was full of expectation for the future, well the future of Television at least. It was a different story when their 'hotly anticipated' second album came out less than a year later. It was bloody awful. I tried to like it, but even the garish red vinyl it was pressed on emphasised the fact that it had been overthought. The life had been produced and polished out of it. A band that I had thought were genius had let me down; it would not be for the last time. Maybe Richard Hell should have stayed after all.

Why do they call it 'musical differences' anyway? It seems like band splits are rarely anything to do with music. It's the people who create and perform the music that cause all the trouble.

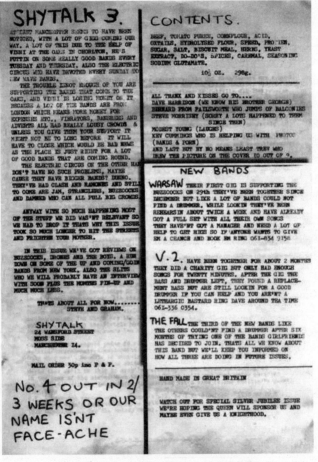

The great drummer shortage of the late seventies was a troubling time.

So, thanks to the wonderful lo-fi publication *Shy Talk*, the name Warsaw had entered my head. It had been checked and filed, and that was more or less that. I didn't really fancy the prospect of another don't-call-us audition.

A couple of weeks after the Television gig I spotted an advert in the *Record Mirror*. It was a bit of a second division music paper. *Melody Maker*, the *NME* and *Sounds* were the main ones, and I thought reading *Record Mirror* was a bit desperate or lightweight at the time. Not something you owned up to reading willingly. But being inquisitive and enthusiastic, I used to read all the papers, including the motleys such as *ZigZag*, *Creem* and *Let It Rock*. It was the only way to keep up with what was happening.

I enjoyed looking hopefully through *Melody Maker*'s musicians-wanted ads – 'Drummer for hot new band with record company interest – must have own gear and transport' – with stars in my eyes, but the reality was I'd pretty much resigned myself to it all being a bit out of my reach. Since the petering out of the Folk Band Whose Name I Don't Remember, I'd concluded that I would forever be a recreational drummer, making a racket in my dad's bedroom. But it turned out punk would change all that.

I wanted to do something, instead of skiving and lurking around Macclesfield, but the *Record Mirror* ad wasn't for a musician. Simple and straightforward, it just said 'Fancy a career as a music journalist? The *Record Mirror* is looking for new writers. Simply write a review of a record and send it to us. The lucky winner will get a chance to become a writer for *Record Mirror*.'

I had recently started and then swiftly abandoned a fanzine of my own. It went by the pretentious name of *Fatal Errors* and was doomed by the office Roneo printer; it wasn't really up to the job, but that might have been because I didn't really know how to work it. My efforts ground to a halt at page 2, with the machine spewing out a mass of inky, illegible pages as I cranked its handle. But my journalistic pretensions were not going to be deterred by a compli-cated machine. Seeing the *Record Mirror* advert, I thought here's an opportunity to become a journalist. You have to remember that, back then, to us avid readers, the writers were almost as interesting as the bands they wrote about.

Johnny Rotten had said (at least according to Caroline Coon's book, 1988), 'Everyone is so fed up with the old way. We are constantly being dictated to by musical old farts out of university who've got rich parents. They look down on us and treat us like fools and expect us to pay POUNDS to see them while we entertain them and not the other way around.'

So I thought, as a writer, I could be an antidote to the old farts and I too could be punk. OK, my parents were reasonably well off, but I had evaded university and therefore a life of musical dictatorship quite successfully. And I was not up for entertaining anyone, espe-cially students.

I quickly bashed out my thoughts on Elvis Costello's *My Aim is True*, which had only just been released, hoping to impress with my up-to-the-minuteness. I slipped it in with the office post and, after a few days, forgot all about it.

On another baking hot day of 1977's endless summer, I was trying to spin out my lunchbreak for as long as possible and set out in search of Macclesfield's largest Cornish pasties. These could only be had (so legend had it) from the pie shop near the train station. (In Macclesfield, pie shops were very high on the cultural agenda; they still are, for that matter.) Pausing for a look at the gear for sale in Jones's music shop on the way down the slope of Queen Victoria Street to the pie empo-rium, I spotted a new handwritten advert in the window.

It said, 'Drummer Wanted for Local New Wave Band Warsaw Phone Ian XXXXXX'. There was that name again – combined with word 'Local' and a Macc phone number, it was too good an opportunity to miss. It was fate, kismet – something of that nature. I made up my mind to have another shot at glory and call that number. I scribbled it on the back of my hand in biro and pushed on to the pastie place.

I called as soon as I got back to my junk-cluttered desk. Ian, the author of the advert, answered.

'Hi, my name's Steve. I'm ringing about the drummer-wanted ad in Jones's window,' I said apprehensively.

'Right, great.' He sounded very affable. I don't know why but I was expecting this conversation to be difficult, awkward or at least to move quickly to 'No, it's all right, mate, we're fixed up, ta' and that would be that, but it didn't.

He explained the band hadn't been going for that long, they'd done a few gigs and he'd got a tape of some songs he could lend me if I wanted to pop round to his house that evening.

His house? His parents', surely?

He said that the rest of the group – Peter and Bernard (Did I hear that right? Sounded more like a folk duo than punk, but who was I to question?) – were on holiday in France till the end of the following week.

I asked where he lived.

'Barton Street, off Park Lane,' he replied.

'Just down the road from me then, I'm on Ivy Lane.' Realising that this didn't sound like an address with much street cred, I added, 'Close to the Weston Estate end.'

'Oh, Debbie's parents live near the Weston. I know it pretty well. Pop round about teatime, half-sixish, and I'll play you the cassette.'

'Right, half-six it is. See you then.'

I settled down to an afternoon of dodging work and letting the monster pastie go down.

Six o'clock rolled round and, not wanting to be late, I scrounged the use of my mother's Austin Maxi and set off down the road for Barton Street.

Ian's house was a double-fronted end terrace on the corner. I parked up and knocked on the door.

'Hi, I'm Steve, the drummer.'

'Ooh hiya, Steve, come in, come in. This is Debbie, Debbie this is Steve. He's come about the advert in Jones's.'

He had blue eyes and a haircut like Augustus Caesar.

'That was quick,' said Debbie.

'I know. Come in here, Steve,' showing me into the blue room on the left of the hall. It seemed that he genuinely did live in his own house with his wife, which was very grown-up. 'The record player's in here. What sort of stuff are you into? Would you like a cup of tea? We've just ate, it's no bother.'

We sat on the sofa and Ian offered a packet of Marlboro.

'Want a fag?'

'No thanks, I've just given up.' This was true. I hadn't had a smoke for two weeks and was feeling quite proud of myself.

'Go on,' he insisted good-naturedly, 'one won't make any difference.'

'Well, I don't suppose it will, will it? Just one, mind.'

I am very easily led.

I gave him an edited CV of my drumming career. Leaving out cabaret and folk bands, it was basically, 'I've got some drums and I think I can play them.'

He told me about the record stall he used to have on the market, prompting a game of what's the rarest album you've ever seen/ bought/sold?

We talked about bands – Bowie, the Velvets, New York Dolls, Iggy – and books we'd read – William Burroughs, Ballard etc. – and found we had a lot in common. He gave me a brief history of the band, that they'd already done gigs with Johnny Thunders and Penetration (Warsaw were credited on the flyer as 'Stiff Kittens' but soon changed their name). I was impressed. He put the tape on and we listened.

'It's not a great recording.'

I thought the tape sounded OK. I'd heard worse. It sounded a lot better than the cassette recordings of Will's band.

Warsaw's origins lay in the now mythical gig of 4 June 1976: the Sex Pistols' first gig at Manchester's Lesser Free Trade Hall. Not so much a gig, more an epiphany. Most of the numerically impossible number of people who claim to have been in that tiny audience were righteously inspired to go forth and form a band in tribute or something. I wouldn't know. I wasn't there. Friday night was a big drinking night in Macclesfield.

Here, some attendees reminisce about the gig. You may have heard of some of them. They may do more of this type of thing later on or they may not: they're an awkward bunch.

They are being treated to a free Chinese lunch one Sunday. I am elsewhere:

TW (Tony Wilson): Who was at the very first gig?
PH (Peter Hook): Me and Barny and Ian. Well, Ian was there on his own. We weren't, were we? He was there . . .
Mary Harron: Was this the first gig they played in Manchester?
PH: Yeah.
TW: This was when there was, there was thirty-five people . . .
PH: 50p.
TW: I was there.
PH: I remember seeing you, yeah.
TW: There was thirty-five people, well thirty-five to forty . . .
PH: What's that?
IC (Ian Curtis): I don't know.
TW: It was arranged by Howard Devoto.
TW: It was set up by Howard Devoto and . . . what else happened that night . . . There was . . . Pete Shelley did the lights. Buzzcocks hadn't been formed at this point . . .

IC: They were advertised on the tickets though weren't they?

PH: Yeah.

TW: Were they?

PH: Yeah.

BS: That was the best gig they played there.

PH: I reckon it was the best gig they ever played.

TW: The very first one?

BS: Yeah, it was great that.

TW: It was funny in that little audience, the very little hall, in this little tiny hall, it was like a very small audience and people were yelling 'Eddie an the 'Ot Rods!' Remember that?

PH: That was because they'd had that fight with them hadn't they?

TW: That's right.

MH: Oh right, right, right

PH: Over the equipment.

IC: Was it John the Postman at the back shouting 'Ultimate Spinach' . . .?

TW: That's right, John the Postman, who's a great Manchester character, was shouting . . . insults, and when someone shouted Eddie and the Hot Rods, John said, 'We're not facking ripoffs!'

PH: Yeah, that's right.

TW: And then everyone was screaming and my favourite moment was when John said, he looked down and said – everyone was going 'urgh urgh urgh!' you know – and he looked down and he said, 'TELL ME ABAHT IT!'

PH: Have you heard the bootleg?

TW: I've got it, yeah, love it.

BS: What's that?

MH: How long after that did it take for a Manchester music scene to start? . . . No thanks.

PH: He'll tell you about that cos I don't know.

TW: It really took four weeks cos then the Pistols came back a month later and played with Slaughter and the Dogs and Buzzcocks.

BS: Didn't think it was as good.

TW: I was away, I was on holiday, I missed that one.

PH: With Slaughter? Slaughter were terrible, they were so posey compared to Johnny Rotten. They dressed up like Bowie and Ronson.

RG (Rob Gretton): Yeah but they could play compared to ... Buzzcocks.

PH: There was a big fight.

TW: Yeah, Buzzcocks couldn't play at all.

PH: All the Slaughter and the Dogs fans had a fight with the Sex Pistols fans.

TW: They always do. Slaughter and the Dogs used to have a roadie called Shed ...

RG: Still have.

TW: Still have. He picks fights with everybody. I once hauled him off Pauline one night. Penetration had finished at Rafters and Shed, 'Right, up for a fight? Your band's crap!!' and this poor little girl, you know, he was insisting on having a fight with her. Is that your lager or mine?

IC: That's my lager!

TW: Is that mine?

Ian, Bernard, Peter and their friend Terry Mason were genuinely at the Lesser Free Trade Hall and, moved by the spirit of punk and a bit of 'if this lot can get away with it, anybody can' sympathetic inspiration, the idea of what would become Warsaw was born.

Initially they were two bands: Bernard, Peter and Terry on one side and Ian and another Ian on the other. Other bands who trace their genesis to that Lesser Free Trade Hall night were the Fall, Buzzcocks and, allegedly, the Smiths.

Ian told me that Warsaw had parted company with the drummer on the tape.

'He's gone off to join another band.'

I didn't ask questions – no point.

'Have another fag,' he said, so I did. We chatted away over coffee about punk bands, the scene in Manchester and Ian's plans for the band. He had ideas, lots of them. We hit it off straight away.

After a couple of hours I left with the tape so I could do my best to learn the songs. He said he would call me once the others got back and to fix up a rehearsal.

Back at home I gave the tape a few more listens. The tracks on it were: 'Inside the Line', 'At a Later Date', 'Gutz', 'The Kill' and 'You're No Good for Me'. And I think 'Reaction' and 'Tension' might have been on there too.

The songs were a bit punk-by-numbers but the band sounded pretty tight. One thing that did strike me was that the bass sounded a bit weird, a bit like a flute somehow.

All right, they weren't the best tunes I'd ever heard but at least they were their own, and the thing about your own songs is that no one can say you're playing them wrong. Well, that's the theory anyway.

I listened to the tape a few more times until I thought I'd got the general idea and waited for a call from Ian, which came the middle of the following week.

Peter and Bernard were back from holiday, and could I do a rehearsal in Manchester, twelve o'clock-ish Saturday afternoon?

I said, 'Pick you up about half-eleven then.' As if I had a car.

Warsaw are one of many recent new wave functional bands; easily digestible, doomed maybe to eternal support spots. Whether they will find a style of their own is questionable, but probably not important. Their instinctive energy often compensates for the occasional lameness of their songs, but they seem unaware of the audience when performing.

Paul Morley, 'They Mean It in M-a-a-a-nchester', *New Musical Express* (30 July 1977)

10

DRUMMER AND DRIVER

'Can I borrow the car again this Saturday? Something's come up' was becoming my new catchphrase. There wasn't much point my mum asking me what that something might be. I was naturally evasive.

Drums and their transportation. I was getting pretty good at packing up and moving an unfeasibly large kit – I did it every night, after all, shifting drums and clattering cymbals from one bedroom to another, stumbling over a percussion mountain if I needed the loo in the night. But cramming them all in the back of an Austin Maxi and setting off for the big city felt like a bit of an adventure.

First stop Barton Street to pick up Ian and his bits of gear. A mic, some leads, a TVM Sound PA amp (made in Manchester) and a pair of Vox column speakers; boot slammed shut and we were off

'Where we off to then, Ian?'

'Do you know the way to Strangeways?'

'What, Strangeways the nick?' I didn't know if I liked the sound of this.

'Yeah, that's right.'

'Er, sorry, no, actually I don't.'

'I said we'd meet them there. I work not far from there so I know where it is, don't worry.'

I was beginning to wonder whether this 'Bernard and Peter's holiday' story might be euphemism for something a little more sinister ...

<u>TENSION</u>

Routine brings me down
drives me to the ground
some kinda life -- makes it easy for more
some kinda strain keeps me screwed to the floor

Useless vengeance breeds
built of last years downs
slow motion without speed
cuts across all concentration
cuts beyond all limits of normal frustration

I'm so tensed up I'm so tensed up,
I'm so tensed up I'm so tensed up.

No escape at all
fugitive of all law
gonna break this life in two
gonna break it up if its the last thing i do

Mother are you ready
to turn me in again
just a test case cut and tried
put down to save your skin
cant you see I'm drowning and youve pushed me again.

I'm so tensed up I'm so tensed up,
I'M so tensed up I'm so tensed up,
tensed up tensed up tensed up.

I. Curtis
(February 1977).

'Tension' – lyrics to an early song.

We whiled away the drive into Manchester talking about music and growing up in Macclesfield. It turned out Ian was another ex-King's schoolboy, just like me, but being older he would have been a year above me. Strange we never met, though. It wasn't that big a place and we had so much in common. He remembered the fuss about me and my friends' expulsion. Ooh, the scandal. Apparently the older boys and prefects had been instructed to keep a lookout for empty cough medicine bottles and to inspect the younger pupils for signs of narcotic intoxication. That made me laugh, though it all seemed a lifetime ago.

True to his word, Ian got us to Strangeways without us getting lost and in record time too. It's hard to miss, really – a bloody big Victorian prison with an ominous tower.

We were a bit early and hanging about outside a prison was a new Saturday afternoon diversion for me. It felt like we were there to spring some old lag. The *Sweeney* vibe went up a notch with the arrival of a Mark 2 Jag, the traditional getaway car of many an East End villain, shortly followed by a Honda motorbike.

'Here they are. That's Hooky's car.'

Obviously I hadn't been paying enough attention as this was the first time I'd heard the name 'Hooky' mentioned. A bearded bloke got out of the Jag. *Ah*, I thought, *Hooky must be either Bernard or Peter's dad or uncle, something like that.* (Bit of an old bloke's car, the Mark 2 Jag, after all.) Call me beardist, but there was no way I thought he was going to be one of the band unless they really were more folky than the cassette suggested. Well, appearances can be deceptive.

We got out and said our hellos. The one on the motorcycle turned out to be Bernard and the bearded Hooky and Peter were revealed as one and the same. Introductions and confusion over, we set off in a Hooky-led convoy bound for the Abraham Moss community centre in Crumpsall. To the casual observer watching us pull out from Strangeways, it may have looked like we were a bunch of ne'er-do-wells off on a job to knock off a bookies.'

We set up my drums and the amps from the back of the Jag in a small room in the modern community centre. After a bit of chat and some amp fiddling, we set to making a racket. I just did my usual stuff of frantic thrashing, which had not won any admirers in the past. But for once it seemed to fit in with what everyone else was playing.

Hooky had an aggressive, driving way of playing the bass and Bernard, the most musical of the bunch, had a great guitar sound. They were a lot tighter than anyone else I had played with and seemed more organised. Hooky and Bernard were both easy-going and I guessed had similar musical tastes to Ian. They'd known each other at Salford Grammar School and consequently had a shared history. I got the impression the band functioned as a sort of democracy. This was how I thought a punk/new wave enterprise should work – it fitted with my old hippie/underground leanings.

We went through all the songs on the tape, had a fag break for me and Ian, another bit of a chat about life and bands, and then went through the songs again.

'Another one from Macc, eh? You'll be all right for a lift home now, won't you, Ian?'

'It's a bit of a greaser town Macclesfield, isn't it? Don't they all shag sheep and that?' was Bernard's take on my home town.

'Only when it's very very cold,' I said.

Apart from Bernard, we had similar office-bound jobs, Ian at Manpower services and Hooky at the Manchester Ship Canal Company. Bernard worked at Cosgrove Hall, the animation studio that produced the kids' TV classics *Chorlton and the Wheelies* and, later, *Danger Mouse*. It was, according to the *Evening News*, Manchester's version of Disney but without the theme park. Working in film production, even if it was of the two-dimensional rodent kind, had to be more creative than shuffling paper and getting bollocked when a delivery driver got lost.

At some point Bernard and Hooky's friend Terry Mason appeared, though I don't think we were formerly introduced at the time. I thought his name was a parody of Perry Mason, Raymond Burr's TV lawyer. His role in the band was a bit vague – that he was something was obvious but not what that was. Time would eventually assign various roles to Terry: guitarist, manager, live sound engineer and tour manager were some of his many job descriptions. Every band has someone like Terry, and their importance should not be underestimated.

Apart from the odd complaint from the community-centre caretaker about the volume, everyone was happy at the end of the day. And as no one else had applied for the job I would have to do. They never told me this. As they hadn't actually sacked me, I assumed I was in.

Driving home, Ian and I talked about gigs and how to go about getting them. Getting in a band now looked like the easy bit – anyone could start a group – but if you couldn't get to play anywhere, what was the point?

Ian had some contacts: Buzzcocks manager, Richard Boon; Music Force, a Manchester music collective/agency set up by Martin Hannett (called Martin Zero at the time) and Suzanne O'Hara; plus he knew a couple of people at RCA's Manchester office.

I didn't even know RCA had a Manchester office. It turned out it was in Piccadilly Plaza, where I used to go to get out of the rain when I was avoiding going to Audenshaw Grammar. I'd spent many unhappy hours sitting in there studying *ZigZag*'s Rock Family Trees and never noticed. I was either a bit depressed or a bit out of it at the time, so no wonder.

Ian would use the phone at his work to pester any likely source for a chance of a gig and, as I had easy access to a phone at the office, it wouldn't be long before I would be doing the same.

Imagine my surprise and delight when a couple of days after the first Warsaw rehearsal I got a letter with a fancy London postmark.

I may have forgotten about the *Record Mirror* job, but they hadn't forgotten about me. The job was surely mine.

Er, well no, actually.

'Thank you for your review, unfortunately you were not successful on this occasion . . .' blah-blah-blah, polite rejection letter stuff, except for '. . . however we would like you to write for us on a freelance basis – please call XXXXXXXXX to discuss this further if you are interested'.

I had no idea what the words 'freelance basis' meant but this was something not to be sniffed at. I would get my name in the papers again, and not in the local crime section for once.

This punk thing (or was it new wave? To the man in the street they were one and the same but there were crucial differences) really was fantastic. Suddenly I had gone from a work-shy 'office employee' to a drummer in a band that had gigs (well, maybe) and now I was a music journalist. My lack of qualifications had not been questioned once. New wave, punk, call it what you like, to me it was the land of opportunity.

Back at work I waited for my fellow office skivers to slip off for a well-earned tea break and commandeered the phone. I dialled the number as instructed in the letter from *Record Mirror*.

The very nice lady at the other end explained that all I would have to do was go to gigs and write a review of what I saw. This they would then publish in the *Record Mirror* and I would receive money.

Fantastic, I thought. 'How much money?' I asked.

Now here it all got a little vague, with much talk of pounds per hundreds of words and such like. I kind of drifted off and imagined myself waltzing into the Rainbow or the Marquee or other such far-flung venues, all expenses paid no doubt.

Er, no.

The gigs in question 'would be in your locality so you shouldn't have far to go. Call us once a week and we will let you know what we want you to do. No, of course you won't have to pay to get in. How silly!'

Well that was something, even though it wasn't quite the marvellous deal I was expecting. It was a start and who knew where it might lead?

Where it led was Rafters, a suitably dark basement club on Manchester's Oxford Street.

I'd kept my eyes on the forthcoming attractions in the *Manchester Evening News*, wondering where my first journalistic assignment would take me. I was obviously hoping for a gig at the Free Trade Hall or maybe the Apollo, or maybe it wouldn't be in Manchester at all . . . bound to be somebody famous.

I rang the *Record Mirror* and a chap in the editorial department said that I should go to see a group I'd never heard of called Ed Banger and the Nosebleeds.

'They're from Manchester and they've got a single coming out this week. We'll put the review in next week. Don't worry about paying, we'll sort out getting you into the gig.'

Thursday 25 August 1977 rolled around and, with a good supply of fags – I was back up to thirty a day again by then – and a pocketful of stolen office biros, I set off for the big city.

'Hello, I'm from *Record Mirror*. I'm here to review the gig,' I announced to the girl behind the till.

'Oh that's nice, lucky you, that'll be seventy pence.'

So with dreams of free admission and the possibility of being blackmailed with free booze more than slightly dashed, I went on down the steps to the subterranean nightspot.

I bought myself a half and sat down at a table next to the dance-floor to take in the surroundings. They were of the dimly lit bierkeller, olde world fake wood beams and red paint variety prevalent in the 1970s. Nice drinking ambience, though.

I was a journalist, I thought, and what I needed was a bit of background. I would have to engage someone in conversation.

The DJ looked as if he would be a likely source of local knowledge. He was playing some good tracks and was chatting freely with the regulars. Spotting my chance, I went over and sort of hovered in the vicinity of the DJ booth. Where I was professionally ignored.

'Hi there,' I said finally.

'Hi,' he grunted.

'Have you got any Patti Smith? I mean I wasn't that sure about the *Horses* record and that. But I think the new one, that *Radio Ethiopia*, is really good, the first track on side one in particular. Why don't you play that?' I spluttered, expecting a critique of the Smith canon to be forthcoming and perhaps eventually a bit of background on Mr Banger and his Nosebleeds.

'Fuck off' was the somewhat harsh response.

Twat, I thought but did not say.

I had just met Robert Leo Gretton, destined to become a rather important figure in my life.

Still trying to look cool but not succeeding, I shuffled back to my table, which in the course of my weighty dialogue with the DJ had been claimed by another solitary lad like myself.

'Er, do you mind if I sit here?' I asked, indicating my chair.

'Feel free.'

A period of awkwardness followed. I finished my half and blurted, 'Hi, I'm reviewing the gig for *Record Mirror*. Would you like a drink?'

'That's nice. Yes, ta, I'll have an 'alf.'

Ice now broken, we embarked on a discussion of the Manchester punk scene – Buzzcocks and Slaughter and the Dogs mostly. The Nosebleed's single 'Ain't Bin to No Music School' was coming out on Rabid, the Manchester label that had released the Buzzcocks *Spiral Scratch* EP. My new friend was a mine of information. The conversation expanded to take in various new bands and, not wishing to seem totally thick, I finally came out with 'Have you heard of a band called Warsaw?'

'Warsaw? Yeah.'

'Any good?'

'All right. Singer's a bit of a nutter.'

Thinking he must have misheard me or something, I let the matter drop. Maybe there was another band called something like Warsaw with an enraged singer. He couldn't mean affable Ian ...

The gig was great. I think they played 'Ain't Bin to No Music School' twice and Ed Banger was what you might call an animated frontman. The guitarist was particularly good.

After the set was over I did a bit of hovering near the dressing-room door at the side of the stage and using the 'Hi, I'm from *Record Mirror*' line yet again, had a bit of a chat with the guitar player. He told me he was inspired by all kinds of revolutionary music and was a genuinely nice person. He said his name was Vini Reilly.

I think I gave them a good review.

Ian and Terry, meanwhile, had managed to cadge a gig out of Roger Eagle, who was manager at Eric's in Liverpool. Well, it was more an audition really. Roger was doing this thing on Saturdays where the bands would do two sets, a matinee in the afternoon for the under-eighteens and a late-night slot for the regular punters. We could come and do the matinee support slot for X-Ray Spex and if Roger liked what he saw he would put us on again.

We squeezed in another quick practice at Bernard's place of work in Chorlton and one late summer Saturday morning I knocked off work early, loaded up the kit, collected Ian, and set off for Liverpool. Ian kindly lent me his Gary Gilmore execution T-shirt for the gig – my wardrobe was a little light on stage wear (it still is). I think my mum shrank it in the wash.

We were hoping to badger our way into doing both slots but, despite Terry, Ian and Hooky's best efforts at persuading Roger and X-Ray Spex's road manager, we had to settle for just the afternoon show. Well, getting any gig was a success.

The gig was the most exhilarating thing I'd ever done.

I think that the assembled Liverpool youth – there weren't that many of them – were impressed by our slightly nervy performance and we left with the promise of a repeat booking from Roger.

By seven o clock I was back in the pub in Macc toasting my Warsaw debut with a pint of bitter. I'd like to think I was the envy of all my chums but the general reaction was more like:

'It won't last, y'know.'

'This punk stuff's just a flash in't pan.'

'You 'avin a safety pin through yer nose then or what?'

That's Macc for you, I thought, walking home with a spliff in hand.

In truth there were very few piercings and leather jackets at the gig. No show-offs, for the most part.

The Eric's gig was my also my introduction to Ian as the frontman. At the rehearsals he had seemed pretty reserved: sitting down, mumbling or occasionally shouting his words into the mic. At the gig he was a lot more . . . animated. Especially for a Saturday afternoon. I remembered the words of the guy at the Nosebleeds gig and, though I couldn't agree with his assertion that he was a 'nutter', Ian was a lot livelier than I had been expecting. In a good way, of course. The sort of way you'd want a lead singer to be.

When starting a band, the hardest job to fill initially is that of singer. It's always a big challenge. You could find a mate – a bit of a show-off maybe – who fancies their chances at the role, and they might be OK in the garage or your auntie's front room when no one is looking, but once the spectators arrive the brash bravado soon disappears like a snowball in the sun. The singer is usually the first thing the audience looks at and, with only a mic stand to hide behind, they are the most exposed.

Assuming that they do get over that hurdle of nerves and can sort of sing, the question is what do you sing? You've got to have words. Gibberish might be OK to get a song going, but the paying customer expects a modicum of intelligibility, or something that sounds like it. Christian Vander's band Magma managed to swerve this by inventing their own language, Kobaïan, but that was a bit over-elaborate. Being French and a bit jazzy, they somehow managed to make it work.

We were very lucky in having someone who not only wanted to be a singer and had the bottle to do it convincingly, but also had the intelligence to write meaningful words.

Get a good singer and you're halfway there. The next difficulty, so I'm told, is finding a good drummer. But I wouldn't know much about that. I was Warsaw's third or fourth drummer, depending on how you counted. It is a standard rock joke, one that is accurately portrayed in the spoof rockumentary *Spinal Tap*, that drummers are the most serial of musicians – there tends to be a succession of them in bands. Are drummers precious and picky, or as my father worried, is the problem that they are typically unstable?

Our next gig would be back at Rafters, of all places. We were playing with another Manchester band, Fast Breeder, and as Warsaw had done the most gigs we figured we would be headlining, a technical term for going on last.

The way this usually works is that the headlining act gets to do a soundcheck first and the support band goes second. This way, the main act get to waste loads of time pissing about with amps, one-two-ing into microphones and flaunting themselves while the support bands pretend not to be jealous or impatient.

So me and Ian got there first, unloaded the car and I set to putting up the drum kit on the stage.

'What do you think you're doin'?'

'Setting up me drums.'

'No you're not, mate. Fast Breeder haven't soundchecked yet.'

I should have mentioned that there was at that moment no PA for anyone to soundcheck with, but I didn't and the moment passed.

Now I might have been new to gigging in the Manchester scene but I did think of myself as a bit of a Rafters regular by now, and there was something about the chap's manner that didn't exactly equate with the chummy notion of new-wave band camaraderie. Also, he was a bit scary. So, seeking safety in numbers, I went looking for Ian to express my concerns.

'It's all right, Terry sorted it out.'

Terry, like Hooky and Bernard, hailed from Salford and had been promoted to manager. He was very funny in a droll kind of way. Anyway he was supposed to have sorted this booking out with Suzanne at Music Force, who had sorted it out with Dougie at Rafters, who had . . .

'Er, I'll have a word,' and off went Terry to fix it, while me and Ian stood at the back trying to look a bit menacing.

He came back minutes later. 'He says we're going on first.'

'No we're fuckin' not,' said Ian. 'Who says we are anyway?'

Events then followed the usual course: a bit tense, then a bit heated, then a bit shouty. No one would back down.

'How about we toss for it?' I suggested.

'Fuck off, that's a shit idea.'

It was what they call a Mexican standoff, only with amps and drums instead of pistols.

Terry went off to a payphone with a load of 5ps to try and call Suzanne or Martin. The Fast Breeders set off with more 5ps to speak to their management.

Christ, I thought to myself, *you'd think this was an argument about topping the bill at the Hollywood Bowl or Wembley Stadium, not a dingy cellar on Oxford Road in the middle of the week. Is it always like this?*

Eventually the Fast Breeder's big gun turned up. A bloke called Alan.

'I'm their manager, I booked the gig and you're going on first. If you don't like it, you can fuck off.'

'No, you fuck off!' Ian was by this time getting truly wound up. He was on his second tin of Breaker and the malt liquor was not having a soothing effect. 'Fucking bastard bastards! We were here first so we're going on last.'

I wasn't going to disagree. We were all feeling the frustration of the underdog.

Each passing hour ratcheted up the tension another notch. The club doors opened and the gear was still piled up on the dancefloor in front of the stage. This was getting stupid.

Finally a resolution was reached and Alan reluctantly agreed we could go on last. Hurray for us! Victory is ours! That'd teach the twats to mess with Warsaw.

Except . . . Fast Breeder turned out to be bad losers and took to the filibuster strategy and went on a go-slow. They eventually took to the stage about half-eleven, this despite Hooky and Terry's frequent exhortations to get a fucking move on.

It must have been gone 1 a.m. when we finally got a chance to play and we were all wound up to fever pitch. What followed was not so much a gig, more a channelling of the spirit of the Stooges live in Detroit. Ian jumped off the stage (more a platform really) and accosted the few punters that remained, turning over tables and smashing glasses in the process. He was wild. We played as though we had something to prove. It was brilliant. It was cathartic. It was us against the world.

And I had seen another side of Ian.

Alan, it turned out, was an actor with the second name Erasmus. Fast Breeder were later joined by Vini Reilly, the guitar player with the Nosebleeds, and Bruce Mitchell, the drummer last seen at Reading 1975, and they became known as the Durutti Column.

The Rafters DJ was so impressed by our anarchic antics that he decided he wouldn't mind being our manager. It took him a while to tell us that, though. Never one to rush things was Rob.

11

FIRST SONGS

So now I had become a player of gigs and discovered that there was more to being in a band than the playing of concerts. There is the matter of the writing of songs to be played when you get there. Hooky and Bernard had learned to play (after a fashion) from a book, nobody had taught Ian how to sing and, OK, I'd had music and drum lessons but I thought they were shit and mostly wrong as they had nothing to do with rock, or music as I saw it. So I was always pretty much making it up as I went along.

So how do you write a song? Let me count the ways. There must be hundreds. How do you write a song when you can't play very well? How do you learn anything? You rely on feeling and intuition. And that's what we did.

One of the first songs we wrote after I joined was a stomper called 'Living in the Ice Age'. This came from a desire to do something that was a bit like the Glitter Band's 'Rock 'n' Roll', which had an infectious drum riff. The Glitter Band were slightly over-endowed in the drummer dept, having two skin bashers – one more than is strictly necessary – but it looked cool and sounded great. (Of course, this was long before singer Gary Glitter was exposed as an evil pervert. Back then he was just an oddly bewigged chap with a permanently startled expression, who wore clothes that looked to have been fashioned from Bacofoil. All the danger signs were there – why didn't we notice?)

I bashed out a Glitter Band drum approximation, only a lot faster; Hooky did a propulsive pulse on the bass that followed Bernard's guitar riff; Ian shouted some stuff about the Ice Age he'd scribbled in his notebook. And in less than an hour we'd knocked off a master-piece, easy as that.

The song's inspiration (apart from the Glitter connection) seemed to come from indescribable ideas or feelings – listening to 'White Light/White Heat' gave you a certain feeling and if what we were playing gave you a similar feeling then that meant it was good. Well, that's how it worked for me and I can only really speak for myself here. My only previous experience in the business of putting together an original tune had been back in the days of the Folk Band and that had been a song the guitarist had written. I just did my best to come up with some sympathetic sort of pattern. The trouble was as soon as he'd finished playing his song to me, I'd already forgotten how it started. No matter how many times we rehearsed it, I still couldn't remember it with any certainty. Even when we went to record it, I was still foggy about when the parts were supposed to happen. I think the technical phrase for this is, appropriately, 'I'm not feeling it, man.'

The problem was that in interpreting somebody else's idea I could always get it wrong in some way. With Warsaw, they were all our collective ideas so who could say what I was doing was wrong? I'd made it up so I could change it. OK, there could be suggestions on how it might be better, but it was still up to each of us to sort out our own parts.

Our songs may have been inspired by our outsider feelings, but we were northern men and talking about feelings was something that men just didn't do in the seventies. Emotions though, like water, will always find a way out eventually and music is as good a way as any. If you suggested something like that to us at the time (or even now, come to that), we would have disagreed very strongly. *Fucking hell, we're men aren't we? None of that namby-pamby shit!*

Emotions were never openly displayed or discussed, but that was not unique to us. Many of my peers have said the exact same thing. I suspect it was a generational thing. My parents, though not miserable by any standards, did not talk about emotions at all. I got the idea that it was a sign of weakness and the best thing to do was keep all that troubling nonsense bottled up in a meta-physical jar in your head – never once considering how much this imaginary container might hold or if it might need emptying once in a while.

Maybe my generation's collective dysfunction was an overspill from the Second World War and the fact that we were now living in a nuclear age with concrete barriers and atomic cataclysm a pervasive undercurrent. Maybe Warsaw and other bands were responding to a constant subconscious awareness of darkness and threat. My parents and their parents before them had accepted that 'the people in charge' would sort things out and it would all be all right in the end, but this was something that the youth of the 1960s had started to question. By the seventies, we knew that the old authority was not always right. That the establishment was bunk and had had its day. That it was time for something new. That popular culture was not just a diversion for potentially troublesome exuberant youth but something that could effect real change in society. This was what I believed.

At our very first rehearsals I don't think we even had a tape recorder so the songs really only lived in our collective imaginations and memory, except when they were unleashed in front of an unsuspect-ing and mostly disinterested public.

Talking of which, one of our next public outings was at the Middlesbrough Rock Garden supporting the Rezillos, a lovely bunch of lads and a lass from Scotland. The Rezillos were a kind of glam cartoon rock-and-roll band on speed, and a really good live band. They had a single out and signed a deal with Seymour Stein's Sire label. They and their manager, Bob Last, seemed to like what they saw in us and asked us to do some gigs with them.

So on Saturday 14 September 1977 we loaded all the gear into the Maxi and Hooky's Jag and set off for Middlesbrough.

It was like driving to the moon. I'd never driven so far in my life, up to Tyneside (almost) – *Get Carter* country. We only got lost once, quite an achievement really. It was one of those Indian summer days. When we finally arrived we did what we thought was our best gig yet to an initially somewhat sceptical Middlesbrough crowd.

It was a bit of a rough venue – what they call vibey when really they mean a dump. We put on a storming performance. If you look hard enough you can find it on t'internet but – without getting the vibe and seeing the good-natured violence of the Middlesbrough crowd at first hand – Ian's spirited performance doesn't come across. Also you can't really see the bit where I set my shirt on fire. I think we did our first encore here. After the gig, we ate some chips and drove all the way back to Macc. I made a mental note that when we did this sort of thing again, if we ever did, it might be an idea to have some speed handy as a bit of a livener.

Our next gig was at the Electric Circus. Manchester's premier punk rock palace was closing down for the first time, and this was one of those events that rightly had a feeling of loss and ending. Anyone who was anyone was going to be on the bill for a series of gigs.

The first weekend in October was the date for the Circus's swan-song, and Terry and Ian had badgered Buzzcocks manager Richard Boon to let us play.

So me, Terry and Ian were in the evening gloom of Collyhurst, standing outside the door of the Electric Circus, arguing and ranting and demanding that we be let in to sort out Warsaw's appearance on the bill for the 'first of the last nights' at the venue. The bloke on the door was having none of this and would only open up a crack. I think he didn't want to let any of the heat out. So, like some party-goer who's expected invite has failed to materialise, we were indignant. Well, Ian was mostly. We'd had a few drinks in the pub across the way and he was not taking no for an answer. So here we were again, having another go at gatecrashing the gig. I was just there as backup and to make sure he didn't get into too much trouble.

'Richard said we could play.'

'Whose we?'

'Warsaw.'

'Don't know anything about it. Anyway, he's not here is he?'

'Well, Richard Boon said it'd be OK. Let us in and I'll get him to sort it out.'

'He's not here.'

'Yes, he is. I've just seen him. Richard! Just let us in for a second, mate, and I'll sort it out with Richard. Richard! It'll be OK, honest.'

The door keeper's resolve weakened for a second and we barged our way past. We were in.

Perhaps emboldened by his blagging entry, or maybe it was the booze reacting with the rush of warm air, we elbowed our way forward into the shortly-to-be-no-more venue. But Ian seemed suddenly distracted. One minute we were searching for Dave or Richard, anyone who could get us on to that stage, and the next Ian was entwined around a passing blonde punkette and locked in an embrace that could only be termed 'serious snogging with tongues'. It was so out of the blue I couldn't quite believe what I was seeing, so I closed my eyes and opened them again. No, they were still at it. After a few minutes feeling like an awkward gooseberry, I decided that this was heading for the 'too much trouble' that I was supposed to be avoiding, so I grabbed hold of Ian and dragged him off. We both carried on as though nothing had happened and the young lady staggered off into the crowd.

I should have reminded him that we had just left Debbie across the road in the pub. That couldn't have just slipped his mind, could it?

Luckily we bumped into some people who recognised Ian – Paul Morley and Kevin Cummins. Paul had written a bit about an earlier Warsaw performance for the *NME* so he was apparently OK. Ian introduced me as the new drummer. 'Stephen's a journalist like you, Paul. He writes for *Record Mirror*. Bit of competition for you there.'

He didn't seem too worried.

Paul then remarked on Ian's black enamel star badge. Paul was wearing the same badge but in the more popular Russian red.

'What's that, Ian? Not a Nazi badge?'

'It's the black star of the anarchists, Paul, not fascists.' It seemed important to know these differences then.

Eventually we were steered in the direction of someone who introduced us to someone else who we could rail and rant at, and eventually we managed to extract a promise that if we came back the next night, we'd be squeezed onto the bill. A successful evening, I thought, and set to shepherding Ian out of the gig and back to the safety of the pub where we could relay the good news to Bernard, Hooky and Debbie.

'He eats glass, you know.'

'What?'

'Paul Morley, he eats glass. Got any fags? I'm all out.'

The next evening we were back again at the Electric Circus and going through the usual 'No, yer not playing', 'Oh yes we are' rigmarole that seemed to go with every Manchester gig. Finally we were shoehorned on before the Prefects.

The way things worked on stage for us at a gig was falling into a set pattern. My larger than really necessary drum kit went sort of in the middle; Hooky on my left; Bernard on my right; and Ian straight in front of me. We normally only had two microphones – Ian naturally had one and Hooky tended to have the other for the odd bit of 'backing singing'. Hooky always seemed to be a bit intimidatory in his stance towards the audience, whereas Bernard would just sort of shuffle backwards and forwards, staring at the neck of his guitar and seemingly oblivious to anything else, while Ian filled up the space in between. There was not much in the way of banter or audience 'interaction', God forbid. Just 'Hello, we're Warsaw' and 'This song's called ...' plus the odd 'Thank you' from Ian, and that usually was that.

The second last night at the Electric Circus, though, things were to be a little different. We turned up and were told to get straight on or

168

we wouldn't be playing at all, so we chucked the gear onstage and started frantically setting up in front of the night's assembling audience. A chap from the PA asked me how many vocal mics we would like.

'Two,' I said.

'Well, the next band's got three so you'll have three too. Won't be a problem?'

'No, shouldn't be a problem at all, thanks,' I said and wondered why he had asked in the first place.

So there were three mics in a line when we hurried on to do our set, but after our first song, instead of ' We're called Warsaw' from Ian, we got, 'Have you all forgot Rudolph Hess?' shouted abruptly but loud and clear from Bernard, one not previously known for his off-the-cuff remarks and witty repartee. It was met with a collective where the fuck did that come from? Undeterred, we did our brief set and went home.

Where the remark came from was a book that Bernard and Ian had been reading: *The Loneliest Man in the World*. It was about Herr Hess and his time in Spandau Prison. There was a picture of Hess on the cover with his prison number '31G-350125', which was the title of the first song we played that night – we would later rechristen it 'Warsaw'.

So that's the 'where' but as to the 'why' Bernard was shouting . . .

'What was that Rudolph Hess thing all about then?'

'Dunno, just felt like saying it.'

As catchphrases go, it's fair to say that 'Have you all forgot Rudolph Hess?' was not one of the greats, but it wasn't as though we'd be constantly reminded of it, was it? Just a spur of the moment thing, a moment in time gone forever. Not the sort of thing that haunts a band for years . . .

We were a bit disappointed with the gig – like a lot of things in life when you have high expectations, the reality never lives up. We

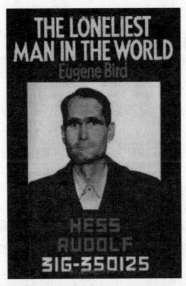

Have you all forgot about . . . what's 'is name?

weren't going to be deterred though. If anything, it just added to the feeling that everyone had it in for us. We were better than them anyway. We just had to stick at it and keep writing, which was what we'd been doing in various upstairs rooms in pubs in Macc and Salford. As well as '31G' (aka 'Warsaw'), we'd written 'Leaders of Men', 'No Love Lost' and redone an old song, 'Novelty'.

In Macc, we rehearsed at the Heyes Hall community centre and in an upstairs room at the Talbot – my favourite pub in the town. It was a shithole really, but the landlord, Tony, was a great Macc eccentric. He owned an ostrich, which he claimed he was going to race. As proof of the bird's existence, the regulars were invited to Tony's ostrich-egg omelette gourmet evenings. They were disgusting. If you're ever offered an ostrich egg dish, my advice is to decline politely.

After all my reading of interviews with drummers, my concept on what drums should do in a band had become distilled down to 'the drummer is the bridge between the bass and the guitar, the thing that glues the two together'. I may have made that up or dreamt it, but it struck me as a pretty good idea to try out.

The problem I had with this idea was in most tunes the bass is playing a simplified version of the guitar part – certainly in the earliest, thrashy songs we did. Either a throb or a very similar part an octave or two down. So what I did was thrashy too. Nothing wrong with that – playing thrashy drums is a lot of fun and a great way to keep fit and healthy – but I played far too many busy fills in an attempt to sound a bit like Keith Moon or Rat Scabies. I mistakenly thought I was being clever and flashy. I wasn't. It just sounded bad. So I stopped. Sometimes it's hard to convince a young, enthusiastic and energetic drummer that less is more. Trust me, with drums usually it is.

In later songs, though, as the tempo slowed, Hooky's playing got more melodic and Bernard's guitar parts became sparser. A space opened up in the music where the drums could be more interesting. I was less of a clock because the entire band was the clock. Somehow Hooky's bass and my drums just gelled instinctively. We never talked about it or thought about it. It just worked. For a drummer, having that kind of understanding of each other's playing is the most important thing. I was lucky, particularly in the early days of Joy Division, that Hooky was such an inventive musician. We locked together and left a space for Bernard and Ian to occupy without it ever sounding too busy or messy.

The drums and bass are to me the engine of the band, its beating heart. The thing that moves the whole edifice while at the same time keeping it together.

The music that I liked best would invoke a picture of the world it inhabited. It sounded like it came from somewhere or had a sympathetic mood. Most progressive rock by the mid-seventies seemed to be all about musical one-upmanship or whimsical concepts. It waffled and said nothing to me.

I judged our music good or promising when, if I closed my eyes, I could see something. It may have been difficult to verbalise exactly what that something was – just a shape or colour, something vague like a blue triangle or green water – but that meant that the sound wasn't a dead end. To have to struggle to see anything meant the song was ultimately a contrived waste of energy.

High-energy rock is about the riff: everybody plays the riff or some slight, harmonically enriching variant, making an irresistible force. (Check out the MC5's *Kick out the Jams* – no solos.) It's pretty simple really and it works, and that was what Warsaw did for the most part.

Virtually every song began:

'What sort of song do we need?' Ian or more likely Bernard would ask.

The answer was (and is) invariably, 'A fast dancey one!'

'Right, Steve, a fast dancey drum riff please.' Or 'A jungly tom riff.'

I would then, hamstrung perhaps by my inability and unwillingness to dance, interpret the direction as best I could. Fast was no problem – everyone knows what fast is – but dance could mean anything. Seeking guidance I would ask, 'Fast tommy? Or fast snare?'

Usually the answer was fast tommy and we were off down the road to 'Ice Age', 'Wilderness', 'Komakino', 'Dead Souls', etc.

No one ever notices the drummer in the band. Maybe that's why I tried to compensate by having too many drums and cymbals piled in front of me. But being unnoticed was part of the attraction of drumming for me. I didn't much fancy the idea of being at the front. Seeing the whites of the audience's eyes. I enjoyed being hidden at the back, going into a kind of trance when I played.

Drummers have an odd relationship with time – they hate being late. I know that sounds like a joke but it's true. Not just in music but in life. Turning up late for an appointment really annoys them. It fills me with a sense of failure. Every drummer I know gets uptight and obsesses about tardiness, as though we are engaged in a constant, unconscious battle with time. As a type, drummers seem quite relaxed, easy-going and willing to experiment. I am one, so I would say that. To most other musicians, the idea of the crazy drummer is the default stereotype, like the prima donna lead singer.

Prima donna drummers, on the other hand, are few and far between. I've heard stories but I've never actually met one. But then I never met Buddy Rich.

Eventually we discovered Tony 'T. J.' Davidson's rehearsal studios in a decaying old mill on Little Peter Street, Manchester. We were put in a room at the far end of the corridor at the back of the building, up a rickety flight of wooden stairs. These rooms had probably been offices until quite recently. They had thin partitioned walls onto which copious amounts of Rockwool roof insulation had been half-heartedly glued to give some sort of rudimentary soundproofing.

It was a medium-sized space with a walk-in cupboard, which we would use to store gear and items of a much less savoury nature. Tins of piss mostly. Our room at the end of the long corridor meant it was also the furthest from what passed for a toilet at T. J.'s. The entire building was more ventilated than heated – it was like spending all day inside a fridge, which didn't help. At rehearsals, the gaps between the songs were spent taking turns to sit on a salvaged electric heater for warmth. So, rather than getting even colder on the long stroll to use the proper facilities, certain members of the group would resort to the use of old soft drinks tins as urine receptacles, which they would then leave in this walk-in cupboard for later inspection. Don't ask me why. They soon piled up, adding to the health-and-safety hazards for which we remember the 1970s so fondly.

Honestly, I don't recall it ever getting physically violent between us, unlike some bands. We were at heart too soft for that. Our major disagreements were about who was playing too loud – a disagreement that has been going on for years. There was one time, in the upstairs room at the Talbot, when things got a bit personal between Hooky and Bernard over how loud the other was playing. It was nothing really but it went on and on, as these things do, and nothing was built into something. In retrospect, it was at that point when what they were playing began to diverge. Around the time of the argument, there was a change where what Hooky and Bernard were playing started to separate more into this-is-my-bit and that-is-your-bit and never the twain shall meet.

We never socialised outside the band and we still never talked about our feelings or emotions with any depth, apart from how we felt about other bands and how hard done by we were. These days, people would say we had a communication problem, and something bad was bound to happen sooner or later.

12

GIRLFRIENDS

Bernard and especially Ian always managed to appear relatively smartly dressed albeit in a slightly ex-army manner. Ian's pride and joy, though, was his pair of black leather pants, essential for the Jim Morrison/Lizard King lead singer look. Not the sort of thing he'd be seen wearing at work, of course. The pair of them looked pretty sharp, Hooky less so.

It was Hooky's choice of footwear that seemed to let him down. He had peculiar taste in shoes, and in particular was an enthusiast of the Western-style cowboy boot. This was quite a common complaint in the late seventies and it would manifest itself upon the most unlikely souls. When the band's piss-taking about his Broncobusters became too much, he moved on to the Army & Navy jackboots, which suited his personality to a T.

Mind you, I wasn't much better dressed. In fact, I was the worst of the lot. I was very self-conscious and found the process of buying clothes an ordeal, so I would wear the same clothes until they disintegrated. Stripy cheesecloth shirts, grey Farrah slacks, brown tweedy blazers with leather elbow patches, and the ugliest footwear of all: Clarks' Nature Treks, or 'pastie shoes' as my bandmates jokingly called them. I topped this ensemble off with glazed-over eyes and a mop of thick black hair that seemed to possess a mind of its own. It was not a good look. And definitely not that of a would-be rock star. Smart I was not.

My fashion sense, or lack of, was a great source of amusement to my bandmates. It is part of the role of the drummer to be a village idiot or willing stooge. I think this stereotype has a lot to do with Ringo; in fact, a lot of band behaviour clichés may have their origins in the Fab Four's projected relationships. The four lovable mop-tops notion of a band has a lot to answer for.

My drug-addled geography teacher look was not one that most members of the opposite sex found attractive either. There was the odd exception. Mostly, these girls were quite addled themselves and we would both struggle to remember what happened and who with the following day. Occasionally this would be a blessing. But as the throbbing pain of the hangover slowly subsided, guilty embarrassment would flicker on and off, accompanied by the wincing, uncertain hope that it may have all been a dream. To be followed later by apologetic phone calls.

My ever-sensible sister was by now at an all-girls' grammar, Macclesfield High School, the female equivalent of King's. Here she ended up acting as my haphazard matchmaker or fixer upper. Hearing someone at her school remark that they loved David Bowie, for instance, Amanda would respond with, 'You'd like me brother, he likes David Bowie too' before adding a cautionary 'He is a bit mad though . . . And he plays the drums.'

Most of the time this was deterrent enough, though every so often it could be an incentive. Drums and madness: what's the attraction?

I despaired at my sister's taste in music – she'd previously been David Cassidy's number-one fan and had by now moved on to Dr Hook and Barry Manilow. This didn't stop her sneaking into my room when I was out and listening to some of my LPs. The Eagles, Bryan Ferry and, surprisingly, John Cale's *Paris 1919* would be found displaced from their rightful alphabetical location, their grooves vandalised by unauthorised fingerprints and mysterious scratches. Sacrilege!

Despite out musical differences, Amanda remained concerned over my love life, or the lack of it. She would trap me, usually while leaving or entering the house, and say, 'Stephen, there's this girl at our school who fancies you.'

Which would lead to awkward meetings at the bus station, followed by even more awkward stilted conversation over drinks in the Macclesfield Arms (punctuated by frequent trips to the loo or jukebox). These generally culminated in an artless stumble back to the bus stop.

'I'll call you.'

These approximations at dates all felt a bit like my numerous unsuccessful band auditions, though I was often confused about who was rejecting who or what and why. Was I that boring? Don't answer that.

A couple of girls stuck it out for longer than that, but not much. It wasn't my interest in drugs that usually ended things. They usually found the guys I hung around with a much more attractive proposition as they were, as a rule, older, more reliable and had their own cars. What the girls didn't understand or didn't care for, even those who had an unlikely initial interest, was my obsession with being a drummer in some weird rock band or other. 'You think more of that band than you do of me' was a common and frequently justified complaint.

My drinking pals, despite being hardcore music fans, were more realistic in their life ambitions: steady job, steady girlfriend or wife and two kids, house, nice car, booze and a spliff at the weekends, and they would be happy. At times I did find myself thinking that they might have had a point. It was the line of least resistance.

I was going out with a girl called Stephanie at the time I joined Warsaw. She was a tall, fair-haired, whimsical fan of Simone de Beauvoir and F. Scott Fitzgerald. Going to pubs for an evening of weak-bitter drinking, smoking and conversation was the chief social activity in Macclesfield and pretty much everywhere else in the 1970s, so when I wasn't gigging, rehearsing or watching other bands, I was out drinking and socialising with my mates. If not every night, then at least every weekend. My doping and drinking pals found the idea of making us an alliterative couple amusing – Stephen and Stephanie, how poetic. She worked for the Inland Revenue.

My friends thought me a bit odd in a tedious kind of way. They frequently yawned when I began to talk about music for instance. But Stephanie was odd in ways that I struggled to understand. She took the being odd thing to a whole new level.

She once called me in the middle of the night: she'd been thrown out and would have to sleep rough on the mean streets of Bollington. Would I come and rescue her? I'd just downed two tins of Carlsberg Special (I found it a great nightcap and nerve settler) and was in no fit state to drive, but being foolishly drunk I woke my mother, who agreed to take part in this outlandish post-midnight rescue mission. She should have told me to fuck off and go back to bed, but mums don't do that sort of thing do they?

Stephanie's story kept changing and unravelling from the moment we found her sobbing at the Bollington phone box. None of it made much sense. Her parents seemed to have transformed into evil zombies of some kind and had chased her out into the night.

It was three on a Sunday morning and Mum and I just wanted to get back to bed. 'We should call the police,' my mum suggested, but past experience told me this was an extremely bad idea and I managed to put her off.

The next morning, the drama had magically dissipated. Stephanie had called home and it had all been a terrible misunderstanding. Apparently it happened a lot.

'Odd girl that, Stephen, odd,' said my dad and I had to admit he had a point.

This sort of thing kept happening. The dramatic SOS phone calls, 'I've got on the wrong train and I don't know where I am' or 'There's a strange man following me and I think he's a rapist' were the kind of things that used to brighten my otherwise dull life.

Things with Stephanie reached a head on 13 October 1977. We had yet another gig at Rafters, supporting the Yachts, and Steph naturally came along. I picked up Ian and then Stephanie. That something was wrong became apparent from the moment she got in the car. Her demeanour was even more skittish than usual. The reason was soon revealed as she produced a half-drunk bottle of some cheap Scotch liqueur from her handbag, took a swig and offered the bottle to Ian. After sampling the goods he professed it was 'OK' but said he would be sticking with Breaker – a four-pack of which was his usual tipple for the journey to a gig.

'Ooh, Breaker! Great. Can I have one?' piped my girlfriend.

'Er, OK. We can always stop and get some more can't we, Steve?'

Another four-pack of malt liquor later and I suddenly had an inkling of what the captain of the *Titanic* must have felt upon hearing the cry, 'Iceberg ahoy!'

By the time we got to my habitual parking spot in the remains of Manchester's once magnificent Central Station, the damage had been well and truly done. The Breaker had worked its pre-gig magic on Ian and he was suitably psyched or vibed up for the night ahead. Steph, on the other hand, was legless – drunk as a skunk and not making sense. My lips were being thoroughly chewed as between us we managed to prise her out of the car.

Somehow we steered her into the gig and I went back to unload the drum kit. Upon my return, I was greeted coldly by Hooky's girlfriend, Iris, with the news that 'The girl you were with, what's her name, has locked herself in the ladies and she's a bit upset.'

What's the saying – out of sight, out of mind? So I set to assembling the bits of wood and metal tubes into something that would pass for a drum kit and hoped things would sort themselves out. I have taken this approach to many problems throughout my life and I can report an almost zero per cent success rate.

The reports came thick and fast and they were not good.

'She's been sick on the floor.'

'She's passed out.'

'You can't leave her stuck in there.'

'The manager wants her out.'

So after a nerve-calming joint, I extracted her from the ladies and bundled her up the stairs, out of the club, and back down Oxford Street to the car park. I left her comatose on the back seat with a plastic carrier bag in case of emergency. This was probably not the wisest of things to do, but I thought, 'It's just round the corner, I'll come back and check at regular intervals.' And ran back to the gig.

This to-ing and fro-ing went on all night. Despite my being a bit more wound up than usual, the gig was OK and the Yachts were a lovely bunch of fun-loving Liverpudlians, who cheated at pool. John Peel played their single a lot and Henry Priestman eventually ended up in the Christians. Oh well.

By the end of the night, I had decided that enough was enough when it came to Stephanie. We broke up.

I didn't do a very good job of it. It became a long drawn-out goodbye. I didn't like upsetting anyone and that only made it worse.

Rejection is never any fun, is it? I'd been on the receiving end a few times and being on the other end of it wasn't a barrel of laughs either. I was much better at getting rejected than being a rejector. I turned out to be just as bad at ending a relationship as I'd been at starting one.

Steph took it badly and began a campaign of suicide threats. I got to know the local branch of the Samaritans very well and became depressed and slightly suicidal myself. I ended up seeing a very unfriendly doctor at Parkside Hospital. As dour a Scot as ever there was – a large man with big bushy eyebrows and piercing eyes staring from below. He never smiled. He had me pegged as a drug addict of the worse kind, a liar and a cheat (his comments are still there in my medical records to this day). He would lecture me on the evils and dangers of smoking pot and he put me on a course of antidepressants. I was to start on three capsules a day, then six, until I was on eighteen of the big orange fuckers every twenty-four hours.

Now, I quite liked the idea of antidepressants – pills that would make you happy, restore the old *joie de vivre*, what's not to like? But no. These pharmaceutical marvels seemed to work by stopping me from feeling anything at all, apart from a kind of perfect blank numbness. This, the glum Scot informed me, was normal and would wear off when I took enough of the pills. Their effect was worse than the brown bottles of barbs I'd swallowed back at Dizz's, worse than a bucket of Phensedyl cough medicine. It never wore off and only got lousier with each dose. I felt like the proverbial nervous wreck. Well, I would have done if my nerves weren't deadened. These pills would not make anyone happy. Not sad either, just empty and hollow inside like my soul had been drained out and flushed away. I felt like I was caught in a dark spiral and being dragged further and further down into a pit.

I do remember being strongly advised by the serious Scot to avoid eating cheese as unspecified bad things might happen. I love cheese. Maybe that was the problem.

Stephanie continued to pop up in unexpected places: trying to jump in front of my car, occasionally going round to Ian's house and locking herself in the bathroom, looking for razorblades; hiding in the bushes outside my widow and screaming. She adopted a diet of rat poison or similar substances. It was not funny at all. She needed help, obviously, help that was beyond me to give, and I am sorry that I have had to drag up her own troubles in order to talk about mine. She later abandoned Macclesfield for life in London and eventually Paris.

In the meantime, I had so many packets of the antidepressants that I thought I would try selling them on, but none of my drug-enthusiast friends found the experience remotely enjoyable. There were no takers. These tangerine capsules were a nightmare. So eventually I pitched the lot on the fire. They didn't burn well either.

I lied to the Highland quack that I was feeling much better, thanks. I just had to cling on and hope that it really would get better, that nothing is ever as bad as it seems, it never is, but that's easy to say and sometimes impossible to believe when you're in a black hole. I found that reading about Buddhism helped a bit –the idea that this too will pass and all that illusory nature of reality thing. I read a lot of Zen, a bit more of Crowley's Golden Dawn mystic hogwash, Jean Paul Sartre and Raymond Chandler, and eventually this did help me lift the old spirits. Maybe not the Sartre.

I really did begin to feel better. Mind over matter. No thanks to the Scot. He put me off going to the doctor for twenty-odd years.

Drumming also made me feel better. It never failed. Alan, an old pal of mine, used to get unhinged on a regular basis unless he exorcised his demons with some violent drumming every once in a while. He'd picked it up in the Scouts. Drumming's a great cure for stress – well, it is for the person doing the drumming, not so much for those nearby. The making of a hellish racket that disturbs the outside world can be a powerful and satisfying feeling.

Existential misery can take root anywhere. I never once thought that my mood swings could have anything do to with my intake of illegal substances. I would have thought the idea ridiculous, a straight conspiracy. In hindsight, I've got to admit that this was more than likely the source. Your troubles are never your own fault. That's how paranoia starts.

My mother was prone to occasional dark moods – it's probably hereditary. She suffered with migraine and would say every so often that she'd had enough of it all and, in the spirit of Virginia Woolf (but without the stones), she was going to throw herself into the canal at North Rode. She couldn't swim. She always came back dry though.

All the doors at Ivy Lane had locks on them – every room. It must have been a 1920s security fad. The keys were kept in a small cabinet by the front door. My mum would sometimes take to locking certain doors in the house to keep me out or to punish me by depriving me of access to my drums. I couldn't really start breaking doors and windows, though I did think of it, as she would call the police. Reasoning didn't work either. So I would grin and bear it. It amused the rest of the band that I was such a wet blanket.

13

'JOY DIVISION, NEVER HEARD OF YOU'

There were two things the band needed to do to get on.

Number one was get a gig in London – that's where everything was happening, wasn't it? Well, it looked like it was happening there or had happened there once. At the very least, that's where the music business was.

Number two was get a record out. Everyone else was doing it. It seemed easy, just do it all yourself. All part of the fuck-the-major-record-labels spirit of punk.

So two objectives, a cart and a horse, a chicken and an egg, but which to do first? We decided to do both at once, just to be on the safe side.

Bands like the Desperate Bicycles had done interviews extolling the virtues and simplicity of DIY record manufacturing, and indie labels were springing up left, right and centre. So how hard could it be?

You may be wondering where all these decisions came from, how they got made and why. It was Ian doing the driving mostly, but not exclusively. We were a democracy at heart. Now before you get the wrong idea that we were like the four musketeers or something –

'I say, fellows, I have a great idea! Let's make a record. What say you?'

'Aye.'

'Aye.'

'Aye.'

'Motion carried! A record shall be made at the earliest convenience.'

It was not like that. It never is. Democracy can be a difficult bastard. Someone is always going to disagree and someone is going to shrug and say, 'I suppose it's OK but . . . What if . . .? Or how about . . .?'

Umming and aahing.

So you compromise. (Or you could just ignore the idea. Say someone came up with an idea that was so terrible that no one could possibly take it seriously – like Hooky's suggestion that we all dye our hair blond for the next gig as a 'gimmick'. We all agreed but only one of us actually did it. Guess who?)

So Ian then – not the easy-going Ian, this was the single-minded Ian, the Ian who believed that we were the best band ever, if only the rest of the world could be made to notice us, if the rest of the world wasn't entirely comprised of twats anyway – would often drive the decisions so we would finally stop all the umming. Ian was ambitious, not purely for himself but for us all. He never considered himself a leader: everything was a group decision so long as you didn't disagree.

That does make Ian sound a bit despotic, which was something he very rarely was. Ian was mostly a gentle soul. He could sometimes be controlling, not in a manipulative hurtful way, but a sort of kind-hearted, helpful manner. In some ways he could even be a bit old-fashioned and overprotective. I am sure he thought he had your best interests at heart, that he could just see things better than you could. With me, he seemed to have taken over from Amanda as being some kind of matchmaker. He would say things such as, 'Debbie's sister fancies you. Just the other night she was saying . . .' This despite the fact that she was recently engaged. Whenever he conspired to create a situation but it went awry or got a bit sticky, he would deny everything. 'No, that's not what I meant. No, I never said that!'

It was here, in this woodland glade, that I would listen to Can and Amon Düül II on cassette — usually in the dark (for reasons that only make sense to a teenager). At the time I was unaware that during the day the Gilbert sisters would use the place for frog collection. *(Author's collection)*

In the 1960s the North West's attempts to enter the space race was plagued with difficulties. The launch site had a number of insoluble health and safety issues. Blackpool in 1967 — my kind of holiday destination — was noted for fresh air and fun. *(Author's collection)*

Every day, instead of going to school, I would (weather permitting) eat my sandwich, sitting on a bench, and read *ZigZag* and Andy Warhol's interview magazine. I would then head to the next record shop for a browse. It was an education … *(Author's collection)*

I used to read this over and over, yearning for ownership of the best value mahogany drums in town. *(Author's collection)*

Hard at work hiding from and simultaneously annoying the general public. *(Author's collection)*

My father was not an egotistical man. So, why did he immortalise himself as a bronze paperweight? Got to have a gimmick, I suppose. *(Author's collection)*

The Ford Cortina Mk3 Olympic blue and rust very rarely let me down. But when it did it was usually spectacular. *(Author's collection)*

Robert Leo Gretton: the flamboyant manager himself in a typical Rob pose. *(Author's collection)*

Trying out for the role of Kilroy. I ticked the box marked no publicity. *(Author's collection)*

This was how Tony Wilson looked when we first met. I turned on the TV and there he was looking just like this, oozing confidence and hip hair. *(ITV/Shutterstock)*

Martin Hannett: legendary record producer and genius. My tormentor seen here with the tools of his trade.
(© Kevin Cummins)

Joy Division in action. I never saw them live myself. I heard they were pretty good.
(Chris Mills/Redferns/Getty Images)

Bernard does a Rick Wakeman: 'Atmosphere' with the Transcendent and Woollies organ. *(Author's collection)*

Ian looking for the lost chord at Bowdon Vale. Love the wallpaper ... *(Author's collection)*

The bar's in here! No, I wasn't wearing those trousers for a bet: they were the height of fashion in 1973. *(Author's collection)*

A picture from the *Macclesfield Express*. Ian wears a lampshade, while I view a candle with suspicion. In my mum's front room if you're interested.
(Macclesfield Express)

The Synare: first ogled in a Manchester music shop window one Sunday afternoon. Its handle convinced me that I had seen the future. Then I saw the price tag. It possesses the meanest-sounding ring-modulator I've ever heard: like a flock of Daleks at a rave. *(Author's collection)*

The Synare 3 was more my price range. My pride and joy. From 1950s sci-fi to '70s disco this could do it all and more. Overzealous pounding was its undoing as the flimsy knobs fell victim to my clumsy thwacking. *(Author's collection)*

The SDS IV: a much more robust device. (You can tell by the thickness of the wood!) Built to last until its promising career was cut short by thieves in NYC Bet it made a nice coffee table if you flipped it over. *(Author's collection)*

The Roland CR-78 CompuRhythm. My first brush with an actual drum machine. Lovely wood again. A classic-sounding beatbox heard on many hit records: Blondie, Phil Collins et al. But not obedient enough for Joy Division. (The hire company sent the wrong switch if you were wondering, and it took years to figure that one out.) *(Author's collection)*

A rare picture of the drummer's face. Look at that array of synthesised percussion. It would never catch on. *(Philippe Carly)*

Gillian's poster idea for Joy Division. Part of a Stockport art project. *(Author's collection)*

Miss Gillian Gilbert. My beloved shows the world how crimping should be done. *(Author's collection)*

Electronics Today International was a wonderful periodical; the Transcendent 2000 a fantastic synth. Don't know about the Stereo 10w Amp though. *Author's collection)*

The Museum Panda: those
sad eyes have seen it all.
(Author's collection)

When I was young I would go and stand beneath these pylons and listen to them hum and fizz. One day I would follow the cables to who knew where. *(Author's collection)*

We needed his self-belief though. Self-belief is all. If you don't think you're the bee's knees, then you'll have a hard time convincing the rest of the world. As well as belief, you need energy. This is what the Folk Band Whose Name I Don't Remember lacked, but we had that, oh yes. Self-belief, energy and enthusiasm. I think the technical term is balls.

Ian was a great believer in persistent 'hustling', as it was then called – now it's 'networking'. Derek Brandwood at RCA in Piccadilly Plaza was among his contacts, and others included Richard Boon, Paul Morley, and if we could get a number for that Tony Wilson off the telly, then he'd be on the hit-list too.

For my part, I completely abused my position at work. I would write up live reviews for the *Record Mirror* as soon as the coast was clear. Despite dropping out of the ladies' typing school, my two-fingered technique was quickly improving. A hour or so of key bashing later, and this week's masterful musical critique (Who am I kidding? They were embarrassingly bad) was ready to be phoned through. I would then take off my pretend journalist's hat and put on my pretend band manager's hat and start calling venues – I got some numbers from a music business directory, others from gig guides in the music papers.

'Hi, I'm from a band called Warsaw, we're a Manchester new wave band and I wonder if you could give us a gig or let me have the number of anyone who might be able to give us a gig?'

That's how my script went, as I'm sure did Bernard, Peter, Terry and Ian's, but abusing the telephone was easier for me, being the boss's spoilt bastard son. For those in real jobs, getting a warning or the sack was a definite possibility.

So there I was, feet on the desk, ashtray overflowing, making my second or third 'give us a gig' cold call of the day. I think it was to a lady who was something to do with booking bands at the Marquee. She listened to my pitch and came back with, 'Well, that's all very nice, darling, but I'm afraid there is no way you'll get on in London with a name like Warsaw. There's already a band here called Warsaw Pakt.

They've recorded an album and they're going to be massive, really big. So really the best thing you could do if you want to play down here is call yourself something else. I'm sorry, darling, but that's just how it is.'

'Thank you very much,' I said and slammed the phone down. 'Snooty fucking cow!' How could she just dismiss us that easily? I'd heard of the Warsaw Pakt. It seemed to me that they were an old London band trying to get a bit of new wave cred by recording and releasing an album in twenty-four hours (as if it was some sort of race), sticking it in a home-made-looking cardboard sleeve, then calling it *Needle Time!*, simultaneously evoking payola/drug abuse/vinyl abuse and just good old-fashioned mental abuse simultaneously. The bastards!

The sleeve was more than a bit like Captain Beefheart's *Strictly Personal* too. On top of everything else, I thought they were rip-off twats as well.

I would make a point of not buying their record in protest. That'd show them.

They'd stolen our name, that was how it seemed to me then. Now, it's just one of life's coincidences. They happen, no point dwelling on them – it will drive you insane if you do, honest it will.

This was bad news indeed, for if the lady from London was to be believed and we wanted a gig in the big city (and we all did), then a change of name was something we would have to consider seriously (and so we did).

There was one bit of good news for me at any rate. One of my father' employees had managed to find himself a better job – I may well have been a contributing factor to his exit. But there's always a silver lining. His departure meant that there was a slightly knackered company car (Ford Cortina Mark III, Olympic Blue, VMA978M) going begging. I volunteered to care for the vehicle to prevent it from falling into further disrepair. In that I was not entirely successful.

I kept on doing *Record Mirror* live reviews for a few months. But it soon became apparent that despite my hints and urgings, they had no interest in me doing a piece about Warsaw, or any other new wave band for that matter.

The final straw was when I was dispatched to do a review of Smokie at the Apollo. I'd given up trying to blag my way into gigs by then. It had only worked once – Barclay James Harvest at the Palace. But having to pay to see Smokie was the height of ignominy, the ultimate humiliation. Fortunately, the Gods of Health and Safety intervened and the show ended prematurely, halted after the support act when the Apollo fire curtain got stuck. Ironic for a band called Smokie, I thought.

I took this as an omen that my days as a music journalist were over. I should quit while I was ahead. The one good thing about the *Record Mirror* job were the huge cheques. Not the amount they were for – all for under a tenner as I recall – but the actual size of the paper. They were from Coutts, the ancient and respectable banking company – the Queen apparently banks with them so they must be quite good. As a result, the staff at my bank started being extra nice to me, well, just nice. I don't think they'd seen a Coutts cheque before and, thinking there would be more of them coming their way in the future, they stopped eying me with suspicion every time I appeared at the end of the queue. Also, I was paying in, not withdrawing. They liked that. They started talking to me about investing for the future, mortgages, insurance. My credit was suddenly good.

Still living at the parental home meant having to put up with the perennial parental gripes.

'Turn that racket down or the electric's going off!'

'You treat this place like an hotel, coming and going at all hours.'

That old one. To be fair, if I had behaved in a similar manner in most hotels, I would have been shown the door sharpish. I abused my parent's hospitality abominably. I was selfish, disrespectful and rude – like most teenagers are. That's no excuse though, is it? I was an oik.

Following in my footsteps, Amanda had lost interest in her piano lessons and we now had an old upright in the parlour going unused. I decided to teach myself to play. Being quieter than drumming, I thought this might go down better. My 'unique' keyboard style – Can's Irmin Schmidt was a major influence – only brought out my mother's inner music critic.

'What the ruddy hell's that you're playing? Sounds like the tune the old cow died on.'

I never saw that particular musical criticism in the *NME* singles reviews. Undeterred, I persisted with my threnody. I had no idea what I was doing but I enjoyed doing it. I'd seen Can on the *Whistle Test* and Irmin's karate-chop style of playing his Farfisa looked both impressive and fun.

If the prospects of a gig down in London had temporarily faded, maybe we could get on and do a record. The guy at Pennine Studios in Oldham (where Warsaw had previously recorded that demo tape) was doing an all-in deal that included pressing up a thousand singles. It was still expensive though – a few hundred quid was an absolute fortune. Ian borrowed some money from the bank, supposedly for furniture or home improvements, and we raised some between us and booked a day in the studio. We had tried tapping up T. J. Davidson for a loan. He drove a Rolls, so we thought he must have a few bob, but no luck. T. J. was more interested in V2, whose line-up included Steve Brotherdale, one of my drumming predecessors in Warsaw, and a couple of lads I vaguely remembered from my unwilling stint at Audenshaw Grammar School. T. J. had plans for V2 and their glam-rock style, and though he was encouraging towards us (we paid him rent, after all), we weren't really his cup of tea.

We were getting to be pretty adept at writing songs and, if calendars and memories are to believed, writing pretty prolifically too.

Three songs in under two weeks is pretty good going considering that we only got together twice a week. We'd got into the swing of writing together and every song we wrote was better than the last. They were evolving, becoming less thrashy, more focused.

The way we usually went about this was by trying to play something a bit like something else we all liked, and we weren't only looking at the Glitter Band for inspiration; '31G' was the Stooges; 'Leaders of Men' came when we tried to play something like the intro to 'Love Is the Drug' by Roxy Music. The song that became 'No Love Lost' was a bit of a funny one as it was two ideas that got glued together – a sophisticated bit of arranging, that one. 'Failures (of the Modern Man)' came out of a long thrashy jam – I think I was trying to play something like John Bonham's riff on Led Zeppelin's 'Rock and Roll'. I failed but somehow it ended up turning into something else, and that was the point. None of our attempts at copying ever sounded that much like the original inspiration. They just came out sounding like us.

Me and Hooky generally starting things off with a rhythm, and then Ian would do some mumbling from his lyric book (he could have been saying anything really, the gear we had for a PA was that bad) until he hit on something that fitted. Bernard either hit on a riff that sat in with the rhythm section or did something a bit melodic that floated on top.

After going on like this for a while, we'd stop, have a fag, do a bit of communal criticism/arranging, with Bernard or Ian going, 'You play two of those chugga-chugga riffs, then a dum-dum riff, then a chugga-chugga again.' And we'd be off again in search of the next bit.

I remember a discussion we had about an interview that the Stranglers had done in NME. They were talking about songwriting, and the way they went about it was that if an idea wasn't going anywhere after five minutes of jamming, then it wasn't to be. There was no point labouring on the idea, just drop it and move on to something else. This seemed like good advice so we tried to follow it. Capture the spirit of the moment and all that. It was all about the song having the right spirit, the right energy, than being musically clever. Though the more we wrote together, the more sophisticated (if that's the right word) the songs became.

'Naming is one of the ways in which the human race demonstrates its power over the environment. In naming we demonstrate our ability to differentiate one thing from another, to create order from chaos, to show kinship with the gods.'

I forget who said that, or something like it, which has kind of blown it, but it's the sort of thing you put in a book to give it an air of sophistication.

Like, 'The act of naming is the great and solemn consolation of mankind' (Elias Canetti, *The Agony of Flies*).

That's better.

Having formed a band, the first big question you're going to be asked is, 'What do you call yourself?'

This is both extremely important in the sense that first impressions count, and unimportant in the sense that whatever you call yourself will take on a new meaning once you (and hopefully your audience) settle in to it. It can be very difficult indeed to come up with a good name or even an appropriate one. So, not something to rush into or to be taken lightly.

As band names go, Warsaw was a pretty good one. One word with a bit of icy resonance. But that was out the window now. It was back to the drawing board.

On the table were the Slaves of Venus, the Out Of Town Torpedoes and the Mechanics, so nothing that really hit you as being a knockout name for a band. None of them had that thing that jumped out, that made you think, *That's a band I would like to hear.*

Coming up with a good name for your band is a tricky proposition. It is something to agonise over and I was not the best person to be asking. I mean, I thought the Sunshine Valley Dance Band was good . . .

Bernard and Ian both liked the name Joy Division. It was taken from the book *House of Dolls*, a novella by Ka-tzetnik 135633 (the pen-name of Holocaust survivor Yehiel De-Nur) that documents the Nazi's sexual slavery of women in the concentration camps. That and the Hess book did give Warsaw's literary taste a bit of a Second World War shock-story bent; Sven Hassel was another favourite author, well, of Hooky's anyway. But to be fair, Hassel's books were pretty popular at the time – they were the sort of thing I had seen men reading on the rail journey to Guide Bridge, that and some SF, usually by Asimov or Arthur C. Clarke. Also, more surprisingly, I'd see someone reading a book by Lobsang Rampa, the 'plumber from Plympton' who claimed to be a reincarnated Tibetan mystic.

Anyway, Joy Division became the favourite for a new name. We decided to try it out on people and see how it went down. In Macclesfield, predictably, it didn't go down too well.

'Sounds like the fuckin' Salvation Army or sommat' was the man-in-the-pub's response, and I suppose he did have a point. But after a while whatever you call yourself, however silly it sounds at first, does take on another meaning. Once it gets tangled up with how you look and the music that you play, it becomes part of your image, but we didn't think of the implications of that. We were a little naive. We didn't think we had an 'image', and we didn't want one, since you're asking.

When the idea of actually doing our own record came up, we had quite a good selection of material. An EP was the obvious thing to do to showcase this. We talked about how the record should sound before we went in the studio, and decided we wanted something a bit like a cross between Bowie's *Low* and Iggy's *The Idiot*. If we told the bloke at Pennine this, he was sure to know where we were coming from.

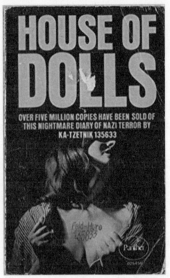

Never judge a book by its cover.

Following on from his drunken encounter back at the Electric Circus, Ian had again been talking to Paul Morley. Paul was allegedly managing the Drones at the time and he'd had something to do with production of their EP *Temptations of a White Collar Worker* and, so Ian said, Paul was interested in producing our soon to be record.

On a dark, rainy morning in late December 1977, I loaded up the Cortina, picked up Ian and off we went to Oldham. Ian had tried calling Paul to make sure he hadn't forgotten his production promise, but there was no answer. I think he was 'a bit ill' or something following a night of intense reviewing. Whatever happened, the upshot was that Paul didn't turn up.

But never mind, who needed a producer anyway? We thought we knew what we wanted and how to do it. We had a good idea of how the tracks should sound at any rate.

Pennine was a bit different from Strawberry, but then it wasn't owned by a chart-topping band. It was a little bit like someone's shed. Not that there's anything wrong with that. Some great records have been made in sheds. I unpacked my numerous drums from their battered cases and starting setting up. Bernard and Ian handled talking to the bloke in charge. I got a 'Blimey, do you really need all those drums? You're not going to hit 'em all are you?' from the owner. A line that I'd heard a few times before at gigs.

'Er, yes, I would like to have a go, if that's OK with you,' was my feeble stock reply.

Bernard asked about the possibility of making the snare sound like the one on Bowie's 'Sound and Vision'. We'd done a bit of research and it seemed that the *Low* drum sound was the result of putting the snare through a harmoniser. What that was and how it worked we didn't know, but it made a snare drum sound great. Tony Visconti, *Low*'s producer, described the Eventime Harmoniser as a box that 'fucks with the fabric of time'. Every home should have one, but Pennine Studios didn't.

'No, not got one of them, mate. I could stick a bit of ADT on it. It's nearly the same thing.'

Ian wanted the vocals to be affected like John Lennon's with an echo/delay thing.

'No, not got one of them either. Could stick a bit of ADT on it, sounds just the same.'

This ADT sounded like a powerful device indeed. I wondered what the hell it was, how it might work and where it was hidden. It turned out it stood for Automatic Double Tracking.

We did the four songs in either one or two takes: '31G' (soon rechristened 'Warsaw' to commemorate our former incarnation), 'Leaders of Men', 'No Love Lost' and 'Failures'.

I think we had only written 'Failures' a week or two before. Ian was still working on the words. 'No Love Lost' was still a bit nebulous too;

in fact it was so vague that it didn't have a title when we recorded it. I think it was called 'the new one', the start of a great tradition.

Of the four tracks I think the intro to 'No Love Lost' would be the one thing that gave an indication of where we were heading musically. The second bit of the song, I pointed out to Bernard and Hooky, sounded a bit like the Doors' 'Changeling'.

'No it doesn't. I've never heard that track in my life so how could it?' was Bernard's response.

You can't argue with logic like that unless you really enjoy arguing.

We knew what overdubbing was – recording another instrument or vocal track on a spare tape track, alongside the tracks previously recorded. Bernard overdubbed a guitar solo at the end of 'Failures' and sorted out the guitar panning effect on 'the new one', on which Ian then did a bit of reading from the *House of Dolls* book he happened to have handy. It filled out a loose bit of the song he hadn't written any words for. This then got titled 'House of Dolls' before becoming 'No Love Lost', with those words coming from the extract he'd read. He got a bit of dubby echo stuck on his voice as well.

By the end of the day, we'd finished our first record – Joy Division's first record. We went away happy having climbed one step up the ladder to who knows where.

At work the next day, I sat at my desk littered with unheeded memos from my father, an overflowing ashtray, empty pay packets, and empty milk and Lucozade bottles, smoking a fag and supping a nourishing pint of milk. I daydreamed about the rave reviews our EP would garner, about the journalists who would flock to interview us.

'Stephen, how would you describe your music?' they were bound to ask.

'Brutal, raw and honest,' I would swiftly reply, stubbing out my No. 6 for emphasis.

'They used to be called Warsaw, now they're called Joy Division and that was really rather splendid, a track from their first EP . . .' I imagined a DJ who sounded a lot like John Peel saying until my reverie was rudely interrupted by the phone ringing under a pile somewhere in front of me.

'Where's my bloody cylinder jackets? You said they'd be here two days ago. I've got customers screaming at me. Pull your effing finger out and get them here, first thing tomorrow!'

'Oh yes, sorry, yes of course, I'll call you straight back but I'm pretty sure they were out on the van today,' I lied and fell back to earth.

A week or so later I got a call of a different nature, some bloke from Virgin records. I thought it was a joke at first (how did he get my number anyway?), but it turned out that two of our songs from the Electric Circus gig has been recorded and they were thinking of putting one of them on an album to commemorate the gig/cash in.

Fucking hell, which one? I don't know why I expected the man from Virgin to be familiar with our repertoire but I did. He said he didn't know what the songs were called but he would send us a cassette of a rough mix of the songs (which they had got Mike Howlett of Gong to mix) and a copy of the contract that we would need to sign.

Bloody hell! A record contract! This was brilliant, maybe they'd put the EP out as well . . .

The two songs were 'Novelty' and 'At a Later Date'. We had only done three songs at the gig but '31G' had got missed off. Bernard's little bit of banter at the end, though, had not. The Rudolph Hess bit was there, loud and clear, now sounding like the introduction to 'At a Later Date'.

The contract might as well have been in Chinese. 'The party of the first part hereafter referred to as . . .' etc., etc. We kept looking for the bit where it said how much we would get paid, but could make head nor tail of the jargon. Terry had a go (I think Terry might have tried asking Richard Boon's opinion), we all had a go, and came to different conclusions. Even though we knew we should have shown it to a lawyer we didn't. One, we had no money, and, two, we would most likely sign it anyway even if it meant we would have to pay the record company, which it probably did. But we would have a song on a proper record label – Virgin, the Pistols' label, good old Richard Branson, what a bloke.

But which track to use? I think I asked if they could go with 'Novelty' but there were some 'technical issues' with the sound (so they said). 'Oh, OK, but do you think you could perhaps lose the, er, banter at the start of "At a Later Date"?'

'Oh yes, of course, no problem,' they lied

'Oh and do you think you'd be interested in putting our EP out?'

Er, no. Good old Richard Branson.

With a peculiar symmetry, on New Year's Eve 1977 Warsaw played their final gig in Liverpool, the city where I'd played my first. The venue was different though: the Swinging Apple.

It was an upstairs club with a hole in the floor. The building looked as though it was about to be condemned. It was a fantastic gig, possibly one of Warsaw's best, but if you can't do a good gig on New Year's Eve there's something wrong somewhere. We ended up doing two sets, possibly interrupted by the chimes of Big Ben. We played every song in our repertoire and they still wanted more, so we did a made-up-on-the-spot spirited version of Iggy's 'The Passenger' and old standby 'Louie Louie', with improvised lyrics.

Then that was it. It was 1978 and Warsaw were no more.

Bands who changed their names:

- The Warlocks – The Velvet Underground
- The Warlocks – The Grateful Dead

JOY DIVISION

BANDTHE BANDTHE BANDTHE BANDTHE BANDTHE BANDTHE BANDTHE BANDTHE BANDTHE BANDTHE I
THE BANDTHE BANDTHE BANDTHE BANDTHE BAND THEBAND THE BANDTHE BANDTHE BANDTHE BAN

Bernard Albrecht-Guitar
Ian Curtis-Vocal
Peter Hook-Bass Guitar
Stephen Morris-Drums

TORY HISTORY HISTORY HISTORY HISTORY HISTORY HISTORY HISTORY HISTORY HISTORY HIST
IISTORY HISTORY HISTORY HISTORY HISTORY HISTORY HISTORY HISTORY HISTORY HISTORY H]

The Band formed in early 77 under their original name of WARSAW.
They gigged around Manchester & the surrounding areas until
July 77,mostly as support band.
After July they decided to take a break to:
A) Find a more suitable drummer
B) Write More material
With both these tasks accomplished,Warsaw returned to gigging.
in August 77,playing the majority of the Norths New Wave venues
including Eric's & the now defunct Electric Circus.
A major problem arose in December with the release of an album by
a band from London with a similar name,and so.to avoid confusion
a name change was decided upon with Joy Division becoming the
band's new name.

IUSIC MUSIC MUSIC MUSIC MUSIC MUSIC MUSIC MUSIC MUSIC MUSIC MUSIC MUSIC MUSIC MUSI
IIC MUSIC MUSIC MUSIC MUSIC MUSIC MUSIC MUSIC MUSIC MUSIC MUSIC MUSIC MUSIC MUSIC
It is difficult to describe the music of any band,without making
misleading comparisons.Suffice to say Joy Division do have a Sound/=
Style that is their own.The enclosed EP gives some idea of the
sound Joy Divison produce.Although the versions contained on the
record are constantly being improved for live work.
PRESENT THE PRESENT THE PRESENT THE PRESENT THE PRESENT THE PRESENT THE PRESENT T
THE PRESENT THE PRESENT THE PRESENT THE PRESENT THE PRESENT THE PRESENT THE PRESE

At Present,the band are rehearsing & writing intensively,improving
constantly & diversifying from the mainstream of "New Wave" music.
Despite this diversity,the band has built up quite a large following
in the North West & it is hoped that this can be expanded in the
not too distant future.

My 'Press Release'.

- The Autistics – Talking Heads
- The Quarrymen – The Silver Beatles – The Beatles
- The Ravens – The Kinks
- The Golliwogs – Creedence Clearwater Revival
- The Hype – U2
- The Detours – The High Numbers – The Who
- The Pendletones – The Beach Boys
- Tony Flow and the Miraculously Majestic Masters of Mayhem – Red Hot Chili Peppers
- Warsaw – Joy Division

14

AN IDEAL FOR LIVING

Being in a band felt like being some sort of rebel – a way to escape the dull workaday routine of life, it showed your rejection of your elders' values, set you apart, gave you a form of freedom to do what you wanted, when you wanted, how you wanted. Then along came the lady from London, well-meaning I'm sure, and oops you have to obey someone else's rules if you want to play the game. Compromise in other words, sell yourself out – OK, in a tiny way – but still . . . There's always the voice of authority lying in wait to trap you.

Three weeks later we were Joy Division, playing our first gig at Pips – number one in Europe, the TV ads used to say – on Fennel Street in Manchester.

Yes, we were playing a disco that advertised on TV. I think Pips was trying to move on from its Bowie/Roxy crowd and attract a new wave crowd.

Another chaotic Manchester gig: Ian nearly didn't sing at all after being thrown out for kicking glass about. He was only being helpful, trying to tidy the place up a bit, as I recall. Hooky, wanting something better than his old EB-o copy, had recently purchased a new bass guitar, a lovely-looking Hondo Rickenbacker copy (I've always liked the shaped of Rickenbacker instruments; they sort of look almost edible somehow). Lemmy used to have a Rickenbacker bass in

Hawkwind so they must be good. But this 'would be' Rickenbacker bass had a design flaw which meant that its low strings would pop out of the nut – a technical term for the bit of wood at the pointier end of things that keeps the strings parallel and therefore playable and tuneable. Maybe it was the way Hooky attacked the bass or maybe the guitar was a bit crap, but either way the bottom string kept springing out in a rather unexpected way. This was mostly either unnoticed or ignored by the small but leery audience (consisting of two camps: the friends of Hooky from Salford and the friends of the support band, who I think were the Stance). The two camps engaged themselves in a brawl that rolled back and forth in pendulum fashion across the front of the stage. They would stop and clap and offer desultory cheers at the end of each song, only to resume their battle as we continued our set. Ian did his best to discourage this but to no avail. The punch-up continued unabated, with Hooky joining in on his mates' side.

Violence apart, there were one or two things of note about this gig. It was the first and maybe the only time we played Kraftwerk's 'Trans-Europe Express' as intro music; and Bernard mentioned something about having seen that bloke from Rafters, that DJ fella, who was going on about wanting to manage us or something. I don't think this was greeted with a great deal of enthusiasm. Maybe it was just not the right time.

We were still after a London gig and a bit of record company interest would be helpful. Other bands seemed to manage it, so why couldn't we? A phone call was probably not enough, and according to the popular wisdom in the *NME*, *Melody Maker* and fanzines of note, sending a cassette of yourself was not the best thing to do either. Too easy to ignore. Every other band under the sun was doing the same, trying to get gigs and a contract, looking for the big time.

So maybe if we turned up on their doorsteps, demo tapes in hand, we could push our way to the front of the queue and get the attention that we felt was rightfully deserved. Maybe even get played/mentioned on John Peel, you never know if you don't try.

The trouble was, the proper job kept getting in the way. All the days off got used up very quickly due to gigs, and a speculative day out would probably call for a sickie. A one-day mystery virus of some sort would do the trick. That was difficult for me though. I had abused my so-called job nearly as much as I could, and my parents might just notice that I wasn't at home in bed with a fever. Still, we had to give it a shot. Nothing ventured . . . so both Terry and I agreed to go to London.

I picked Terry up bright and early from Irlams o' th' Height (no, that's not a silly made-up name; it's an area of Salford). Armed with the addresses of several likely record companies and some cassettes, we the boarded an Intercity at Piccadilly Station, bound for Euston. All set for a day of no-nonsense record-label bartering and schmoozing. I should emphasise here that the addresses and the tapes were Terry's managerial responsibility.

We'd been rehearsing the night before at the Big Alex in Moss Side, an old hotel that seemed to have a band practising in every room. It was cacophonous. You had to wait for a gap in the racket before you could have a conversation. The deal was that each band would have to perform before the pub's clientele in exchange for a reduced rental. I think we only stuck it out there for one night.

So, with cassettes in hand and a potted history I'd banged out on my typewriter, me and Terry did our tour of record company offices: Virgin, United Artists, Polydor, EMI, Rak, CBS . . .

Ask for the A & R man. That's what the guide to the music business said you should do.

The A & R (artist and repertoire) man, it explained, was the bloke whose approval you had to seek. He did the signing of bands for massive advances and paid for expensive dinners. He knew where to get the best drugs. They also occasionally turned up at gigs looking

AN IDEAL FOR LIVING

for bands to sign up and throw money at, so the guide said. They were all blokes, and we even knew some of their names, or thought we did. Each visit elicited a similar response from the girl who opened the door. They were always girls, skinny girls with sleepy eyes.

'No, he's not in today,' or 'He's in a meeting, leave your tape and we'll get back to you,' or 'Who? No, he hasn't worked here for years.'

The other thing these groovy hit factories had in common was outside each one was the same bit of graffiti.

'Wise up [insert company name here] sign the Banshees.'

This looked like a good bit of promotion and we could have added 'and Joy Division' to their graffitied appeal, but we didn't bring a marker pen with us. We didn't even bring a pencil.

Of all the bands emerging in this era that would later be christened 'post punk', but was now just known as 'new wave', it would be Siouxsie and the Banshees to whom I most felt some kind of affinity. The same line-up, the bass-led rhythm, the way first drummer Kenny Morris (wonder if we were related) played mostly toms. In interviews, Siouxsie would claim the sound of cymbals was forbidden in her group and you couldn't avoid the impression that the band were *her* group, contrary to the way that Joy Division were not Ian's band. The Banshees had that gothic, foreboding sound, somehow sketching out the future from the dark of the past. Siouxsie's singing sounded nothing like Ian's, of course, but hearing the sessions they'd done on John Peel's show and reading gig write-ups in the *NME*, I had to admit they sounded interesting. Anyone who began their career doing a version of the Lord's Prayer would have to be a bit different.

'Fucking bit of a fool's errand this, Terry,' after the fifth or sixth door closed in our faces and the charm of Soho was wearing a little thin. I was beginning to suspect that London was, if not cursed, then home to something malignant that did not want me there. This feeling was only encouraged by Terry's insistence that I wait outside in the dripping streets of Soho while he ventured inside to try and charm the disinterested girls with his cassettes.

When we were standing outside the magnificent white elephant that was Centre Point, I was beginning to feel distinctly nauseous and out of sorts. It really felt as though London's record companies harboured some virus that was slowly infecting me. But Terry's attention was elsewhere. It had been caught by a young lady who was campaigning for equal rights for pandas or whales or something.

'Just one donation, however small, could change these poor creatures' lives completely.'

'We're in a band . . . from Manchester.'

'Ooh, from ooop North, that explains your really healthy complexions.'

'Very healthy lads us, aren't we? Bit of a rosy glow you've got there, Steve, eh?'

'Feel a bit queasy, Terry.'

'We're down here visiting record execs. We're after a deal.'

The panda (or whale) woman looked impressed. Tel had that look that said, 'I'm in here.'

But it was not to be, the sickly gooseberry that I had turned into made sure of that.

'For fuck's sake, let's just go and see if we can get a gig at the Marquee and piss off home.'

The Marquee Club was closed.

We pissed off to Euston and got the last train home, me feeling more and more ill with each passing tunnel. By the time we got back to Piccadilly, I was feeling like death. I remember grimly driving to Terry's house and dropping him off. My feverish solitary journey back to Macc was punctuated by waves of extreme wobbliness verging on blackouts. I narrowly cheated death and avoided writing off the Cortina as I slipped under the sea of sickness.

The next morning I awoke sicker than a dog. My head felt like it had been hit by a train and my 'healthy complexion' had turned into a mass of red spots. My made-up excuse of a serious illness had turned into a prophesy. I was laid up for days.

The rejection letters soon started turning up. Standard stuff.

'Not what we're looking for, etc., etc.'

Only one showed any interest at all and that was from Andrew Lauder – I think he was still at United Artists then but perhaps he had already set up Radar Records. His letter, unlike the others, seemed positive and he asked us to send him any further recordings we might make. He also returned the copy of the cassette we'd been hawking round with us. Which when played turned out to be a bit of a revelation and not a terribly good one at that. The music on the tape was virtually inaudible, being drowned out by the clatter of knives and forks, snippets of conversation and dialogue from an episode of *Coronation Street* – pretty avant-garde stuff.

It turned out that Terry had copied the tapes from one cassette player to another by sticking a mike in front of it while eating his tea and watching *Corrie*. Ian was furious. But I thought that Andrew Lauder must have really keen hearing and an acute ear for talent if he could make out anything at all from the muffled Woolworth's cassette we inflicted on him. Either that or he had rather unusual and eclectic tastes.

Our next disappointment was when we finally got the copies of the EP, which we had titled *An Ideal for Living*. I went round to Ian's and you could hear it halfway down Barton Street. It sounded great if you played it at maximum volume on a Dansette, which was Ian's hi-fi of choice. But when you played it at normal volume and compared it to other records, it sounded really tinny and quiet, and not that great at all. Oh shit, we'd got a thousand of these fuckers;

spent a bleeding fortune making them too. Most of which Ian had borrowed.

The worst thing was when we all trooped into Pips and demanded that the DJ play it there and then.

He got about halfway through one track before realising that this was a floor clearer par excellence and swiftly replaced it with the Clash. It was not how I'd imagined hearing my first record in public would be and we quickly skulked out, most likely shouting abuse at the poor DJ and calling the club's sound system crap. It wasn't our fault!

There must have be something wrong with the copy we gave him. Maybe it was just a few copies that sounded bad. I checked a few more at random. All the same. I had to face facts: the EP sounded dreadful. And we had a thousand of them.

We had decided that we would put all four tracks onto the record making it (of course) an EP. This happily avoided us having to make a decision as to what to leave off. We weren't completely ignorant about the process of manufacturing records and everyone knew the longer the playing time, the more the sound would deteriorate.

By doing a bit of rough calculating, we worked out it would have about six minutes a side. Now I was pretty sure that EPs went on for longer than that. I flicked through my records for confirmation and, sure enough, Nick Lowe's *Bowi* EP had a side longer than 6 minutes, *Spiral Scratch* had one side about five minutes, as did the Albertos' *Snuff Rock* EP. A minute couldn't make that much difference could it? We'd be fine, of course, we would. The guy at Pennine who sorted out the pressing as part of the deal told us it'd be OK and he should know. What I hadn't spotted was that most EPs played at 33 not 45 RPM. Having spent nearly all our (Ian's) money, there wasn't much we could do about it anyway.

Then to make matters worse I discovered that there was already a record company called Enigma – the name we'd given to our non-existent label.

Could it get any worse? Now we'd got a bunch of crap-sounding records with another record company's name plastered all over them.

Thankfully Enigma were a classical label so the chances of them getting wind of it were slight but with our luck . . .

We still hadn't sorted out what we might do with the records once we had them. I'd spoken to Bob Last, Terry had tried Richard Boon and Ian was daily pestering Derek at RCA and T. J. Davidson. But no one was interested. My hints to Virgin had gone nowhere. Maybe things would change once we had the sleeves done.

Bernard did the designing of the, er, slightly 'controversial' sleeve (a member of the Hitler Youth banging a drum), and I figured that a 14 x 14 inch sheet of paper folded into quarters would get rid of the need of any gluing – all it would need was a little origami. I arranged for the sleeves to be printed at a little shop in Macclesfield. One Saturday afternoon, everyone came to Ivy Lane and, to a soundtrack of Neil Young's *Zuma*, we set to work paper folding and record inserting. All that work and for what? A pile of shit-sounding records in slightly controversial sleeves.

I went round the record shops in Macc to see if anyone would take a few copies off our hands, but with no success. I tried selling them to mates, who naturally expected not to be charged. This usually ended up with a bit of bartering – only Phil Swindells (my drummer friend of cabaret fame) coughed up the full amount and later collared me to say he thought it was really good. Most demanded a refund. I tried selling them down the pub, resulting in even more bartering.

'How much without the sleeve then?'

'I'll give you 50p and a pint now but if I don't like it you'll owe me.'

Somehow I didn't think David Bowie did much of this.

Once again it was us versus the rest of the world. Through no fault of our own (obviously), we were doomed.

Then one day Ian came up trumps. His persistence and charm had paid off. Richard Searling and Derek Brandwood at RCA's Manchester office had a friend, John Anderson, who ran a northern soul label, Grapevine, which was thinking of branching out into new wave.

The plan was that John would pay for the recording of an album, and then Richard would put it out through RCA with a licence deal, or something of that nature. This was brilliant. An album was better than an EP. When do we start? There was one small catch, however: as part of the deal they would like us to do a cover of a northern soul hit in a new wave/punk rock styling.

First, we would have to meet with John Anderson and hear, from the horse's mouth as it were, what exactly the deal was going to involve. So one sunny morning, Ian and I set off in the Cortina bound for King's Lynn.

An odd place for a northern soul label to be based, I thought, *surely Wigan would have been more like it?*

I knew a bit about northern soul thanks to Geoff, the youngest recruit to Cliff's office staff. He was a Wigan Casino regular and explained that northern hits were frequently extremely obscure or extremely rare old American tracks whose true identity and origins were masked by the DJs. They were given new names and lineages, or sometimes rerecorded to disguise their pedigree. Well, that's the way I understood it anyway. It seemed a bit murky but ... in the light of what Richard and John were proposing it made some sort of sense.

Basking in another nefariously gained day off, we journeyed east to Norfolk. The Cortina's unpredictable radio was behaving for once and Dee D. Jackson's 'Automatic Lover' got frequent plays on Radio 1 to the approval of the east-bound travellers.

'Good this, innit?'

'Yeah, she sounds a bit dirty.'

'This synth bit's good.'

The radio packed up just outside Grantham.

We were two lads off to the seaside. We smoked and talked about the future of the band, what we should be doing.

Ian's old mate Toz was doing Art at college, 'Really good, weird stuff. We should get him to do something.' I'd thought about art school once but an unfortunate glue-related incident had rendered me an undesirable pupil.

Other bands, of course, we invariably talked about bands – that was always the meat of the long-drive conversation. Ian had been reading about Genesis P-Orridge and Throbbing Gristle and their industrial experimental approach to sound. Reports of the Throbbing Gristle live experience seemed to intrigue him, particularly the bit he'd read about them charging over a thousand pounds to play.

'That's what we should be doing.'

We talked of the old jobs we'd both had in the mills of Macclesfield, Ian's salvaging of balls at Prestbury golf club, the current plight of our 'day jobs', the time-off wrangles; we talked about writing songs and books we'd read and films we'd seen. Happy-go-lucky driver and navigator fare.

John Anderson was welcoming. We got sandwiches, but really should have pushed for fish and chips. He gave us some of his records, northern soul 12-inchers mostly, and some Casablanca singles, which had been done by John's US partner, Bernie.

That went down well, free stuff always did, and he told us a bit about his plan for the record/label.

He was thinking of calling it 'Sourgrapes'. What did we think?

'Yeah, that sounds great,' I lied nervously as Ian choked on his third or fourth sandwich.

The track John and Richard wanted us to cover was by N. F. Porter and called 'Keep On Keeping On'. We listened to it a couple of times – it had a driving beat and a cool guitar riff. How could I not have heard it before? It was really good! But it didn't sound much like us. That didn't matter, apparently, if we just stuck to the bare bones of it. I think John was unaware of the exact level of our musical competence but we nodded and enquired about further sandwiches. Ooh and any crisps? We were easily bought. I doubt we played the free records more than once.

Most musicians can, after hearing a tune once or twice, knock off a pretty good version of it. Well, if not good, then something that bears a passing resemblance to the original.

None of those musicians were members of Joy Division.

Our few attempts at covers were notable for the way they sounded nothing like the song that they were supposed to be.

There was 'Riders on the Storm' by the Doors – that one got a public airing once to the sound of Jim Morrison's remains rotating in a Paris graveyard.

'7 and 7 Is' by Love – that one never got out of the rehearsal room. In fact, we only got as far as the first chorus before we knew we were facing defeat.

'Louie Louie' by the Kingsmen wasn't that bad. It helped that John the Postman, with whom we mostly jammed it, knew nearly all of the words and at least two of the three chords.

'Sister Ray' by the Velvets was something that sounded a bit like a rambling jam anyway and so long as we got somewhere close with the riff, artistic licence could justify the rest.

Much, much later there would be 'Wooden Heart' and 'Are You

Lonesome Tonight?' by Elvis (the King) Presley, and 'When I'm with You' by Sparks, but I'm getting a bit ahead of myself there.

Don't get me wrong, I'm not saying this failing was a bad thing. No, not at all, quite the opposite in fact. It showed imagination, if anything. Creativity, you know?

We set to trying to cover N. F. Porter's track, but the one thing that stuck out was the guitar riff. In trying (and failing) to copy the feel of the track's rhythm, we ended up speeding it up a fair bit. Ian wrote some new lyrics, nicked a title from William Burroughs (or from a Manc sci-fi fanzine, which had nicked it earlier), and after a couple of evenings work at T. J.'s 'Interzone' was born. *Pretty good*, we thought.

It was more than that really. With the benefit of hindsight, perhaps this was the beginning of a style. Ian's Ballard-like lyrics evoked some decaying cityscape of the near future or the recent past. Cold like a foreign film, it almost sounded like it had subtitles. It didn't have a chorus (not much of our stuff did), just a kind of refrain that relieved the wound-up tension of the verses. We may have had different backgrounds but the one thing we did all have in common was that we wanted to get out, to escape, and music seemed to offer a potential route.

It was the first of our songs that I could see as existing in an unreal place, like a scene in a movie, or a landscape passing by a windscreen. A world that Ian described, Bernard punctuated, Hooky steered and I propelled us through. A world from inside our collective heads, not really real, not thought out, just bits of stuff, made up and let out.

Whether this was the sort of thing Richard and John were expecting was something else. If it wasn't, there wasn't much we could or would do about it.

We had a couple more meetings with John and Richard in Manchester. Did we have enough songs for an album when our live sets just shaved twenty minutes? Course we did. Anyway, we weren't going to let a little thing like that stop us.

Great things were promised over a drink. The then legendary EMI Paris was mentioned as a possible recording studio.

'Fantastic-sounding room,' said John.

'Paris?' I spluttered in a funny high-pitched voice, much to the amusement of the rest of the band, especially Hooky, who still finds it funny to this day. In my head I was picturing myself being asked (in French of course), 'Are you going to hit all those drums?' 'Mais oui, mon ami,' I would reply, 'mais oui!' as I lit up another Gitanes.

It was, of course, the beer talking and, strange to say, we ended up in Arrow Studios, Jackson's Row, Manchester, in May 1978 for a couple of days. Not the more upmarket Parisian equivalent for 'as long as it takes'.

I must admit that I found it an interesting experience. I was learning what mics got used on the drums and the way that different sorts of rooms affected the sound of them. You could read all you wanted about this studio stuff, but until you started actually doing it . . .

John and Richard were nominally producing and Bob Augur was doing the engineering. Things started off swimmingly enough, but pretty soon it all went a little bit pear-shaped. I think John and Richard wanted a mutant soul record but getting Ian pissed on Scotch and John urging him to 'sing like James Brown' was like throwing petrol on a barbecue. It did not end well. To say there were musical differences would be an understatement. Transporting the pissed and enraged singer home and explaining to Debbie how he got in that state was challenging too.

That we went along with this deal – only Hooky had reservations – just shows how mad for a record contract we were. RCA was especially attractive: being on the same label as Bowie, Iggy and Lou Reed said something, carried a bit of weight. Ian was convinced that RCA proper (rather than Grapevine) would pick up the album once they heard how good we were.

Looking back, we must have been crazy.

You don't need a lawyer to tell you it's there in Black and White.

'We want all the publishing on their tunes.'

We weren't *totally* ignorant of what a contract meant. But one area where we were completely in the dark was music publishing. Rather than asking John and Richard what exactly publishing was, we guessed that what this meant was the world of sheet music. Who bought sheet music in this day and age? Can't be much money in that, can there? The fools! Let John's company have the music publishing. Ignorance is bliss.

Music publishing, as it turns out, has very little to do with sheet music. It's about assigning copyright and is in fact a complicated business. Even more complicated now in the twenty-first century with new technology, making downloads and music streaming as important as the sales of physical records.

We would also, in giving away the publishing, be giving away the right to exploit the songs (not the recordings we had made, but the rights to the actual songs themselves). We would potentially be giving away ownership of our music.

The actual royalties rate for the record (the amount we would make on sales of the record) is kind of straightforward: 4 per cent of 90 per cent of record sales after recouping (i.e. paying back) the cost of actually making the record in the UK, and 4 per cent of 90 per cent of 50 per cent overseas.

That's not too bad is it? we thought.

Ignorance is not only bliss, it is also very dangerous.

The record we made for Grapevine/RCA was never officially released but it is generally available these days on a bootleg with various names – 'The Warsaw Album' is the most common but we were actually thinking of calling it 'Abstract Music' – and it's OK at best. Mostly it sounds rough and unfinished. Most likely this was because we ran out of time. That's not to say we didn't have a plan as to how we were going to go about recording the songs and how we wanted them to sound. We'd put a lot of thought into it as these notes from the time show.

The notes will probably intrigue and confuse the trainspotters among you – myself included – for a couple of reasons, which I'll do my best to explain.

The song called 'Conditioned' is, I think, an alternative title for 'Novelty' hence '(Nov.)'. We did have another song called 'Conditioned' from July 1977 and were probably recycling the title, having binned the song for some reason.

'Soundtrack' in this case refers to the song aka 'No Love Lost', which had been recorded for the *An Ideal for Living* EP but not yet widely released.

I can still remember every word of that jingle, unfortunately.

All of us, but Hooky and Ian especially, were easily irked. Any little setback quickly became disaster. More proof that our group paranoia was justified.

We felt we were outsiders. I liked that idea. I wanted to be outside. Inside was being controlled and suffocated, starved. That's what we thought *they* were doing to us. The bastards. We felt collectively persecuted and that is not a good way to make friends – people will think you moody bastards. Quite a few did. Quite a few still do.

In our world, we were not moody bastards. Far from it. We were easy-going, happy-go-lucky, practical-joke-loving types – looking for a life of fun and frolics, but thwarted at every turn.

*　　*　　*

I'M LIVING IN THE ICE AGE: approx.2.50. *1*
  Back up Vocals,Ring Ending, Echo on drums? o/*Oule cmple ton vm* / *CLAPPING!!*

INTERZONE: app.3.20 *2*
  Dead finish. *piue - Huon/oeue enter + Harisom* / *CLAP.* /

LEADERS OF MEN: app.2.35 *4*
  Back up Vocals, Echo on Drums, Ringing finish, use of background tapes as introduction & low dub.
  Guitar- Normal with high volume for sustain.

CONDITIONED (Nov.): app.4.00 *5*
  Bang Finish, Emphasis on build ups and climax on build up, after quiet verse.
  Guitar - Normal Vol.6½.

SHADOW PLAY: app.4.00 *7*
  Straight forward with extended lead fade finish. /*OVER DUB DRUM HULL/DRUM cymbals*

Failures: app.3.30 *3*
  New Beginning, attention to Rhythm Track and extra dub on first part of riff, speed up and echo on finish.
  Multitack vocals or use of Octadivider or Phlanger.

Walked in Lines: app3.10 *4*
  Back up Vocals, with intense recording, with ringing finish. *O/O RYTHAM GUITR ON BEARS*

Transmission: app.4.00 *3*
  Back up Vocals on Dance Chorus, Lead beginning, into melody lines, 1st Dance Chorus Low Chord Riff 1, Verse with high Chords, Dance Chor
  Ring finish on Guitars with drums continuing and slowly stopping.   Low 1.

Soundtrack: app.3.45 *Bass?* *5* - *7 CLAP !! on drum*
  Backing Vocals,   Intro: Random Chords first, then on second Digital notes and Harmonics, 1st Drum riff all way through with second riff
                                                                                        dubbed on top on second part.
      Main Song: Alternate Riff first, then simple riff on second part. Background tapes to be tried on both intro & main song.

Warsaw: app.2.25 *6*
  Backing Vocals, Ringing finish, Multitracked Guitars, Attention to Vocals.
  Try claq ton-tom. II

The Drawback(win): app 2.00
  Backing Vocals, Ring Finish, attention to Chorus.

Abstract Music

The two memories that stay with me from those sessions are getting the keyboard player from Sad Café to come down with his Minimoog and add a synth bass line to 'No Love Lost', and asking him if it could make other noises apart from the one he was playing. He took it well, though. I just liked the noises. We probably wanted some noise as a substitute for the 'background tapes' we wanted to try. Contrary to popular belief, I don't think we were averse to using the Moog (well, I wasn't) but somehow our dissatisfaction with the production of the record seemed to muddy the waters a bit. Were we ever satisfied? Will we ever be?

The other was arriving slightly early one day to find a small, ever-so-camp chap recording a jingle for a football pools company.

'Who the fuck are you?' Ian probably thought this was John's idea of getting some backing vocals on the record.

'Bob, Bob, Bob, there's people in the studio. Bob! I can't possibly work with this sort of pressure. Get them out right this minute, if you please,' the little jingle songster pleaded.

If you do anything often enough you will either get better at it or realise that it's not for you and never will be, but at least you tried. Either way, you will have learned something important about yourself.

By dint of repetition, I was making progress in the art of persuading people I had never met (and largely never would) to give us gigs. These were mostly in the pubs and clubs of West Yorkshire and took place, without fail, on those dead nights in the middle of the week. So they weren't the best-attended events, but the theory was that, by word-of-mouth, things would get better. Sometimes, though, there didn't seem to be any words coming out of any mouths.

At one gig in Oldham there was literally no one there, just the caretaker, Hooky's girlfriend Iris and her chum Pauline – making a surprise hanky-panky inspection to check up what mischief went on with this earth-shattering band. Oh, and there were two punks who interrupted our set to ask, 'Are the Prefects on here tonight?'

Enclosed please find Joy Division pics., biog.,
+ E.P. as mentioned in the previous letter, 18/2/78.

The E.P. was originally intended for release on
our own label - ENIGMA - but after the records
had been pressed it was discovered that another
record company existed with the title ENIGMA, so
once again we are in a "HAVING TO CHANGE THE
NAME" situation.

At present no distribution channel has been
finalised and any advice/help you could give us
on this would be appreciated very much.

We hope to be able to play London quite soon,
the reason we have not done so before is that we
were told by a Major London Agency that no-one
would book a Band with a name similar to "Warsaw
Pakt".

As and when we do play London we would hope to have
the opportunity of meeting you.

Yours sincerely,

(Steve Morris)
pp Joy Division

P.S.
Unfortunately the enclosed E.P. is minus the Sleeve, as they
have not yet been returned from the Printers. As this is a
special folding Sleeve which turns into a 14x14 full colour/
black-white poster, - a real treat for all "Collectors item" fans.
We will send one as soon as possible so you don't miss out
on this "unique" opportunity!

A slightly bitter press release.

On hearing our negative reply the pair then enquired, 'Do you
know where they *are* on then?'

Then they were gone, and the wind continued whistling and the
tumbleweed blew across the empty hall.

You would have thought that we could have managed to get
ourselves a gig in Macclesfield. I mean, we'd played in Manchester so
Macclesfield should have been a shoe-in. But getting anything done
in my home town is never easy.

In the spirit of the times, bands had started playing live music nights at the Travellers' Rest pub and Moreton Hall community centre. There'd even been a bit of a festival on at the Moss Rose football ground featuring local rock legends Orphan and Silverwing. But phone call after phone call trying to get us a gig anywhere in town drew a blank. So one Friday night I decided to take the bull by the horns and set off with Ian to corner a promoter in person and persuade him that it would be a good idea to give us a gig.

'Thee don't like that punk rock, new wave or whatevreet's called business in Macc. Come back when yuv dun a few more shows, got a bit more experience like, and I'll 'ave a see abowt getting yer on or sommat' was his response.

That's Macclesfield for you. The Beatles played here once, you know. They never came back.

With the response from the man in the pub to the EP, I shouldn't have been surprised.

One gig (technically two as it would turn out) we did manage to get was arranged by Hooky in Salford: Wednesday night in Little Hulton at the local working men's club, a lovely modern affair with the extremely bright fluorescent-tube lighting that was a trademark of such venerable institutions. This in itself was not too bad. It was more that it turned out to be 'Talent Night' that marred things.

'I thought you said it was a New Wave Night!'

'Nah, I said it was Rock Night, well it was last week. Ay, mate, what happened to Rock Night?'

'Didn't go well with the regulars. They preferred Talent Night, so we changed it back.'

Ian, Terry and Bernard were soon engaged in a fierce competition of their own, taking it in turns to try and charm the lovely lady songstress who was the act after us. I think we were on after the comedian.

Accompanied by a cover of Huddie Ledbetter's 'Black Betty' that was then riding high in the charts as unrequested intro music, the club compère announced, 'If yer like yer Ram Jam, then yer'll like this lot . . . local heavy-rock band . . . the Joy Divisions!'

After the first song, the compère looked uneasy. By the close of the second, he was bellowing in my ear, 'Wind it up! Next one's yer last. Get off, for fuck's sake, yer'll 'ave me sacked.'

In the embarrassed silence that followed our brief set, we apologetically scooped the gear off the stage, chucked it into the waiting getaway cars and sped off into the night. We didn't bother staying to see if we'd won. My money was on the lady songstress.

I don't remember whose idea it was – Ian would be the prime suspect – we ended up driving to the Ranch, a Manchester punk hotspot adjacent to local drag queen Foo Foo Lammar's nightclub. Like some pirate-raiding party, we announced that, like it or not, we were going to play. We would redeem ourselves.

Whether it was because of the gig's spontaneous nature or, more likely, that we were all more than a bit wound up from the earlier debacle, this was a fantastic gig, filled with dangerous energy and spirit. Ian nearly took my head off with a badly aimed pint-pot throw – he was, of course, angry and wound up the tightest. The Ranch's crowd were surprised and impressed, even if they still thought we were called Warsaw. We had seized victory from the jaws of defeat. Ace.

After that night, you'd have thought we'd have given anything vaguely resembling a talent show a wide berth.

15

HOW I MET YOUR MOTHER

Bored teenagers of Macclesfield: Julie, Gillian and Jill.

In the little room up the wooden staircase and at the end of the corridor of T. J, Davidson's rehearsal mill, I am set up in the middle of the back wall with the door to my right. I like having a wall behind me. I worry that my drum stool will give way and collapse, and the yellow,

Rockwool-insulated wall will cushion my tumble. We've tried peeling the hairy material off in places. It's too great a temptation to resist.

There are two ancient, second-, third- or maybe fourth-hand electric heaters, one either side for warmth. Only one works reliably.

Hooky is set up on my left, with his big, square, yellowy-green single speaker cabinet and amp. Bernard, on the right, has a Vox UL715 series amp and cab with a chrome tube frame – the sort the Beatles used.

The tuning of strings. We have to go through this before we can do any serious playing. Bernard is the only one of us who has the gift of guitar and bass tuning. He is also the most naturally musical.

'Third fret.' Iiiiiiing. Bonnnng. Iiiiiiiiiing. Biiiing. 'Fifth.'

It's a ritual.

I roll a joint and find an empty Tizer tin to use as an ashtray.

Ian is set up facing us, with a wonky Vox column cab on either side of a newish-looking Carlsbro Viper PA amp. He is sitting between the door and the right-hand speaker cab, trying to light up a Marlboro with an expiring disposable lighter.

'Ian? Here ya are, catch!' as I toss my Bic lighter over to him.

'Fucking hell, did you see that film on BBC2 the other night?'

'The one with the girl with big . . .?'

'Yeah, that one! Fucking hell . . .'

Something like that is how it usually begins.

Not much talk about the music. Just this and that until there's nothing left and we'd better play something then.

As time progressed, the four us became more proficient musically and became better songwriters. No one told us how to do it. Together the four of us learned how to be Joy Division. Who else could we be?

Wednesday evenings and all day Sunday, that was our rehearsal routine without fail. There were interruptions from visitors.

T. J. Davidson, the rehearsal-mill owner (his dad really owned the place, truth be told) turned up with glamorous lady casino worker in tow.

'How's the motor, Tony?' Hooky would ask. Hooky was keen on cars and scrapyards, from whence our faulty room heaters and some of Hooky's cars were scavenged. ('I'd like to run a scrapyard of me own one day.')

T. J. would ask how we were doing, what gigs we had coming up. We'd ask how his label was doing, and he'd feed us bits of other resident band gossip.

'Buzzcocks have booked a month in one of the upstairs rooms.'

Then his by now bored glamorous croupier companion would remind him that her presence was required elsewhere, and they would be off to her tables in his Roller.

Michael Gorman was another regular feature of life at the mill. He was the place's caretaker and nightwatchman; we usually had to go and find him if we wanted to get into our room. Irish Michael (never Mick) and his big bunch of keys lived on the premises in a small room on the first floor that he shared with Woolly, the guard dog. They made an odd couple. Conversation with Michael was difficult to follow at times and was perhaps only truly understood by Woolly who, despite living up to his name, was not the most lovable of animals. Guard dogs aren't as a rule.

'Da Daags iz up da taap and da Cacks is com'n in layter an,' Michael would say.

There were the other bands too, the ones more on our sort of level. Not big like Buzzcocks or Slaughter and the Dogs, who kept themselves to themselves. But Emergency, who had their own PA. They were OK. We would try and persuade them to leave the PA in the walk-in cupboard in our room so we could borrow it on the quiet. Marc Riley – he'd been in the Fall – popped in a couple of times, just looking or after borrowing a lead, and the Inadequates, to whom we were yet to be introduced, were in the room at the other end of the corridor from us, on the way to the toilets. Though pissing in empty Tizer tins remained Hooky and Bernard's preference.

Assuming you were to make the usually icy trip to the conveniences, or if you were nipping out to Burgerland for a spot of lunch, it was only natural to have a look through a half-opened door at what your neighbours were up to.

The sound of female laughter. That would certainly pique your interest.

'Them at the end. They've got a bird in there!' was Ian's sit-rep and we would revert to naughty schoolboy mode.

'Steve, you go and ask if they've got any spare drumsticks. Say all yours are broke.'

'Fuck off!'

'All right, Barney,' everyone always called Bernard 'Barney', 'you go and see if they'll lend you a guitar lead. Say you forgot one or say your amp's bust or something.'

In the end it would nearly always be Ian, trying a bit of a blag. Like a nosey neighbour spying on the new arrivals next door with a proffered cup of sugar, off he would go to investigate.

On this occasion:

'There's three of them,' like they were stray ponies or something. 'They're from Macclesfield. It's them three that were in the *Macc Express*.'

The *Macclesfield Express* was my home town's premier purveyor of local gossip and scandal. My mother, a keen reader, came a close second; her knowledge of scandal was encyclopaedic, and her specialist subject was the obituary. The *Macc Express* was the sort of paper that carried stories such as 'Local Man Abducted by UFO' accompanied by a photo of a local man looking slightly bemused and pointing towards the heavens. Every town had one. They'd done a front-page piece accompanied by a picture of three girls holding a copy of *Never Mind the Bollocks* and looking suitably bored. You can imagine the photographer's exhortations.

'Reet reet, that's it. Lovely, girls. C'mon, look a bit more cheesed off, like. That's it, love it! You, the one in the middle, think Johnny

Rotten. How about a bit of spitting, love? In't that what you punks do?'

The story was that three local girls were forming a new wave group – sisters Gillian and Julie Gilbert and their friend Jill Barker were the local girls in question. Gillian played guitar and Julie and Jill did backing vocals, along with Chris Whitehead, also on guitar, 'Tony' on bass and an anonymous (at least to me) drummer.

The *Macclesfield Express* would later do a piece on Joy Division titled 'On the Mark with Much Joy'. Not exactly 'Freddie star ate my hamster' is it? The piece had a similar grainy snap of me and Ian in the parlour of Ivy Lane. Ian looked to be wearing a lampshade on his head.

That three girls wanted to form a new wave band was big news in Macclesfield but I have to admit I dismissed the article (as I did much of the *Express*'s output) with a cynical sneer that said, 'No chance!'

Just goes to show how wrong I can be. For here they were, the self-same three local girls, just two doors down from us, wailing away a Sunday afternoon in Manchester.

'Go and ask them how they're getting home,' Hooky said. 'Say they can have a lift with you and Steve.'

So Ian did and that night sisters Gillian and Julie and their friend Jill squeezed into the Cortina between bits of drum and cymbal. They giggled and oohed while me and Ian did the shy-boy chat-up stuff as we ran them back to, of all places ... Gawsworth Road, Macclesfield. The street of my childhood.

It was fate, divine intervention, synchronicity – whatever.

The Gilberts had moved to Gawsworth Road from Stretford in April 1963, just around about the time I was destroying my Beatles guitar. Their house was less than a hundred yards from mine. I must have gone past it on my bike hundreds of times. How had I never noticed? (Probably too preoccupied by plastic model planes and glue.) It is indeed a small world.

We had a lot in common, Gillian and me. Living on the same street for how many years? We were bound to have. The sweet shop down the road, the fields around the back and the pond where I'd planned my den. She couldn't recall hearing the music of Can and Terry Riley echoing across the pasture in the dead of night, though. Must have been the wind. It was the beginning of a relationship that forty years later is still alive.

Her new wave band the Inadequates, though, is not. They lasted a couple more rehearsals at T.J.'s and one gig at a party in Heald Green, their one and only public performance.

I would meet Gillian in Macclesfield on my lunch break as I trawled Macclesfield's record shops (I wasn't hard to find), and the Cortina taxi service expanded to lifts to gigs, then the odd nights out in the pub. There really wasn't much else to do in Macclesfield. We'd spend most of our time playing on the Space Invaders machine. Jukeboxes were on their way out and massive cabinets with screens that took money as they bleeped and squawked were on the way in. Those machines were mesmerising – the 2D 8-bit aliens' inexorable march ever downwards, going faster and faster as I tried to defend Earth with the puny laser. This was the future with its bleeping, shrieking, white noise explosion soundtrack. The one I loved best of all was Missile Command, with its track-ball aiming and the strobing nuclear explosions. The fear was that this might actually happen in real life. A nuclear wipeout.

Game Over.

Gillian, Julie and Jill were collectively referred to as 'the goshes' by the rest of the band – they did say 'Gosh' a lot, I have to say – and I think Hooky fancied his chances with Julie. They'd come to the gigs in Manchester. I was only allowed to transport them to 'home' gigs: there was a girlfriend embargo on anything further afield. I forget who came up with that rule. Something to do with telling tales, anyway. Joy Division could be a bit sexist on occasion.

The goshes were viewed with suspicion by the rest of the band's wives and girlfriends. They were interlopers, harlots and most likely groupies! They would be after their men, and I was a fiend anyway for dumping that Stephanie.

I was shocked that Gillian had never heard of the New York Dolls and took her to see David Johansen, the band's singer, perform solo. She wasn't impressed. So we spent the night just walking around Hulme instead.

Gillian was artistic. Unlike me she could draw and paint – obviously useful for an artist. She made badges, experimented with photography and designed mock-up cassette covers. She liked the Pre-Raphaelites, who I thought were a band, and Gustav Klimt, who I guessed was a German.

The Gilbert sisters stood out with their futuristic barnets. I knew nothing of the science of the styling of hair (I remain an ignoramus still), but along with her de rigueur lapels filled with band badges, Gillian's tresses impressed. She had a crimper – 'A what?' I asked – and she knew how to use it. I supposed Kate Bush must have had one. Arlene Phillips's Hot Gossip were devotees of the crimping iron. It went well with stark lighting and a glossy-lipped pout. Apart from the shared frizz, the Gilbert sisters looked, well, like sisters and to the unfamiliar they could seem identical. Not identical twins (or triplets: there were actually three of them), but there were enough similarities that could confuse the slightly pissed.

Gillian's parents made a living making children's clothes and selling them at local markets, Wythenshawe mostly. Their house was full of sewing machines and stacks of kid-sized blue jeans and orange shirts. Gillian and Julie worked on the market stall selling Day-Glo kids' clothes and ladies' undies. West Indian cricketer Clive Lloyd was one of their customers allegedly – maybe not for ladies' undies. Their middle sister Kim did not take part in standing round in the cold and rain collecting change. Kim was fragile and liked disco, preferring the boogie nights at Macc's Silklands Suite to new wave gigs in Manchester.

We would sit on the floor in Gillian's kitchen listening to the John Peel show, waiting for Joy Division's session to come on. (Yes, I am getting ahead of myself here. Joy Division hit the big time. Sort of. Sorry to ruin the surprise.)

'The drums sound fucking shit!' I would invariably exclaim.

The trap of vanity springs shut, for as a musician you begin to forget to listen to the song as a whole and instead focus on your own particular bit, which for you is the most important bit in the whole thing. If the drums sound shit then the song sounds shit. See where you end up? Before you can say Jack Robinson you've turned into a moaning musician or, even worse, a temperamental artist or, worst of all, some sort of perfectionist, leading ultimately to your transmutation into a rock arsehole.

It happens, not overnight of course, but believe me it does seep in and twist and corrupt and ... Bob's yer uncle. (Who were Jack and Bob? Were they related? Anybody know?)

I would grumble.

'It sounds fine,' Gillian would say, for she was hearing more than me.

I would haughtily and patronisingly tut and think to myself, *What do you know?*

Sexist pig, she thought, for I could read her mind and she, of course, could read mine.

Life in the band meant whatever social life I might have had took a back seat. Nights out became few and far between and, honestly, they were boring compared to the excitement of playing a gig or the satisfaction of working out a new song.

We all had day jobs to hold down and, although turning up for work half asleep wasn't too much of a problem for me, for everyone else it was. Most bosses' sympathy will wear thin after a bit. As will relationships.

'You think more of that band than you do of me' is a difficult argument to counter with any degree of apparent honesty. As is the question, 'What do you get up to at these gigs then?'

'Why can't I come if it's so innocent?'

That one was dealt with by the 'there's no room in the car' and /or 'it's not me, it's Steve/Ian/Bernard/Hooky/and later Rob' (the answer depending on who was doing the lying). In truth, the band embargo on wives and girlfriends coming on these outings was more to do with spoiling the chances of copping off than any more spartan or logistical reason.

Doing gigs therefore involved coming up with creative excuses for work and girlfriends: we were creative in deceit, as young men can be. Though sometimes less than plausible.

'Always tell the truth: just miss out the bits you don't want them to know': the band philosophy of the time.

The blueprint for a good life in the 1970s was:

- Go to school
- Get a good job
- Meet a nice girl
- Get married
- Have kids
- Die

That was about it. Hopefully the good job would provide enough cash to pay for your burial after the last bit. But there were no guarantees. I'd already done a pretty good job of trashing the first in the list. The second, employment, wasn't looking that great either.

This order of living was handed down like a mantra from one generation to the next and no matter how progressive or forward thinking a young man was in the seventies, it was imprinted on him from an early age.

If you did nothing, just drifted along, this is what would happen, like it or not. There would be no escape to the world of the folk on the telly. We'd never had it so good.

'Oh, one day you'll meet a nice girl.'

OK then, on to the third – meet a nice girl. What was that about?

In the office where I bided my time and skived the day away were several girls. Most of the time, they outnumbered men five to two.

I got on with them very well; and I got on with their sisters pretty well too. They were very nice.

And there it is, that 1970s northern man's patronising arrogance. It may seem alien and wrong in the twenty-first-century LED light, but bathed in the fluorescent strip light over my tray of neglected filing, it was ubiquitous and inescapable: hot-blooded young chaps didn't want Linda from next door but one. They wanted Babs or Dee Dee from Pan's People.

'Phoar,' as Reg Varney of *On the Buses* might have said at the time. 'Look at the . . . on that one!'

Women in the seventies – an allegedly liberated age of equality, or so we thought at the time – were by and large treated appallingly badly. Mostly by men who thought they were following in the footsteps of their fathers, so where was the harm in a little good-natured misogyny? As the Nuremberg defence goes . . .

Get a bunch of high-spirited lads together, maybe in a rock band or something, send them off on the road and left to their own devices, and who knows what might happen? Well, I think you can predict the answer to that one easily enough.

If you were steadfast in the avoidance of the 'proper job' that your mother and father wished upon you, then there was a pretty good chance that 'nice girls' would not be the thing that you were after.

'Tales of Rock-and-Roll Mayhem and Sexual Hi-Jinks' were pretty high on the list of incentives to become a rock star, probably higher up on the list than 'untold riches' and more often than not just as imaginary.

It's a glamorous business.

One of the great things about punk was that women could break out of the stereotypes that showbiz had them typecast for. Gaye Advert, Siousxie and Debbie Harry weren't typical chanteuses, the Slits were not the Three Degrees. There were the Raincoats, Tina Weymouth, Poly Styrene, Joan Jett, Patti Smith. The thing that went under the umbrella of 'punk' was nothing if not a great leveller, an equaliser and something that definitely broke down the preconception of what role a woman in a group might have.

At T. J.'s rehearsal mill, women, though, were still a rarity. Hence the interest in the arrival of the Inadequates. Later, when we moved up in the world and got the bigger room – the one that's in the photographs and the 'Love Will Tear Us Apart' video – we found ourselves neighbours with Manicured Noise (mentioned by Siouxsie in a couple of interviews, so interesting); the all-girl rhythm section certainly appealed to some.

The Inadequates protesting at the lack of music
venues in Macclesfield. Nobody listened

Funny that, looking at this photo, nobody looks overtly like a 'punk rocker' but that was how it was. The only signifier of affiliation was the collection of badges and the odd safety pin or dog collar. The tartan bondage trousers and spiky Mohicans were rarely to be seen in the early days of north-west DIY bands. It was only later, with the second wave of 'oi' punk bands such the Exploited and the Angelic Upstarts, that we really began to see the stereotypical uniform and wearing of dyed and spiked-up hair, which now features on holiday postcards of King's Road punks. As jolly old London as jellied eels or the Changing of the fucking Guard.

PART 3:

TOMORROW'S WORLD

Roll up, roll up to the Stiff Test/Chiswick Challenge, 14 April 1978.

Before shows such as *The X Factor*, *The Voice*, *Wherever's Got Talent* and God knows what else passes for twenty-first-century gladiatorial light entertainment, there was *Opportunity Knocks*, a show that, unlikely as it seems, had been running since 1949.

Opportunity Knocks was fronted by the ever-so-slightly weird but more-than-slightly faux-sincere and staunchly Thatcherite Canadian expat, Hughie Green. It did exactly the same thing as today's search-for-a-star reality pap. Aspiring stars were given the chance to do their act before a TV audience who would pass judgement by applause volume, before the viewing public got their say with an unriggable postal vote. The show ceased in 1978, and by then it already had a rival in the form of *New Faces*, which had tarted up the format for the seventies audience with the inclusion of a panel of four celebrity judges. The idea really wasn't that new – the search for raw and cheap talent to exploit had long been a part of the showbiz food chain. A tradition ripe for lampooning and sending up.

The Stiff/Chiswick talent show was a new wave homage or piss-take of this variety genre. It would tour the UK, visiting musical hotspot cities. Local bands turned up and did their set and the 'best' artistes would be given the opportunity to record for either Stiff or Chiswick – it was unclear as to which. What was also unclear was the method of judging who the winner might be. Hughie Green used a clapometer but I doubt that would have been much help here. I guess the assumption was that some representative of that branch of the record companies' A & R department would do the job – it was theoretically right up their street, what they were bred for: identifying talent.

You would have thought that going off our previous brush with the talent show back in Little Hulton, we would have learned our lesson and avoided anything featuring the word 'talent' in its title. In justification, I guess that there was an ironic use of the word here. That there would be no magic acts, ventriloquists or lovely lady singers seeking approval from Stiff or Chiswick was guaranteed. No, definitely no novelty acts at all, you would have thought. What could possibly go wrong?

It was only a matter of time before the Stiff bandwagon clattered into the north-west and parked itself in Manchester city centre.

The venue for the fateful night in question was to be Rafters, yet again: the scene of both the debacle with Fast Breeder and the inebriated girlfriend incident. How we got on the bill for this one I can only imagine. We certainly didn't just turn up and expect to play like we had at the Ranch, so presumably Terry, as our notional manager, had something to do with it. The gigs we did at Rafters (and I may be imagining this) all seemed to involve Dougie James (of Soul Train fame), who worked upstairs at the swisher Fagins nightery, so he may have had a hand in getting us on the bill. It is also more than likely that Alan Wise, doctor, scholar and legend of Manchester's gigging world, had some input. He usually did. He appears in most tales of Manchester venues in some capacity or other.

However it happened, we turned up for the shindig and were given a piece of paper with a vague running order of ten, fifteen or more bands on it. There was V2, Spider Mike King, the Yo-Yos, Prime Time Suckers and a band called the Negatives. Of course, there was no mention of Joy Division – or even 'Joy Davidson' as we had once been billed at Rafters. (I found this out when, unsure as to exactly the date of our next gig, I rang up the venue pretending to be a curious punter, and asked politely what live acts would be performing in the coming weeks, only to be told 'next Thursday we've got a lady vocalist, the lovely Joy Davidson'.)

Past experience having taught me that getting two bands to agree the running order could be a tortuous ordeal, I had a pretty good inkling that this was going to be a very long night – a long, fractious squabble-filled night. Ah, the camaraderie and comradeship of musicians in the seventies Manchester new wave scene warms my heart.

To pointlessly pass the time during such occasions, I had acquired a pot of Slime to play with and relieve the inevitable stress. Slime is a wonderful invention: a tub full of snot-like disgusting fluorescent green jelly that could be squished, squeezed and juggled. Simple pleasures, simpler times. It is difficult now to explain quite what the appeal of this was. The target audience was the under-tens.

Even in my twenties, I loved toy and model shops. They always seemed places of happiness and fun, and Slime looked to me like it could be a lot of fun. The question most right-minded folk would ask a twenty-year-old carrying a tub of useless green jelly would be, 'What on earth have you got that for?' or 'What have you been wasting your money on now?'

I got asked this all the time.

I still do.

There were no electronic gadgets to waste money on then so maybe that explains it.

On the night in question, Gillian and I discussed the many potential uses of Slime. What I thought was a hilarious plan formed. What if we engaged someone – the victim – in conversation or some other diversion, and while he or she was distracted, slipped a large dollop of this green goo down their shirt? Or even better, into their pocket . . . for later discovery. Boredom, the mother of puerile invention.

Elsewhere in the venue, the potential impact and the logistic problems of the sheer number of bands was beginning to dawn. It was minor at first: everything would simply get moved a bit later. (When did anything ever get moved earlier at a gig?) But as Joy Division didn't have a time to start with, what did this mean for us? Hooky and Terry were doing their best to sort this out, but so were about fifteen other bands, all expecting this gig to be 'the big one'.

So, as to be expected, things were from the outset quite tense and the close proximity to large quantities of strong lager (Holsten Pils) would only exacerbate that.

The running/billing negotiations took a turn for the worse when Hooky, Terry or Ian raised the question of why the Negatives were on the bill at all.

'They're not even a proper band, just a bunch of fucking *NME* hacks taking the piss.'

The Negatives were loosely comprised of Dave Bentley (the Drones' manager), Steve Shy (of *Shy Talk* fanzine), Paul Morley (*NME*), Kevin Cummins (who also worked for *NME* and perhaps wisely would stick to a career in photography), plus girlfriends on backing vocals. Predictably, their presence would only inflame things further.

Now you could take a Situationist point of view on this (which perhaps the Negs did) and argue that they had a perfectly valid right to be there, and that top of the bill was the only acceptable slot for them seeing as how they felt they were the most archly anarchic and new waviest bunch there.

We, of course, disagreed and cried foul. What began as a good-natured bit of banter on both sides gradually bubbled and fizzed with alcohol-fuelled belligerence as events ground on.

Band after band dumped their gear on the tiny stage (or borrowed somebody else's gear to speed things up), played the microcosm of a set (time was tight and getting tighter) and trundled off, while the next lot argued the toss about whose turn it was now.

Sometime around about V2's glam set – still featuring former Warsaw drummer Steve Brotherdale and someone I seemed to remember from my brief spell at Audenshaw Grammar (Mark Standley) on guitar – Gillian, who has always had a great knack for identifying a face in a crowd, spied Tony Wilson at the end of the crumbling mock-Tudor half-timbered bar area.

'Let's slime Wilson!' I said. His position as man on the telly with a bit of an arty-farty outlook made him a prime candidate for the role of victim in this ridiculous scheme.

Gillian, closely followed by a slightly tipsy Ian, went to engage the luminary and TV presenter in conversation while I readied the Slime.

Ian was many things (too many things possibly), but one thing he was not was violent. He could (very quickly) get wound up and he would let frustration spill over into rage in a Basil Fawlty manner. But at no time was anyone's wellbeing ever at risk. Even if their name was Anthony and they worked for Granada TV.

'Hello, Tony,' began Gillian demurely, 'when are you going to have Joy Division on "What's On"?'

To which Tony commenced his usual reply, 'Darling, I get—'

Only to be interrupted as our singer steamed in with . . .

'Yeah, Tony, when are you gonna put us on? You've had V2 on, you've had Buzzcocks on. What about us, ya cunt?'

If Tony was taken aback in any way, he didn't show it at the time. 'You'll be on next, darling, I promise.'

'Yeah, fuckin right! Ya twat.' A final salvo from Ian, and schmoozy conversation was thus curtailed – all before I could get a chance to unleash the green goo.

As V2 trooped off, I said hello to my glammed-up predecessor, who informed me that V2 would soon be embarking on a lengthy US tour. I wished him all the best as he sauntered off with a spangly-dressed lady friend.

Meanwhile, stage left, the Negatives v. Joy Division skirmish was showing no sign of abating. The night was turning into a déjà vu of the Fast Breeder gig, only even more annoying. The same 'yes you can, no you can't play', the same 'everyone's against us' paranoia. It was getting to be a habit.

A full-on goading competition was now taking place between the Negs and Ian, ably supported by Hooky and Terry. We must have been past band number ten by now, and the heat and the frustration were getting dangerously high.

Eventually a compromise of sorts was reached; we could go on after the Negatives, who were still drunkenly arguing for top billing, but we had to be off the stage by 2 a.m.

After the Negatives' much-delayed exit from the stage – they really were taking the piss – we hastily threw our gear on and played as though our lives depended on it.

We didn't win the contest (it was Spider Mike King, who was pretty good) but, and I may be biased, I honestly think we got the best reception of the night. Maybe everyone was just relieved it was all over and they could go home. But even Tony Wilson came back and congratulated us all. As he raved about how great he thought we were, I was quite glad he didn't have a load of Slime in his pocket.

And that DJ was there again.

One lunchtime, back from record hunting, I was at work, feet on the desk, on the phone speaking to Bernard, discussing the time of the next night's rehearsal, when he suddenly began to sound very agitated. He was in a phone box in Spring Gardens.

'Oh fuck, it's that bloke from Rafters again. The DJ. He's banging on the window, hang on, hang on, what should I tell him? I'll have to call you back in a minute, Steve.'

The phone on my desk rang again and after the 'beep beep beep' tone of two pences being poured into the slot, Bernard's voice continued.

'It was him again, he's still going on about wanting to be a manager. I told him to come to rehearsals and he can ask us all then.'

That phone call I can remember quite vividly. Rob Gretton coming through the door of our room at T. J. Davidson's that very first time is a wee bit hazy though. It must have happened, but perhaps it's shrouded by a cloud of hash smoke. That seems likely.

And maybe we went to the pub, the City Arms, the one across the road from the intriguing International Marine boat showroom on Whitworth Street. International Marine and another place under the bridge in Salford, Interarms, seemed to hint at some Manchester-based corporate global conspiracy, something out of Burroughs or Ballard. The blank exterior of Interarms' building seemed to be hiding something.

Yes, the pub, that's what I think I can remember. A pint of shandy for the driver. That's me.

'I'll get them in, what you having?'

Rob smoked. Now there were three of us, lighting up, 'Give us a fag then. Fuckin' 'ell, Ian, not Marlboros, give you a bad throat, them. I'll have one of yours, Steve, thanks. Christ, No. 6, a bit better, not much.'

Somebody must have given him a lift back to Chorlton.

So that would be me then. It was on the way back to Macc.

Rob didn't drive. Just me, Hooky and Terry; Barney still had the bike.

From the start, Rob seemed older than the rest of us. He was slightly, but the age difference seemed much wider than it was. He was confident, maybe it was that, or perhaps the streak of grey at the front of his otherwise dark tidy hair. Or was it the spectacles that did it? Made him look somehow wiser.

Whatever it was, we didn't take much persuading. He was like us and not like us. Anyway, nothing ventured, nothing gained. He became our manager. We didn't um and ah about it much, not then.

He called us daft as we told him about the records, the Electric Circus thing, the EP and the Richard and John RCA album. He called us lemons and said that people thought we were Nazis, did we know that?

'Oh yeah,' we laughed.

'Have you signed anything?'

Er, mmm.

We were the stupid kids and he was the grown-up.

He said something about working with Slaughter and the Dogs. He'd grown up in Wythenshawe, so they were a local band. He'd been managing the Panik (hadn't Ian been in the frame for that band once upon a time?). He'd put out a single for them. He'd give us a copy.

'Got loads left.'

Rainy City Records was the name of his label. Good Mancunian name.

Here's an interview with Rob in which I think he somehow manages to mix up memories of the Fast Breeder gig (with Warsaw) and the Stiff/Chiswick contest (Joy Division) and skips a few weeks. Or maybe it's my faulty memory.

Whatever, I always found it best to let Rob have the last word. He would anyway.

Anyway Fast breeder decided to go on before them because they were running so late. Fast Breeder went on at say . . . half twelve. Well a lot of people started going home after that time. So Warsaw got on at about half past one, twenty to two, y'know. And that's why . . . and all the equipment broke down and all that. And they had a really bad time. The PA didn't arrive 'til nine o'clock or ten o'clock. That's why they were all running late. And erm, that's why he went smashing glasses and that. I thought it looked really weird. Ian looked really weird then. Like he had his hair cut up to here and, er, leather pants on. They looked like little rich boys but dead weird. S'like you just get fed up of going to gigs and seeing that . . . I don't know, it just fuckin' amazed me. And I went up and telling them at the end, and telling them how brilliant I thought they was. And the usual thing . . .

'FUCK OFF. NO BASTARD'LL SIGN US THOUGH! EVERYBODY'S AGAINST US. WE WERE LUCKY TO GET ON.'

And Tony Wilson . . . And I went in the dressing room and told them after. Well there wasn't really a dressing room. Round the back. And told them how great I thought they were. And Tony Wilson came in and said, 'I thought that was absolutely brilliant.'

I was raving about them all the next day. Raving absolutely. Woke up in the morning and – they're great they are. I could remember the songs as well. It was like a flash. I thought they were very threatening. They threatened me. I don't know whether it was the next day or a couple of days after. Say that gig was on the Friday, I think it was on the Friday. The next Monday I was phoning, I was phoning someone up and in the next . . . you know in Spring Gardens where all them phones are by the Post Office . . . in the next one was Bernard.

And er, I went and asked him, 'Do you want a manager?' And I thought he was a really weird-looking character as well. He looked really weird.

And he said 'Well we've signed this contract and we're going in the studios to record an album tomorrow.' Which they were. He just said 'yeah' when I asked. And well, he said 'Come down the rehearsal rooms on Sunday and we'll talk about it.' But apparently he never fucking told anyone.

And I walked, I went down the rehearsal studios, walked in.

'Hang on, who the fuck's that?'

'Oh I forgot to tell you . . .' Which is his usual . . . 'This is our new manager.'

Anyway I talked to them, became their manager, and they've never looked back.

16

THE SOUND OF THE FUTURE

Funny the stuff that sticks with you, isn't it? And the stuff that doesn't . . . I can't be certain but I guess it was sometime around now that Bernard bought a synthesiser. Well, a potential synthesiser.

Found in the pages of *Electronics Today* magazine were circuit diagrams and assembly instructions for the synth. They began 'Despite the high complexity of this project, its construction should pose no ELECTRONIC problems to the competent hobbyist . . .' before descending into solder-ese. Designed by Tim Orr, the Powertran was available by mail order for a bargain price of £172 plus VAT.

What you got for your money was a bag of electrical components, circuit boards, keys, knobs and switches, all in a box proudly labelled 'Powertran Transcendent 2000 Synthesiser'. This may seem quaint and charming (hell, these days it's vintage and valuable as well) in today's age of smartphones, iPads and laptops, but back then in the good old, bad old days of yore, most affordable technology arrived this way. In a box of bits.

The DIY electronics kit trade, an odd amalgam of radio hammery, home organists and early practical computing enthusiasts, attracted single men with a passion for soldering and few female friends. It became a big business.

Sir Clive Sinclair, before he was a Sir, of course, sold most of his stuff (calculators, pocket TVs and eventually microcomputers) direct by mail order as a bag of components and an instruction sheet. That some of these technological marvels failed to work on completion could be put down to the sometimes puzzling and often confusing sheet labelled 'guide to assembly'. No problem for the seasoned assembler of Airfix kits.

By the mid-seventies, I was already sold on the idea of anything electronic, and particularly digital. In 1975 I became the proud owner of a digital watch like Kojak on the telly. I began purchasing digital gizmos and whatnots like there was no tomorrow. These were all pretty useless calculators with a bit of spin. Biorhythms were a popular fad in the 1970s – by entering your date of birth into the calculating device you could discover if today was a good one for doing any work or if you were likely to be in a bad mood and should avoid stress. Hocus pocus, really, but I thought because the biorhythm information was built into a calculator, then surely it must be true? With one of these you could be some kind of digital swami to your friends. Who needs horoscopes when you've got technology? A triumph of pseudoscience.

I began spending as much time in Dixons and Currys (in the electronic knick-knacks dept) as I did in record shops, eyeing up every gleaming new device to appear on their shelves with the word digital in its name. These things were, I thought, a boon: life enhancers, answers to prayers, and problem solvers. If only I could figure out how they worked. That each one failed to live up to my expectations of its largely imaginary potential did not deter me from my obsession. For it was becoming exactly that. I'd just keep buying them until I found one that did what I wanted it to.

Which was what exactly?

To be honest, I'd not given the practicalities much thought. But I had faith. It was only a matter of time until I found a gizmo that would improve and enhance my life.

*   *   *

The synthesiser had been around in one form or another since the 1930s. They were supposedly capable of producing an infinite range of sounds, from imitating 'real' instruments to sounds no one had ever heard before. That was the theory. My interest in synthesised sounds probably began with the tune 'Telstar' by the Tornados, closely followed by the weird soundtrack of *Doctor Who* made by the BBC's Radiophonic Workshop. That music was definitely interesting: the icy sounds of other worlds and the terrifying metallic voices of the Daleks and the Cybermen.

That early synths looked more like pieces of laboratory equipment than anything capable of producing music made them all the more appealing to me. In the late 1960s Wendy (at that time still Walter) Carlos had used the first Moog synths on his recordings of Bach and Beethoven. I didn't find them particularly appealing. Given the choice between Bach's *Brandenburg Concertos* and Kraftwerk, Bach was bound to lose out no matter what it was played on.

Synthesisers quickly caught on with prog bands and pretty soon any self-respecting ivory tinkler would have one piled on top of the mountain of gear that was the trademark of any keyboard wizard worth his salt in the 1970s.

They could often be seen noodling away on one of Robert Moog's inventions. That these marvels could only perform one note at a time (as opposed to multiple notes simultaneously) was not seen as a problem considering the wide range of sounds they could produce.

For me, it was in Germany where synthesisers were being used in a more inspiring way. Krautrock bands such as Tangerine Dream, Cluster and Kraftwerk were using synths in a rhythmic or more atmospheric way, rather than trying to mimic the sound of acoustic instruments. In 1977, Giorgio Moroder's synthesiser pulse on Donna Summer's 'I Feel Love' was irresistible, even though I still thought 'disco' was a dirty word. That was more like it. Moroder went on to produce Sparks' 'Number One in Heaven', which was sublime, but he also wrote 'Son of My Father', which was not.

I'd always liked the repetitive sounds that machines made. The clattering rhythm that the looms made during the brief spell I spent working at Uncle John's mill was loud and hypnotic. If I could make a sound like that somehow, that would be cool. There was no chance it would ever actually happen though. I had no idea how a synthesiser worked, much less where to find one. Not in Macclesfield, that was a dead cert.

Machines that made music were surely going to be a big thing, I thought, but not everyone agreed. Synthesisers were viewed by some with the sort of hatred and distrust that Ned Ludd had for the spinning jenny. 'No synthesisers' was a slogan on Queen's early LPs. They gave the impression that using technology to make music was cheating, as though any fool could do it.

I had a conversation on the subject with another drummer, a bit of an old pro, a cabaret, show tunes, end-of-the-pier kind of guy (probably a mate of Doug and Dave), who said, 'They're all right them synths, in their place, but you've got to keep yer eye on 'em or they'll take over.'

Crikey, he made them sound like the Daleks. *Great*, I thought, *where do I get one?*

I was, as always, looking for musical short cuts and this new and potentially dangerous instrument sounded just right.

I was labouring under the mistaken belief that these things would make life easy. Make me a better drummer/musician. That they were for cheats who wanted to be clever but couldn't be bothered putting in the hours to acquire sufficient knowledge.

It didn't turn out to be quite that simple.

There was one thing in 1975 that had a big effect on me and that was Kraftwerk's appearance on *Tomorrow's World*. They performed

'Autobahn', which had been out the year before and which at the time I admit I thought was a bit of a Krautrock novelty track, a synthesised German Beach Boys kind of thing. I suspect that at the time my reticence towards the song was more likely due to its chart success. How dare they get played on Radio 1 alongside the Osmonds, Showaddywaddy and Windsor Davies and Don Estelle. It was an outrage! What were they thinking, making a popular record? (That didn't stop me from dancing to it though. I got my head kicked in by a bunch of skinheads for dancing to 'Autobahn' at a Judas Priest gig at Poynton Civic. My dancing frequently offended.)

Despite my reservations, seeing the enigmatic and reclusive Kraftwerk on *Tomorrow's World* was a revelation. It was the most un-rock-and-roll thing I'd ever seen and all the more enticing because of that. Electronic drums played with knitting needles, that got my attention. I might never be Keith Moon, but I could see myself doing something like that. Above all, Kraftwerk looked very weird – hang on, they looked a bit like me. My mid-seventies geography teacher look was suddenly fashionable.

Another nugget from the future came to me courtesy of the magician David Nixon. He was Basil Brush's first straight man, if that's any help.

When he wasn't pulling rabbits out of hats and making glamorous ladies vanish from boxes, David had an interest in a revolutionary keyboard musical instrument that could reproduce any sound by means of a series of tapes stored in its innards. An orchestra at your fingertips.

This was generally known by the company name, Mellotron. Mr Nixon was an investor in the company and could clearly see the appeal of every family having one of these in their living room. One of the keyboards was offered as a prize on a 1960s quiz show and he was on hand to demonstrate the machine's potential. One minute he was playing what sounded like a full orchestra, the next he conjured up the sounds of planes, explosions, car horns and machine guns. I don't think the bemused contestants were much taken with 'tonight's star prize'. They were probably hoping for a car. What use was an organ that sounded like World War Three had just broken out in your living room? But it was the explosions that sold it to me.

I've never come across anybody else who can remember this particular TV gem. But I'm sure it happened. The idea of an instrument that could make any sound imaginable being played by a man with a talking fox for a friend? That's not the sort of thing you just make up, surely.

The Mellotron accomplished its feat of sonic mimicry by having an eight-second loop of magnetic tape connected to each of its keys. Press the key and, hey presto (as only old magicians say), the sound recorded on the tape plays back. Of course, the tape wears and stretches over time and it's this that gives the Mellotron its own peculiar sound. A kind of haunted gramophone tonality. In the 1970s, you couldn't really get yourself taken seriously as a prog band without owning at least one Mellotron. Just ask Robert Fripp.

Seeing Kraftwerk reminded me of an odd incident from my childhood back at Gawsworth Road. I had a friend called John Shufflebottom who was two or three years older than me and was the proud owner of a BSA air rifle, which I coveted. So any excuse I could dream up and I would cycle up the road and knock on the Shufflebottoms' door.

'Is John playing?' I would plaintively ask, meaning let's get the gun and go shooting.

So one afternoon I knocked on the door. There was no answer, but there was this weird sound coming from somewhere. It was musical but in an odd, mechanical way. Thinking that perhaps they couldn't hear me, I made my way to the back door. The sound was definitely getting louder and weirder – an odd nicky-nocky-click-click-boom rhythm and some sort of throbbing undercurrent seemed to be coming from the Shufflebottoms' back room. I ventured further round the back and peeped through the patio windows, and was startled to see that the back wall of the room was taken up by a monstrous wooden multi-keyboarded electric organ resplendent with many switches and flashing lights. It was like finding the lair of a sophisticated supervillain in a Bond movie. Then I spotted, to the right of the organ, John's dad, Charlie, playing a brand new Fender Precision Bass, providing the throbbing undercurrent to the organ music. He was engrossed while I was spying on him, but for some reason he looked up and spotted me staring wide-eyed through the patio glass.

'Crikey,' I said in my best *Just William*-type voice, 'I'm for it here . . .'

But Mr S just laughed at his discovery.

'John's not in, Stephen. Would you like to come in and wait?'

I was rewarded with a tour of Charlie's organ, no pun intended, and it was the drum machine or rhythmic accompaniment section that I found compelling.

The cartoony tick-tock robotic sounds were magical and otherworldly, and I thought, *When I grow up I'll definitely have one of these in my living room.* It was the stuff of *Thunderbirds'* Tracy Island.

After my tour of the keyboard, I wasn't that interested in the bass, to be honest. I lost all interest in waiting for John and his air rifle, and cycled home as fast as I could.

A few months after Kraftwerk's appearance on *Tomorrow's World* I was walking past a music store on Manchester's Oxford Street and there in the window it was, the instrument of my dreams: the Synare 1. A percussion synthesiser.

Four square black rubber pads, a whole section of sliders and switches that probably did marvellous things and the one thing that caught my eye the most: a handle! Like a futuristic attaché case, the

Synare was effortlessly portable compared to a gazillion-piece drum kit. And it didn't have all those bolts and pipes and nuts that always went missing or came loose mid-song. This thing seemed to have no downside. I had to have it.

Luckily it was a Sunday and the shop was closed.

For I had failed to notice the price of this marvel was around £1000. You could get a car for that – two cars if you weren't too choosy.

Synthesised drums actually existed and in Manchester too, but they were slightly out of my league for the moment.

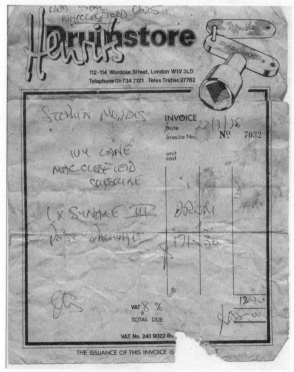

Never throw anything away. You never know when
it might come in handy.

By 1978 things had changed. Electronic drums were in, the prices came down and I was finally able to get into drum synthesising myself, courtesy of the much more economical Synare 3.

Like Barney's DIY Powertran Transcendent synthesiser, it was a mail order purchase and cost almost exactly the same: £171.30. No soldering required, though. The Synare 3 came ready assembled ... just stick in a couple of 9-volt batteries and you were off.

If you wanted something that sounded like a real snare, forget it. Luckily it was sounds from another planet that I was after. I was off to the future with this matt black flying-saucer-shaped instrument. I spent hours and hours figuring out how the thing actually worked, in the process transforming my tiny bedroom into Ivy Lane's ear-splitting equivalent of the Radiophonic Workshop. The neighbours were terrified.

I loved the Synare 3, and we used it for the sci-fi whup-whup siren intro in the live version of 'Disorder', noise washes in 'Shadowplay', chi-chi sounds in 'She's Lost Control' and, more alarmingly, for the disco drum and ray-gun blaster break on 'Insight'. On a good night, it would sound like ray-guns. On a bad night, if I got the switches wrong, it sounded like a flock of enraged pigeons.

Using the Synare live was challenging. Adjusting the tiny knobs and switches while still playing the rest of the drum kit was difficult with only two hands. I soon discovered it was easy to dislodge or break a control knob with a bit of overzealous pounding. Collateral damage.

This was the first stage in what would years later become an unhealthy case of gear addiction.

Meanwhile, we were all a little sceptical as to the successful outcome of Barney's foray into the world of DIY synthesiser construction. Hooky's bet was that it would end up stuck in a bin bag under Bernard's bed, never to be mentioned again. Being a habitual fence sitter, I'd have given you even money.

I think Hooky felt ambivalent towards Bernard's Transcendent synth project. I guess he thought it unnecessary as he was under the impression we were in a rock band. To Ian, it was all magical hocus pocus. Ian was not one of the world's most practical people. He knew synthesisers and computers were going to be the future, but as to how all this might work in practice, he had no idea. It just would and it would be great.

Bernard's soldering project proved to be a great success. The Powertran actually worked. Better than that, it sounded incredible. It looked like a pretty simple synth but looks can be deceptive. It was a lot more sophisticated that it seemed and it was easy to get confused by its innocuous-looking switches. But back then it was absolutely fascinating. What did an oscillator do exactly? What did VCFAD mean?

Bernard used the synth to make some ambient background music for the launch party of *The Talking Parcel*, a Cosgrove Hall animated film he'd worked on. It sounded very sophisticated, and I remember being really impressed. It certainly didn't sound like someone pissing about on a synthesiser they'd just made from a kit.

Bernard had also acquired an Akai two-track reel-to-reel tape machine, which Ian thought we would be using to record our rehearsals. Ian was annoyed when that only happened very occasionally. To be fair, I don't think Ian thought of the practicalities of carting a large tape recorder around on the back of a motorbike. We were all still ferrying our gear to and from rehearsals every night. But logistics did not figure largely with Ian Curtis. He remained miffed.

A friend of mine, who worked in Terry Blood's record shop in Macclesfield's shopping precinct, heard of a Tandberg two-track tape machine that was going for a reasonable sum in Upton Priory if we were interested. Well I was, and with Ian in tow just in case it was very heavy, I acquired the machine and began ferrying it to rehearsals in the Cortina. Problem solved. Happy Ian.

I also got an accounts book, which I suggested we could use to record our expenses, gig money and so forth.

'What do we need that for, you daft bastard?' (meaning the book not the Tandberg) was all the thanks and encouragement I got from Bernard and Hooky.

1 Tandberg tape machine £45

4 tins of coke £1.50

Those were the ledger's only entries before it was consigned to a cupboard of wasted dreams for eternity.

Things were changing. Ian in what I guessed was an attempt to provide some company for Debbie while he was out gallivanting bought a puppy. A black and white bundle of fluff he named Candy. A sheepdog of sorts. A bundle of fluff with remarkably large paws.

Now I'm no expert but I did know one thing about dogs. Large paws equals large dog.

Ian thought otherwise.

'No, the kennels said it's only a miniature. It won't get much bigger.'

It didn't take long. The animal expanded exponentially. Over the next twelve months my weary dawn drop-offs at Barton Street were lightened by the sight of Ian reappearing from his front door moments later. A freshly lit Marlboro in his mouth, his long mac flapping as he was dragged from the house by the eager and ever expanding hound, Ian would laugh and wave to me while struggling to keep up with Candy's pursuit of the milkman.

My mother, who was an expert on all things canine, remarked at hearing of the singer and sheepdog combo.

'Be a baby next.'

17

THE MANAGER

What are my ambitions? My ambitions are never to work again. When I was twenty-three I decided that working was pretty boring anyway. So I decided to give up working.

Rob Gretton, in *Play at Home* (1983)

When young people looking to get ahead in the music game ask me for advice (yes, I know that seems unlikely), I usually respond with, 'Get yourself a manager, it will save you a lot of grief in the long run.'

This advice is generally not what they're looking for and is universally ignored because young people always know best. They want me to point them to the secret unmarked door that leads to success and lend them the key.

A manager is the band's helmsman and navigator. You work out your destination collectively and he or she gets you where you want to go (or once thought you wanted to go). Managers also tend to serve as emotional punchbags, functioning a lot like the artwork in Dorian Gray's attic: they age and wither with worry while the band members themselves remain young, virile and ostensibly carefree, though they are constantly thinking of new ways to torment their theoretical handler and each other. Managers, in short, are the designated adult in the outfit, though adult may at times be pushing it a bit. The band will take the credit for all the manager's good ideas, and the manager and the manager alone will be blamed for all the disasters.

Rob Gretton was naturally competitive. He loved sport and he loved to bet and he hated to lose. He would keep on playing whatever 'game' he was involved in until either he won or every other participant gave up or fell asleep. This competitive nature, combined with his charm and outgoing jovial hooligan personality, meant he was the perfect pack leader. Ideal manager material. I couldn't help but respect someone much more confident, outgoing and possibly crazier than me. That Rob had a generally optimistic outlook counterbalanced our 'the world's against us' attitude. He was not fazed by anyone or any bizarre predicament. He was the definition of self-belief in a nutshell. He was also very smart, certainly smarter than you would credit if you went off first impressions.

Rob had seen a bit of the world. He'd worked for a time on a kibbutz in Israel, and he told stories of being questioned by the secret police in Cold War Yugoslavia. I respected Rob and trusted his judgement – I didn't always agree with it, but that's usually the way with bands and their managers.

We should be a 'cult' band, Rob informed us. That was enough of an aspiration for me. Going on *Top of the Pops* and global domination felt like a waste of time and energy. The Velvets and the MC5, along with pretty much every punk band early on, were all culty in appeal, unusual, not for everybody, at the fringes of normal. That would definitely do for me.

The idea here was to quote Rob, 'Never peak'. Just keep steadily working, getting bigger and better. To succeed by doing cool things and clever things, not large splashes of 'we are the next big thing' hype. Hype was to be avoided at all costs. 'Grow virally' I suppose you'd call it today. Rob would never call it that though.

The manager as the fifth member of the band. Where we went, Rob went. He would turn up at rehearsals, listen to what we'd done and give his appraisal. At gigs he would stand with Terry, by then doing live sound at the mixing desk, and tell him what to turn up. He would sit in at interviews, interrupting and usually saying something more inciteful than us.

'You lot are basically a bunch of idiots so don't say much. Just try and act dark and mysterious. Especially you, Hooky. For fuck's sake, button it.'

Most of the time it was Rob who did *all* the talking; Rob loved to talk, as did Tony Wilson. Hooky, at times, also had difficulty keeping quiet. Me, I gave up trying to get the edgeways word in. It's always the quiet ones you've got to watch.

Rob had exceptionally good taste in music. All the best groups on Factory were Rob's discoveries.

We would have meetings with Rob at rehearsals. He'd pull out his notebook and tell us about our future. We've been offered this, so and so wants you to do that. He was always talking about the next thing. It's the next thing that keeps you going. The thrust that drives a band. The next thing is always going to be better than the last thing, and that was good so this'll be mega. The next song we write has to be better. Onwards and upwards, that's the trajectory.

But like the perpetual motion machine, sooner or later entropy sets in and eventually bands reach a peak, squabble and stall. Which usually means coming out with statements like:

'I felt like I needed a new challenge.'

'I've always wanted to work with other people.'

'I wanted to break out of the closed shop of the band structure and try new things.'

It's the biggest cliché going: the singer goes solo. Occasionally (though very rarely) to greater success. Usually it's self-indulgence that lets down these solo endeavours. Dealing with a group of musicians can be a tricky business. They by nature have an 'artistic' temperament, which if pandered to can be encouraged to grow to an uncontrollable size. There are no two ways about it. Success can do terrible things to a personality. The nice boy next door can easily transform into a monster – fighting with journalists, cancelling gigs willy-nilly, falling over at awards ceremonies – you know, the stuff you love to read about in blogs and gossip columns. All because the 'artist' has been denied his rattle.

It's a manager's job to keep a lid on all this, ideally to stop it happening in the first place. When I first met Rob, he had a small patch of grey hair in the front of his short fringe. In time this would bloom until it covered his entire head.

We were all friends. We were not businessmen and we were all doing it more for fun than the thought of any eventual financial reward, though that would have been nice. I wasn't in it for the money. So long as we could do what we wanted – write songs, play gigs, make records and have fun at the same time – I was happy.

Rob wanted, above all, to be fair. He would do his best to be as even-handed as possible with us. He got the best deal anyone could get for the band from Tony. He believed in us absolutely.

Rob would not do anything that was blatantly commercial. We would much rather do quirky or interesting gigs than the ones that paid the most. Rob and Factory were, if anything, anti-promotion. Factory didn't advertise or, in the early days at least, use any record promotion at all. Rob thought the idea of band T-shirts corny (although he did get some Joy Division badges done).

We would not be marketed. If you don't like it fuck off.

That was Rob's catchphrase.

He'd worked in the insurance game when we first met, so I figured he must know a bit about the risk business.

RG (on seeing Tony Wilson in cowboy boots): God almighty!

BS: It's like that clown.

RG: Oh no, now what am I . . . how am I gonna . . . I've been trying to get Hooky to stop wearing a pair of cowboy boots for the past two years! And then you wearing 'em . . . oh God almighty.

TW: You've got no sense of style! That's right, which is why the *NME* described him once as being 'flamboyant'.

MH: You? Described you as . . .?

TW: Him. HIM!!

MH: Flamboyant?

RG: Wear one of these on yer head as well, yer style . . .

TW: The *NME* described him as flamboyant – look at those flamboyant corduroys.

MH: Ha ha.

RG: I'm thinking more of Hooky, y'see. I'm going to have problems with him.

IC: He's easily influenced.

RG: He'll say well, I'm the new Tony Wilson you know, and he'll start walking round with these cowboy boots again.

TW: Just tell him that Peter Saville started it, that'll put him off.

RG: Have you seen this?

TW: Aren't they good, eh?

RG: Took your breath away, hasn't it? . . . Too polite, this lad.

TW: Too polite to say anything nasty, ooooooh.

RG: So where're we going then?

TW: Well we can go to the Bella Napoli, which is the nicest, if it's open, and if it's not then there's the all-day one up by Piccadilly. It's not that far to walk. Five minutes . . . Do you want an Italian or is there anything else you fancy?

RG: I don't mind, I'm not bothered.

TW: Do you prefer Mexican?

IC: Ooh err, where's the Mexican? Hooky won't eat anything that isn't absolutely plain on account of . . .

BS: Doesn't like tomatoes, doesn't like . . .

TW: Well, there's a Mexican takeaway, but you can sit down in it. It's great. I mean it's a bit cheap.

RG: Nah, I don't thin . . . I think you'd be better with the Italian with Hooky.

IC: Where is it?

TW: It's up by Whitworth Street bus station, it's a really good Mexican takeaway. It's excellent.

IC: Must remember that. Is it open on Sundays?

TW: It's open late night . . . Like a taco? Do you know what a taco is?

TW: Taco is like the little kind of like bent over kind of er bread thing with mincemeat, refried beans, bit of cheese, bit of salad and a bit of hot sauce on it. 39p! It's really cheap.

RG: Hey, trying to take us for a cheap meal out here now! 39p's no good.

MH: Ha ha.

18

THAT MAN OFF THE TELLY

I was and I am very clever and I'm very arrogant. Put the two together and you become a very unpleasant person unless you behave like an idiot. Like an idiot, rather like Shakespeare's fools, who are the idiots in the play and are always very stupid and stuff. But at the same time they are the only ones who have read the play. From the very beginning of the play they always know exactly what's going on. They're always the cleverest. But to avoid being persecuted for that cleverness you behave like an idiot. It's like being in the bath with you now. It makes me appear less awful and arrogant and elitist and extremist than I am.

> Tony Wilson, being interviewed in the bath
> by Gillian Gilbert for *Play at Home* (1983)

So how come Tony Wilson is suddenly a big part of the story, threatening to force-feed 39p tacos to members of Joy Division and their manager? And what's all this unexplained Factory stuff? How did all that happen? I'll squeal the rewind and give you the precious details later, but first let me tell you a little bit about Tony . . .

In the late seventies, Tony Wilson was 'that trendy bloke off the telly' to the watchers of *Granada Reports*. Bob Greaves, the older, safer, more traditional TV presenter, was usually his straight man. Tony, ever so trendy and full of himself, was the perfect fall guy for the quirky and slightly dangerous spot after the serious biz of the news was done: the 'And finally . . .' slot, where it might involve the intrepid reporter in a bit of 'dangerous' hijinks.

'Are you sure it's safe?'

'Of course it's safe, Tony.'

How we laughed when he came a cropper.

At the time, the world reflected back to us through our TV screens seem to consist almost entirely of old people.

In real life, too, everyone in sensible jobs, such as doctors or dentists, seemed old. Even if they were only twenty-five or thirty, they wore the uniform and carried the demeanour of a fifty- or sixty-year-old. They stuck to the script of the 1950s with the odd nod to the crazy young people of the recent 1960s with their wild ways, long hair and flared trousers.

Tony Wilson was different. With his long locks and with-it shirt collars, he looked young, but you could tell just from the way he read the news that he was confident in his own cleverness. This cleverness was of an arty bent, as demonstrated in his 'What's On' entertainments section. That the section was all his idea, of course, seemed to radiate through the tube. (I can't watch Chris Morris on *The Day Today* without being reminded of Tony at his most serious and pretentious.)

Through this tiny slot of TV airtime his love of subversive rock bands and obviously Manchester's new wave contingent was manifest. Admirable as this was – and it was a lot more than that – there was also a strong suspicion that he was showing off, and no one likes a show-off. So he was loved and hated in almost equal measure, usually by the same person at the same time.

'He has some good things on that show of his, that Tony Wilson, but he's a bit of a twat if you ask me!' was the man in the pub's begrudgingly considered opinion. I could see his point. Tony had new ideas and a not-from-round-hereness about him.

```
24th February 1978                                    JOY DIVISION
                                                      Steve Morris,
                                                         Ivy Lane,
                                                      Macclesfield,
                                                      Cheshire


Tony Wilson,
"Whats On",
Granada TV,
Manchester 3

Dear Tony,

Sorry to have not written before,but unfortunately,as you were
no doubt told,we had to collect the tape we lent you.

At the moment things seem to be looking up for the band-
Virgin have been in touch & are putting a track of ours
out on the "Live at the Electric Circus"LP & we've finally
managed to get the EP out.

Enclosed is a copy of the EP (minus sleeve I8m afraid) & a
biog sheet on the band.We hope to recommence gigging soon
& look forward to seeing you as I when the opportunity arises.


                        Best Wishes,



                    pp Joy Divison/Warsaw
```

Think I ran out of Tipp-Ex writing this one.

Me, I learned to like him. Though he never seemed to talk the same language as me. He was magnetic and funny and clever (he always made that very clear), and anyone who got the instrumental intro from 'LA Woman' on the box at teatime was OK with me. He was a celebrity though. Untouchable and unreachable, I imagined, ex-directory at the very least, but he was still an obvious target for letters from my typewriter while I was pretending to work.

Unlike the BBC, ITV had never really had a proper heavyweight rock show. There had been *Ready, Steady, Go!* back in the sixties. Then there was Muriel Young's *Lift Off*, which was really just a glammed up version of 1960's kids' fave *Five O'Clock Club* (though sadly without that show's stalwart, Bert Weedon, who was probably living the high life with the royalties from his great big lie of a book, *Play in a Day*).

Lift Off was no competition for the late-night serious music spot monopolised by BBC2: first *Colour Me Pop*, then *The Old Grey Whistle Test* with Richard Williams and later Whispering Bob Harris. Bob Harris starting to get all bitchy when the Dolls and Roxy Music were on in 1973 was a sign of things to come. When the show did not offer punk a warm welcome – they tried to justify its curious exclusion with the explanation that the show was about albums and punk was about singles (bullshit) – I'd had enough.

A gap in the market then – a breach that Tony filled on ITV with *So It Goes*, a legendary TV show if ever there was one. Where else would you see Soft Machine, the Pistols' TV debut, the Ramones, Buzzcocks, John Cooper Clarke, Jonathan Richman, that ace archive stuff of Sister Rosetta Tharpe *and* Clive James? It was fucking brilliant. I was never too sure when it was on exactly – it kept getting moved around in the schedule, almost as if the Granada bigwigs were trying to bury it. It was ahead of its time and gloriously doomed from the start. They say it was Iggy getting a bit sweary that got the show cancelled in 1977, but the erratic scheduling didn't help.

So, Tony Wilson was one of us. Well musically, at least, it looked like he might be. A man to mither at any rate. He'd put all those other bands on the box, so why not us?

Getting yourself on the telly is a must, I thought, if you want to get anywhere in this game: stars of stage *and* screen, as they say. Overnight success would be pretty much guaranteed. Those (despised and envied) idiots wouldn't bother miming like prancing poodles on *TOTP* every Thursday if it didn't do them any good, would they? Yup, getting on the tube was a *big* must.

Mixing music and television is a tricky business. TV has its own set of rules and ways of doing stuff, and these usually clash with those of the would-be rock star of tomorrow. Take the miming business for a start. From the musician's point of view, it's shit: you're a musician, you play live, you perform, you keep it real, man. You don't pretend, you don't act, you don't deceive. 'That's tantamount to selling out!' the inner hippie shrieked. But still the TV beckons you with its glamour, so compromises have to be made in the name of what they call 'promotion' today.

So the rock band and the TV studio are uneasy bedfellows. Now I should make it clear that I'm talking about TV as it was in the late 1970s and the 1980s, and that in the twenty-first century most of the technological difficulties of accommodating a pain-in-the-arse band that wants to play their new song live can be easily overcome.

In the era of Joy Division/early New Order, there was, on the part of most TV shows, little will to allow a band to do a live performance. And if there's not a will, there's always a drink. The highlight of our rare and usually not too successful appearances on *TOTP* was the trip to the upstairs bar at the BBC, where you could see household names getting three sheets to the wind on subsidised booze.

When you did get to perform, amplifiers were apparently a problem. 'You're too loud for the cameras, darling!' a man with a headset (aka the floor manager) would say. 'Do you think you could turn it down just a touch? Thank you.' The old 'You don't hit all those drums at the same time do you?' would be heard again.

So the begrudging compromises begin. You are a fish out of water in somebody else's pond. Trying to pretend it's a gig at the same time as trying hard not to fuck up. Sometimes having a dozen or so guests or extras that make up the pretend audience helps, gives things a bit of a vibe, but they are usually as flummoxed by what's going on as you.

'And three-two-one, go!'

'Hold it, hold it!!'

'Ready camera and three-two-one. No, hold on! Sound's not ready, there's a buzz coming from somewhere.'

The tension and unease mount. Still, it will all be worth it when your mum sees you on the telly or the man behind the bar banters 'Saw you last night on't box. What the fuck was that about then, eh? Jesus, what's that singer on?'

You're a band, after all. Why should you understand the whys and wherefores of a television studio?

Tony did though. He understood the game and he was very good at it. When I wrote this not quite begging/nagging letter, it was with the hope that he would perhaps mention us, say that we had a record out or a gig or something, maybe turn up at a Joy Division gig himself. I like the pompous bit about recommencing gigging as if there was some organisation or great plan involved, not just me ringing up randomly and saying, 'Give us a gig will ya?'

What I didn't expect was that in two months' time a pissed-up Ian would be haranguing Tony in Rafters, calling him a cunt for not putting us on TV. In short, making the sort of impression that my whiny letter fails to do.

That night at the Stiff/Chiswick show in April 1978 was the real start of my relationship with Tony Wilson. A month later, we played at one of his first 'Factory' nights at the Russell Club, Hulme, and from that point on the story of Joy Division/New Order, and that of Tony/Factory, would be entwined.

Tony gave the impression of being always on the move, either off to interview someone with an important-sounding name or just coming back from some far-flung meeting. He possessed an infectious enthusiasm, laughed like a seal and saw solutions not problems. He was a great conduit or catalyst for putting people together in situations they would not normally think of venturing into.

I suspect he liked the idea of being a rock star but did not want to have to go through the hassle of writing, playing and hanging around with other musicians in the messy arena of band life. No, let others do that shit, he would direct and channel like some benevolent emperor. I always thought he would have liked to end up as the Emperor of a twenty-first-century Manchester structured like a Modernist version of ancient Rome, with grand buildings, civic pride and Latin mottos carved in Helvetica and designed by Peter Saville or Ben Kelly.

Tony was intelligent (as I've said, and as he said himself many, many times), and like Rob was a Great Thinker. Those terrifying words, usually Rob's: 'I've been thinking . . .' The doing was generally down to someone else.

Tony became friendly with people in the biz whom he felt trod a parallel path – Mo Ostin, Seymour Stein, Malcolm McLaren, Geffen – and he loved to name-drop.

'As P. J. O'Rourke said to me just the other week . . .'

Or,

'As A. J. P. Taylor said . . .'

Or, famously,

'As Trotsky once said, "Though we fight to change life, let us not forget the reasons for living."'

Did Trotsky actually say that or was Tony putting words into his mouth?

Tony borrowed ideas and references from Guy Debord and the Situationists. Books on them decorated his coffee table. At the time, I thought they were just another bunch of French performance artists with groovy posters and clever slogans.

I asked him about the Durutti Column, the name of Vini Reilly's band, which Alan Erasmus and Tony were managing.

'It's from the Situationist manifesto, darling. They were roving anarchists in the Spanish Civil War.'

I had a hard time imagining Vini and Bruce Mitchell roaming Catalonia, armed with rifles, with maybe Orwell and his missus in tow.

Mostly I found Tony's intelligence intimidating. He came from a world I had avoided. He had been to university. I bet he was good at games too. He used words that I only half understood and did that thing called 'oozing' confidence. That he was articulate was not surprising. He was a journalist, and his ability to talk while juggling a biro, with which he would write notes on the back of his left hand (Tony's personal organiser), combined with boyish floppy-haired youthful looks, made him a natural for TV.

Me and most of the Factory music co-workers were not lexicological maestros, but we were all – what's the word? – dedicated. And Tony needed us to be dedicated, to give it everything so his Factory vision actually had some content and could be writ large.

Maybe an uneasy division of labour developed because of that. To carry on further in the life of a band meant giving up the financial security of the day job. That moment comes to every fledgling band: fly or fall. Initially, at least, the trajectory takes a downward path and many a disgruntled Factory musician would say to Wilson, as he was becoming known by the staff, 'It's OK for you, you've still got a job with Granada while I'm fuckin' signing on.'

Tony always came across as a benevolent Svengali, though, and a Situationist-inspired catalyst. He would come up with some apparently crazy suggestions that you went along with just because he was Tony. You knew it was bound to be OK.

An early example was in summer 1978. Tony called me and Ian out of the blue and asked if we could play cricket. Being unerringly noncommittal I answered, 'Sort of.'

'Good,' he replied.

He'd promised to field a cricket team for a local village match:

264

celebrity friends of Tony's versus the village regulars. I along, with Bernard and Ian, had been 'volunteered' to play a game that, even on my best days, I found confusing and boring beyond words.

TW: What happened was ... I had to ... the local village cricket ... in fact it's like tomorrow, I've got to play a charity cricket game. For weeks I'd agreed, six months ago, to do a ... to get a charity team together for my local village and I'd forgotten all about it and I'd been ill the week before and I started panicking and these lot came along and er ...

BS: Almost won the game.

(Hooky arrives after parking up the car.)

TW: Almost won the game ... Let's go this way ... I'll try and hide the boots ... don't mention 'em.

RG: Ask him where he wants to go for something to eat.

IC: Don't ask him, tell him!

MH: Did he offer to get you the meal as a thank you?

IC: Yeah, ha ha.

TW: Where we going? You don't want to go?

MH: What?

TW: Do you?

PH: I don't like tomatoes.

MH: Have something without tomatoes.

PH: There isn't anything at an Italian restaurant!

RG: What about chicken? They do things like ... yeah, wait a minute ...

MH: Yeah, you can get a steak.

RG: They do things like chicken and ...

MH: Get a steak or chicken or something.

RG: Steak?

TW: Let's have a look at the ... Let's have a look at ... oh my
   God.
IC: He doesn't like tomatoes
MH: I've never met anybody who doesn't like tomato.
IC: Causes a lot of problems.

As well as being clever and intelligent and a bottomless font of
knowledge, Tony knew people, important people in Manchester.
People who in the normal course of events would not give Joy
Division the time of day, but for Tony? That was different. But he
never could persuade Hooky to eat tomatoes.

Or play cricket.

The cricket match, predictably, was awful. We were all out for a
duck except for Bernard who surprisingly managed to hit the ball
and almost saved the day. Almost.

Full of surprises, Bernard.

Many years later, Tony had his own radio show, *Sunday Roast*, and he
invited me to be part of it. He confessed that he loved Glen
Campbell's 'Wichita Lineman', which pleasantly surprised me. He
then went on to confess that he hated Bowie's *Low*, which was a
complete shock. How could anyone not like *Low* or at least realise
that it was a fabulous and innovative record. I never would have
thought that of Tony.

But back in the 1980s ...

GG (Gillian Gilbert): Factory Records, what's it all about? The
   truth.
TW: I could give you eighteen different truths or loads of
    different stories. But they all come down to praxis. You
    know what praxis is?
GGL Praxis? No.

TW: You ever heard praxis makes perfect? Praxis is the idea that you do something because you want to do it. And after you've done it, you find out all the reasons why you did it. I could give you a hundred great reasons – political, ideological, aesthetic. I mean, I liked the friends I made in punk working as a journalist in '76 and '77, didn't want to lose them. I'm trained as an academic, I wanted to do experiments – laboratory experiments – in popular art. Experiment with people like you, you see. You're experimenting with me in the bath. I wanted to make political experiments as to how you could function politically in the marketplace. All those things which I might say were the reasons. I've only found out they were the reasons for doing it by doing it. You just do it. I mean everything we did, everything you've done, everything we've all done – just cos you wanted to do it. I can think of great reasons afterwards but it'd be dishonest . . .

GG: What are your ambitions? Where do you see Factory going in the future?

TW: To do more Factory. To be Factory in more places. I mean every year, it's rather like farming, in that every year we have a crop, which normally includes your album and then there's Vini's album and A Certain Ratio album, whatever. Every year there's a crop of albums and after we've struggled to get there and get them all out, then three months later the money comes in and we pay all the bills. Then for another couple of months there's a bit more money and every time we have a bit of money then we can do something interesting, like we did the Haçienda last year, the video unit the year before that. Next thing I'd like to do is get the office in New York buzzing. Thing after that, I'd like to build lofts in Manchester. The year after that Gretton wants to buy Manchester. There're millions of things one could do, but to do things that are valid in the marketplace and valid in the political textbook and moral textbook at the same time. And also valid as art, in terms of style, all those things which we've done already, but to do them in other areas.

Play at Home (1983)

19

A FACTORY SAMPLE

Rob took up the baton of persuading anyone who might listen to give us a gig. The obvious first port of call was Tony, who had finally given *An Ideal for Living* a TV plug on 'What's On'. He was now beginning to look more like an OK sort of guy instead of some trendy pseud and member of the Manchester Music Mafia. Who were basically anybody else in Manchester who were not part of our slightly dysfunctional musical gang.

Rob, being Rob, got on well with Tony. They had a Catholic upbringing in common, and Rob's fuck-you attitude impressed Tony the same way it impressed me.

The Russell Club, Hulme.

I found the Cold War dystopian edifices of Hulme fascinating. The area was sandwiched between leafy old-world Didsbury, Moss Side, Trafford and the empty warehouses of Manchester city centre. It was a herald of the future city. A city that, like jetpacks and flying cars, never materialised. Still, Hulme had an atmosphere that came to be indelibly associated with Joy Division, largely through Kevin Cummins's snowy photo of us on the bridge over Princess Parkway for the *NME*. It would become, whether we liked it or not, part of our image . . . an image that we denied existed, of course.

Nestling somewhere in this brutalist concrete fortress was the Aaben, an independent arthouse cinema – an oasis of culture (in many ways the forerunner of the Cornerhouse and now Home). It showed the best films, unseeable elsewhere. *WR: Mysteries of the Organism* was nearly always being screened, as was *I Am Curious (Yellow)*. I saw *Steppenwolf, Siddhartha* (bit of a Hermann Hesse season), Herzog's *Nosferatu, The Enigma of Kaspar Hauser* and *Fitzcarraldo* and Lynch's *Eraserhead* – all the greats. Joy Division loved weird films. Ian particularly loved the films of Herzog and Lynch, and Bernard liked *The Tin Drum*. We went for anything with an unusual atmosphere or story. This was when seeing a film was a bit of an event. We were all regular moviegoers – Lindsay Anderson's *If* was a perennial favourite, as was *A Clockwork Orange*, despite its ban. But the all-time movie classic by a mile was *Apocalypse Now*. The soundtrack is a masterpiece.

Tony Wilson and Alan Erasmus wanted to do a series of new wave nights, called 'The Factory', at the Russell Club in Hulme, an entertainment appendix to the brutalist tower-block fortress of the Hulme Crescents that dominated the landscape.

At the start, Factory wasn't just Tony. It was Tony (the thinking) and Alan Erasmus (the actual doing), to be joined later by Peter Saville (the overall look) and by Martin Hannett (the sound), and let's not forget Manchester music legend Alan Wise, who took care of the door at the Factory.

I liked Alan Wise. He claimed to be a doctor (of theology). A true Mancunian character – he was a larger-than-life Manchester music veteran and knew all the greats, so he said. His tales of the acts he had worked with were always extremely entertaining if occasionally implausible. He was the only promoter who ever let me in to gigs for free. He also ran the other gig nights at the Russell that weren't specifically 'Factory nights' – it was the other Alan (Erasmus) who first came up with name. He was always a bit of a blur, Alan Erasmus. Never stopping in one place for very long, always on the move. In later years he would take to doing a Sunday-morning bagel run.

Suddenly and without warning, he would appear on my doorstep for a chat, a smoke and an update before leaving as abruptly as he'd arrived.

The four initial Factory gigs in May and June 1978 were a success and it became a regular gig for us. Alan and Tony, spurred on by this success, came up with the idea to do a record.

'Hey, let's start a record label!'

Everyone was doing it – Rabid, Stiff, Bob Last's Fast Product. Post-punk indie labels were springing up everywhere. How hard could it be?

Even Joy Division had had a go.

Tony had been hanging out at Rabid Records in Withington, making friends and getting ideas. Forging a blueprint.

The whats and the whos of what would become Factory's first record were a bit nebulous at first. Roger Eagle from Eric's in Liverpool had been mentioned, and the idea of doing a London/Manchester EP had also been mentioned but that never worked out.

In the end three bands, Joy Division, the Durutti Column and Cabaret Voltaire, would end up contributing two tracks each, along with three by comedian John Dowie, presumably for light relief. Martin Hannett would produce both us and the Durutti Column.

The sampler EP was not a new thing. Stiff, Chiswick, Sire and Berserkley had all used the format. Not quite a single and not quite an album. A bit like brunch. The sampler EP was an ideal halfway solution.

Martin had produced Buzzcocks' *Spiral Scratch* EP on New Hormones, and Slaughter and the Dogs' single 'Cranked Up Really High', not forgetting 1978's Manchester pop smash hit 'Gordon Is a Moron' by Jilted John for Rabid, where he was the resident producer. He was the obvious choice for producing. Being the only producer in town helped. Rob had a connection with Martin though Rabid and from his Wythenshawe days with Slaughter and the Dogs.

We'd had a bit of a run-in with Martin previously when he was part of the Music Force collective responsible for occasionally booking bands at Rafters and the Band on the Wall.

Song wise we were in pretty good shape and we were on a bit of a roll songwriting-wise. Latest additions to the set were:

'Digital' – this one came about through the suggestion of doing a four-on-the-floor kind of disco beat, like 'I Feel Love'. Horrified by the D-word, I played it in a jerky, stilted manner, which I thought would put most people off the scent of disco. At the time I had no idea what syncopation actually meant but I was damned if I was going to do it. But 'Digital' was the future – we all knew that, as did most fools at the time.

'Glass' – the title may have been one of Rob's suggestions but most likely Ian's. It was made up of two or three bits, which we shifted between, going off Ian's vocal cues. This was one of the first 16s hi-hat songs that usually came about by my trying to get a bit of an Isaac Hayes 'Shaft' vibe going (first started with 'Interzone'). This was pretty much a jam thing at the time, though me and Hooky were a particularly tight rhythm section and we were all good at musical telepathy.

The Germanic one later titled 'Exercise One' – this came about from Bernard's idea of doing something a bit like Carl Orff's *Carmina Burana*. I know this sounds like we were listening to highbrow classical music, but the tune was widely known at the time as the music from the Old Spice aftershave TV ad and was used in *The Exorcist*. Anyway, it is dark, weird and scary. The title came from Bernard too. The ever-innovative Bernard couldn't see why we had to keep coming up with different titles for the songs. Why couldn't we just give them numbers instead – 1, 2, 3 or 4 for example? Just as an experiment. 'Might get boring after a bit,' said Ian tactfully. 'Exercise One' was a compromise. There was never an 'Exercise Two'.

'Wilderness' – this featured 'I've got a lot of toms so I'm going to use them but not all at the same time' drumming. I tried using a tom as a ride cymbal. I think Rob thought this one was a bit cornball – maybe it was the stop-start instrumental bit. He liked the lyrics though.

These, then, were our shortlist of songs for recording for the *A Factory Sample* EP.

Rob brought Martin Hannett and Lawrence Beedle – another partner in Rabid Records – down to T. J.'s practice rooms to get acquainted, which we did over a couple of spliffs. This meeting was speculative in a couple of areas.

We were meant to be sounding Martin out as a potential producer – he'd seen us at Salford Uni the previous year and had been taken with the rhythm section's ability to improvise through technical malfunctions – something that we were all becoming pretty adept at doing.

Lawrence was there because Rob was working on a way of getting the *Ideal for Living* distribution debacle resolved. He was hoping to persuade Tosh Ryan at Rabid to pick up the many unsold copies of the EP and distribute them. This was complicated by Rabid's belief that we were probably a bunch of Nazis. The sleeve of the 7-inch did nothing to dispel that misconception. Rob's plan was to re-press the EP as a 12-inch – which would sound much better – in a new, less controversial sleeve.

I took to Martin straight away. He was a man after my own heart: a sci-fi dope fiend and old hippie. He smoked Gitanes probably just to be anti-social. He reminded me of the sort of people I would end up talking to at gigs while trying to score.

We then set about running through the shortlist selection from our repertoire. Our favourite, possibly because it was the one we had only just finished and so still fresh, was the Germanic one. Martin wasn't that taken with it and Rob wasn't a fan of 'Wilderness' either so that left 'Digital' and the still slightly nebulous 'Glass'. The choice was made easy by that simple process of elimination.

Next stop Cargo Recording Studios, Rochdale, which I'd heard of as being somehow connected with hippie legends and DJ John Peel favourites Tractor, who'd released albums on Peel's Dandelion label back in 1972. So that for me meant it was cool, man.

On 11 October 1978, with our gear once again crammed in the Cortina and Hooky's jag, we set off for Rochdale and straight into a can of worms.

The first problem was that Tony had negotiated the session with Cargo's owner, ex Granada cameraman and *So It Goes* sound recordist John Brierley, and in the process may have given him the impression that John, and not Martin, would be producing. Possibly in exchange for some Factory involvement, in lieu of cash. This made things a little awkward from the word go. A phone call to Tony smoothed things over with John, but there was a bit of tension all day between him and Martin. This would turn out to be par for the course for any Hannett session. Martin seemed to thrive on tension, but we didn't know that at the time.

'Not got a Prime-Time, John? That's a quality American device, you should get yourself one of those' was Martin at his most helpful.

I'd taken the Synare 3 because, you never know, it might have been useful. Martin wasn't too impressed.

A further inconvenience for John was provided by Martin in the form of his recently acquired black box. This was an early AMS DMX 15-80 Digital Delay (made just up the road in Burnley of all places), which would have to be wired into the mixing desk.

This futuristic device, with its glowing red digital display and keypad, looked magical. It was Martin's pride and joy. We didn't know it, but the future had arrived.

Neither did we know that this would turn out to be a blueprint for a method of recording that we would end up using time and again.

Martin had *ideas* – he wasn't just going to record a song as well as possible given the time and resources available. He was going to add to it, process it, change it, give it a setting. He would refine the raw material and make it shine in an eerie light. What Martin did was to transform the song into a proper-sounding record. The trouble was that he didn't seem to speak the same language as us. He spoke a kind of university techspeak, interspersed with odd bits of musical terminology – off beats/chords/bars – which, although we were aware of, we only vaguely understood. 'Muso shit' was the name Hooky and Bernard disdainfully gave it.

The handclaps on 'Glass' were our idea. Rob, keen to get on the record, was the first volunteer but the worst handclapper going. He never got any better even after years of practice, but always insisted on having a go.

Martin made some changes to the song arrangements, telling us to play that riff two more times before changing to the next part, which made no sense at the time but we gamefully did as we were told.

Ian liked the vocal sound that Martin got for him – it somehow sounded to me like he was channelling Elvis.

I think it's fair to say that we thought that with Factory and Martin, we had found people who were on our wavelength (even if we couldn't always understand them) and who probably weren't just in it for the money.

We packed up and went home reluctantly. As we'd gone over the time we'd booked – another future tradition – Martin and Tony sorted out an evening's studio time to come back and mix the two tracks (according to Martin, it was imperative to mix at night – for the vibes, apparently). Martin wanted to mix the tracks at Strawberry, scene of my earlier half-baked musical recording endeavour with the Folk Band Whose Name I Don't Remember. I thought that might be difficult as Strawberry was a 24-track, and we'd just recorded on a 16-track machine.

'Not a problem,' he said. 'We'll change the head block.'

Martin insisted he could only mix in rooms that had been mixed in for generations – places with pedigree. Some mystical quality sonically imprinted within their walls.

We were all a lot happier with the end product of the *A Factory Sample* session than we had been with *An Ideal for Living* and the RCA record-that-never-was. I thought it sounded fantastic in a way I never thought it could. It sounded like the sort of record I would buy.

However, there still remained the homespun/bedroom indie method of actually producing the finished article. Peter Saville had designed a fancy double 7-inch sleeve in keeping with the original Factory poster for the Hulme gigs. In terms of Factory creations, that poster was 'FAC 1' and this was 'FAC 2'. The sleeve required encasing in a plastic wrapper so, like the *Ideal for Living* sleeve-folding party, we were co-opted into a heat-shrink-wrap party at Factory HQ: Alan Erasmus's flat on Palatine Road. Nathan McGough, future manager of the Happy Mondays, also turned up but he kept breaking the heat-shrink machine. (It turns out that there must have been many of these dope-smoking, finger-burning, sleeve-making sessions of which we were unaware. The number of people I come across today who say they were press-ganged into heat shrinkage is starting to rival attendees at the Pistols' first Free Trade Hall gig.)

Malcolm Whitehead, a friend of Rob Gretton's from his days working the bags at Manchester Airport, proposed the idea of making a film about Joy Division with his Super 8 camera. We would be following in the fifties/sixties tradition of bands making films – *Expresso Bongo*, *Summer Holiday*, *A Hard Day's Night* – although the inspiration was to do something more like Godard's *One Plus One* on the Rolling Stones rather than anything that Cliff might have appeared in. We, of course, loved the idea. Malcolm was easy to get along with and shared the same sense of humour.

The basis of this film was footage of us performing at the Bowdon Vale Youth Club on 14 March 1979. (As Bowdon Vale was just up the road from Altrincham, Malc's place of residence, the venue was most likely his idea.) This would be intercut with other contemporary footage to form a ten-minute semi-documentary.

It is a very good representation of what we were like live just prior to *Unknown Pleasures*. We all look incredibly young and fresh-faced, and the flock wallpaper gives the place an authentic seventies feel.

Typically we weren't happy with some of the additional footage Malc had edited in.

'Fucking hell, Malc ... Not Hitler! Jesus, you'll have to get rid of that!'

Over the years, Malcom would revisit the film and send us the latest director's cut. Although he did resolve a few of the film's technical problems – playing at the wrong speed being the main one – he never did come up with an edit without the Nazi bits. Or, in fact, change the edit in any major way.

Malcolm was the founder and guiding light of Factory's video department, Ikon, which put out a wealth of cool stuff in the halcyon days of VHS. I would spend many hours with him in the cellar at Tony's house, learning how to edit and make videos on the cheap.

In late 1978, Factory were not the only fish in the sea; Rob would weigh up our options, as managers do. In the course of sorting out the distribution of the *An Ideal for Living* 12-inch, which was released on 10 October under our own label, now called Anonymous, Rob had spoken to other labels/indie music-biz folk about exactly what our next step forward might be. There was Chris Parry, manager of the Cure, and his label Fiction, Bob Last, Rough Trade and Martin Rushent, who had been with Andrew Lauder at United Artists (Buzzcocks' and my old hippie fave label). Andrew had set up Radar Records (a pseudo indie backed by Warners) and Martin Rushent set up a new company, Genetic, as a Radar spinoff.

I drove Rob down to London for meetings, and the upshot of talking to Martin Rushent and Anne Roseberry at Genetic was that we were booked into Eden Studios for a day to record some tracks with him producing. He was a veteran – a nice enough bloke, pretty tech-savvy – but nowhere near as mad-scientist-like as the other Martin, Hannett.

He was also suffering terribly with haemorrhoids on the day. Always a problem in the producing game.

Options duly weighed, Rob decided the best deal in town was with Factory. The great thing for us about doing this was that we wouldn't be tied to Factory. The deal was simple: the revenue would be split fifty-fifty (*Brilliant*, I thought), there would be no actual written contract and the band could walk away at any time and take their songs with them. The band would retain the copyright on the songs. Unheard of! Perfect! After the Virgin and RCA/Sourgrapes debacles, this sounded like a sure-fire winner. No small print. In fact, no print at all. (Not strictly true as there was the infamous note signed in a pinprick of Tony's blood.)

We would be based in Manchester (which Rob thought was great as he was never a fan of southern bastards). It was all upside for us.

It was the worst business model for a record label ever, but that was neither here nor there in 1978.

Tony summed it up best when he said, 'The bands on Factory have complete freedom, the freedom to fuck off.'

As is the way with these things, it didn't take long for the majors to get interested in this new indie thing – they scented a profit and bands began to get hoovered up left, right and centre. We, and that includes Factory, didn't really take them seriously – sure the big guys had money, but it wasn't about the money (it really wasn't – oh, the folly of youth). Later, Warners wanted to sign Joy Division and, as Tony and Alan were busy that day, Martin Hannett and Peter Saville, as partners in Factory, were dispatched to Claridge's in London to handle the negotiations. According to Factory folklore, the story goes something like:

'We want a million, not a penny less.'

That was Martin's opening (and closing) gambit. Peter, I suspect, agreed, possibly adding, 'And complete artistic control.'

Bob Krasnow, Warners' vice president, unsurprisingly choked on his scone, made his excuses and left.

Crazy Limeys, he probably thought as he hailed a cab. *Who do these guys think they are?*

No wonder the big labels always thought Factory were a bunch of Marxists.

Had the band been present or known anything about this meeting at the time, they would probably have said something similar, but for a million pounds, who knows? We might have joined Bob in the cab.

Whatever Factory was, it was not a record label in the traditional sense of the word. Berry Gordy probably wouldn't have understood Factory.

Yes, Factory put out records, great-sounding records, great-looking records too. But it was the way that they did it that was the thing. They had a style that nobody else had. OK, maybe some of that style was borrowed – isn't it always? – but the ethos was totally original.

TW (to Gillian Gilbert): Well, you see, the record business functions by securing your investment, which is to secure your talent. So you sign people for seven-year deals and stuff. But we're only doing this for fun. In the end ... I mean, it's an old Jake Riviera thing, that's all it's about – fun. And you're doing it for fun with integrity and stuff. Now, if we had a contract with you, what's that gonna do? It means you're signed to us. What happens if we all go off each other? You should be able to go away. So there's no point in having a contract. As long as we're all friends you're going to stay; long as we're not friends you're going to go. Which seems the right way to look at going and staying.

Play at Home (1983)

20

THE NIGHTMARE JUST AFTER CHRISTMAS

So we now had a manager, we had caught the eye of Tony Wilson and both our 12-inch EP and *A Factory Sample* had just been released. Just when things are beginning to look up and the feeling that good times are indeed just around the corner gets a hold of you – this is when the gods intervene and the whole house of cards comes tumbling down.

Finally we had a gig in London. We'd had to change our name, but we could go down there and prove everybody wrong.

The cellar of a pub in Islington may not be the most auspicious of venues, and who in their right minds wants to go out on 27 December anyway? The dead time between Christmas and New Year. A Wednesday at the black end of the year 1978.

I was getting used to these marathon drives. Going down corridors of twinkling orange lights looking forward to the long straight fast bit just after Coventry on the way back. The start of the Midlands, the end of the South, that meant I was nearly home. At times, the drives were enjoyable. A hypnotic odyssey with Rob's conversation and wit for company. Hooky had invested in a well-worn Transit. (Every band needs one: it's another tradition.) Hooky drove the rusty van with Terry and the gear, and I had the Cortina with Rob, Bernard and Ian. Our regular roadie and Salford friend, Twinny – real name Carl Bellingham, though never used – would travel with him and Terry. A little bit of speed and a lot of fags to help the journey. The heater in the Mark III Cortina was a not a guarantee of toasty warmth at the best of times and, in the depths of a soggy English winter, to describe its output as a mild breeze of tepid air would be pushing it.

To placate my passengers' requests for warmth, I had taken to carrying a brown nylon sleeping bag on the back seat to try and stave off the threat of hypothermia. Unzipped it would accommodate two at a pinch.

Things did not get off to the best of starts. Bernard was ill, suffering with the flu, and needed all the heat the Cortina could provide. He had augmented the back seat comforter with a sleeping bag of his own. Post-Christmas cheer was a bit thin on the ground.

What was it about London? It almost seemed as if there were some kind of psychic force field around the place, infecting us with some plague whenever we tried to reach its holy grail.

I think the rain stopped around Birmingham as me and my not-so-happy crew squelched our way south on the M6, Bernard groaning and moaning from the back seat, cursing the smoking bastards who disturbed his rest and threatened his health. He wound down his window a crack to vent the cigarette fog, making the car feel even more chilly and damp.

It was dark by the time we found the Hope & Anchor, our venue for tonight. Rob's navigation had unerringly got us there, though whether by the best route was always a matter of dispute. We were relying on an old and battered *A–Z* from which a few pages were missing. We occasionally had to go round the houses to compensate for the vital missing pages.

'The load-in's down the hole,' said Terry as we pulled up.

I thought he was joking but no, the gear had to enter the premises the same way as the beer barrels: down a metal chute into the depths of the Hope & Anchor's cellar.

'It's going to be fun getting it all back out later.'

Whatever we had been expecting, we didn't get it.

We played well enough considering Bernard's depleted state, and the meagre crowd didn't seem too dissatisfied. But it was one of those things that I'd built up in my mind, dreamed of, struggled for – this was the 'big one' – and when the day finally dawned . . .

'Is that it?'

The gig could have been packed to the rafters, the audience could have cried for more, and it would still have fallen short of the imagination. Expectation always beats realisation, every time. Onwards and upwards though.

Bernard still grumbles about this gig. Apparently my overzealous (I felt 'passionate' would have been a better word) bashing of the ride cymbal caused him serious physical discomfort and torment. He has held a strong dislike and distrust of cymbals ever since and looks quite disgusted whenever I hit one.

We (well, Hooky, Terry, Rob and Me) humped the gear back out up a flight of stairs and through the punters still enjoying a pre-New Year's drink upstairs in the bar, got back in the Cortina and hit the North Circular.

Ian was unhappy. It was his turn to moan and as the last few minutes of John Peel's show struggled to be heard over the radio's static, he'd found his rhythm. 'Fucking bastards. Fucking, fucking bastards!'

Rob's attempts to placate him only wound him up further.

'Fucking cunts!'

By the time we hit the M1 it was getting a bit tedious.

'Give us a bit of the sleeping bag, Ian. I'm fucking freezing here.'

Through the rear-view mirror I could see a tug-of-war in progress between Ian and Bernard, fighting over the sleeping bag.

Ian was in the seat behind me. I could feel him banging his knees and kicking the back of my seat. This was getting ridiculous.

'Fucking hell, Ian, leave it out. I'm trying to drive here.' The kicking in my back only got worse and more frequent. 'For fuck's sake, give it a rest.'

Then there was an animal snarl.

'For fuck's sake . . .

'Steve, pull over!' said Bernard.

'Why? What the fuck's up?'

Rob leant over the back of his seat to help Bernard.

'PULL OVER!'

By the time I realised this wasn't a joke and swerved the car onto the hard shoulder, we had just passed the Luton turn-off.

We got out and helped Bernard pull the thrashing Ian out as gently as we could. I fetched the sleeping bag.

I think we all knew by then what was happening.

'Mind his tongue.'

'He's having a fit! Turn off the hazards, Steve – strobe effect!'

I was quite surprised that the hazards were working and that I had remembered to turn them on.

What to do in times of crisis like this? Well, the first thing that sprung to mind was, *I need a cigarette as a matter of urgency.*

Rifling through my pockets turned up nothing but empty packets. Bits of cardboard kept for roach material.

My friend was having a seizure on the hard shoulder of the M1 and all I could think of was nicotine. I was a heartless bastard but maybe it was shock.

'Rob, see if he's got any cigs. Get his fags.'

'Fuck off. We've got to get him to hospital.'

The fit had subsided slightly but Ian was still only semi-conscious. We laid him on the back seat and I took off in the wrong direction for Luton.

'Slow down, Steve, you'll fucking get us all killed.'

How the hell we found Luton and Dunstable Hospital I'll never know, but probably by stopping a couple of times, winding down the window and asking an unsuspecting nocturnal pedestrian out walking the dog.

'Hospital, mate? Which way?'

We ushered a still not-entirely-with-us singer into A & E with Rob doing the rundown on the drama of the last forty-five minutes.

'Think he's had a fit, he's in a band . . .' As though being in a band made one prone to this.

A nurse took Ian away while the three of us waited in the glare of the strip lights.

'Er, did you get his fags, Rob?'

We were in for a long wait.

Ian was finally released with a bit of paper and instructions to see his GP first thing in the morning without fail.

'What was it then?'

'He's had a fit of some kind—'

'Give us a fag, Ian!'

We resumed our moonlit slog back up north, shocked and subdued.

That night, everything changed.

Maybe I'm reading too much into it, but after this Ian's lyrics, which had previously seemed inclusive – about more than just himself, about people living in some world – became more about departure or confinement. Yes, I am probably reading too much into it, but I'm not alone there. His lyrics were personal to him and we never talked about what they might be about, except in general terms that lyrics could be the script of a film, tell a story. They were important though, very. Ian downplayed that a little.

*　　*　　*

MH: Sorry to get mixed up but who writes the lyrics? You write the lyrics, you have control over a lot then if you write the lyrics.

IC: You don't have control over anything, do you?

MH: Don't you? In a way, I mean the lyrics define what the song's about.

IC: No I always put the lyrics in after. After the song's been done, I get a vocal line for it . . .

RG: Not always, sometimes.

IC: We have been doing lately, the way we've been working lately.

TW: What do you mean, you get a vocal line?

IC: Well, the way . . . the melody, a vocal melody and some of the lyrics that I'd have to sing at the time when we did the song. I may keep others, I may not.

MH: What, you make them up as you sing?

IC: Yes.

PH: (referring to an earlier Interview with Sounds' Dave McCulloch) Flipped when we told him.

RG: He just couldn't believe that it all just fell in place. He said well, you must sit down and say we're going to write a fast poppy type one or a slow . . . didn't he? And we said, no we just play and it just comes.

PH: Just rehearse, yes.

IC: I don't usually keep the ones that I make . . . What I do is usually I get the vocal melody. There's usually some of the words that I've sung at the time I do keep. I write more to go with it, to fit the mood of the song, fit the mood of the rest of it.

MH: So you will create the mood of the song?

IC: Yeah, that's basically what it is.

BS: You just feed off it . . . we start with something small and each of us feeds off it till it grows into a song.

All of this is perfectly true: the music came first, then the words. I can't imagine a situation where you would get a set of lyrics and then write a tune around them. I'm sure someone must work that way but to me it seems a bit weird.

We distrusted journalists, felt they had the wrong idea about us. Paul Morley, as someone we'd known a long time, was OK. He had done a proper piece about Joy Division in the *NME*. The one with Kevin Cummins's photographs of us in the snow in Hulme. He had mentioned Warsaw in passing previously, but having a write-up in the *NME* was a big deal. Somehow I expected that seeing us in print would magically make us look like a proper band. It was a bit of a let-down. Compared to the rest of the bands in the *NME* that week, we just looked odd. We didn't really look like a band at all. To me, the four of us, Ian, Bernard, Hooky and me, looked just, well, odd. My geography teacher blazer and stripy woolly jumper was about as rock and roll as a mug of Horlicks. Forty years on, the same photographs say something else. Now, we look like a band with something to say.

When I asked him how he was, Ian said, 'I'm OK,' and I willingly believed him.

In January, the doctor confirmed that Ian had epilepsy and would have to moderate his lifestyle; he would need medication to control the seizures.

Doesn't sound too bad, does it? Moderation and some tablets? A few early nights, swallow some pills and it'll all go away.

I heard what I wanted to hear.

'I'm OK.'

'Great, let's have a smoke.'

The pills began benignly enough but were ineffective. So they tried something stronger but with more potential side effects.

*   *   *

A panacea? There isn't one.

It's really up to you.

You are now leaving the town of Frying Pan.

Welcome to Fire (population 1). Please drive carefully.

Of all the 1970s' many taboo subjects, mental illness was possibly the most misunderstood. I know that there is a difference between what is termed mental illness and epilepsy, but to most people in the seventies it was one and the same.

'Off his bloody head that one.'

Best kept in a dark cupboard and ignored by polite society.

In Macclesfield an ailment of the mind was the domain of the men and women of Parkside – the Funny Farm. I'd been there myself a few times. The most recent hadn't really been that long before Ian's first seizure, when I'd got severely depressed and ended up on the antidepressants with very unpleasant and honestly more depressing side effects.

Those pharmaceutical side effects would be trivial compared to those that Ian experienced. His was heavy-duty medication. A 'normal' life would be just about possible. What we were doing was not normal by any stretch of the imagination.

I've said it before and I'll say it again – not that it matters, as hindsight holds no virtue – but we should have stopped there and then, or at least paused for breath. Ignored the 'I'm OKs' because he was as far from OK as he could get and would get further away from it the more successful Joy Division became.

That's not to say we weren't deeply concerned. Of course we were. We stopped flashing the lights at gigs, but we just didn't know or understand exactly what his illness meant (or might mean). It could have been a one-off event, might never happen again if you regulated your lifestyle or, on the other hand . . .

So the New Year got off to a shaky start, but Ian for the most part was soon back to his usual self. Like it or not, the unspoken fact remained that the future of the band now lay with one person's ability to cope with something we couldn't comprehend.

Most of the time, you view success as something that will make life easier. It will arrive in tiny measures and gradually take some of the pressure off. It's never that simple.

As you work your way from aspirational amateurs playing and writing for the fun of it, to the point where someone actually pays you money to do the same, there is a critical point. A fork in the road. Turn back or press on. Your eventual destination is not guaranteed.

The promise of life in a successful band is one that is free of responsibilities. A Peter Pan-like world that suspends the need to become a grown-up. Be a big kid forever. But to get there involves an investment in responsibility, pressure and strife that may not produce any short-term gain or any gain at all – but so long as everyone's happy, where's the harm?

The degree to which this affects you and those around you will depend on your personal situation and your ability to juggle. It will impact each of you at different times depending on circumstances.

It was Ian who felt it first.

House + Wife + Job on the financial certainty side had to be reconciled with potential income from gigs and records in the unpredictable column.

He and Debbie needed money and what started as a reasonable band meeting on how we could accommodate this slowly boiled over into one of Ian's petulant but hilarious rants, during the course of which he raged about the rehearsal room wearing a drum case on his head.

Ian, of course, didn't find it funny. For him it was very serious indeed. The crux of the argument, as I recall, was to do with the puzzling phenomenon that having being paid a week in hand would now leave him one week out of pocket, if he was paid the Gretton way.

Rob tried to explain rationally, but once Ian had an idea fixed in his head it could be difficult to dislodge it with reason. You had to bite your lip and ride out the storm.

It is a situation that all musicians find themselves in at some time or other and needs a leap of faith to overcome. One by one we would have to go through it; we didn't earn enough from the band. We were all sympathetic to his predicament. It didn't stop us laughing at him, though.

'You don't fucking understand!' he wailed from under his black drum-case helmet. Maybe we didn't. For a start, we didn't know Debbie was pregnant. Ian was going to be a father.

Ian seemed to keep bits of his life compartmentalised. Maybe we all did.

There was an example of this in October 1978, not long after the Factory Sampler session. My twenty-first birthday was fast approaching and I'd had a bit of cash saved up.

Never having been twenty-one before, I thought it might be an occasion to celebrate. Gillian and Julie were keen on this idea and suggested maybe we could have an old-fashioned party. Jellies and trifle might be a bit of a laugh. We'd hatched this tipsy juvenile party plan on the way back from the Factory the week before the big day, without giving serious consideration as to where such an event might take place at short notice. It was a nice idea but a little bit impractical. Why not just have a slap-up dinner and a night on the tiles instead?

The Gilbert sisters still championed the jelly plan; Gillian was in for a more conventional soiree.

We'd played Leeds with the Cabs on the 24th and I mentioned to Ian that I was thinking of going out that Saturday and did he fancy a night out with Debbie?

'Oh yes, fine, be great.'

Saturday night rolled around and I gave Ian a call to arrange a time.

'Oh, I'm a bit tired. I've been at Barney's all day.'

I was a bit surprised by this. Debbie had just passed her driving test and surmised that perhaps it had been a bit of a practice outing for the Curtises' recently acquired green Morris Traveller. I was no longer Ian's only chauffeur.

Not to be deterred, and unable to take a hint, I suggested he have forty winks and I'd be round about half eight. My vague idea was for us all to go out for a few drinks and a nice meal with Gillian, maybe a Chinese. I knew Ian had very strong feelings about Indian food. We'd then have a few more drinks and go on to one of Macc's two nighteries, Images or Krumbles. I knew he was short of cash so I had come at the ready.

I arrived at his door. 'You two up for it then? I've got sixty quid to spend tonight.'

'Oh no, I'm still worn out. I had to be Barney's best man. What a palaver. I'm knackered.'

Was I hearing things, '"best man"?'

'Yes, him and Sue have got married.'

Now I may have neglected to mention that Bernard is full of surprises. I apologise for that, though mostly logical and analytical Bernard's capacity for the unexpected never ceases to amaze me. This one surely took the biscuit. I was flabbergasted, I had no idea. Had I missed something? Not that I would have expected an invitation or anything. You think you know someone and . . .

Even Debbie looked surprised. I finally took the hint.

Feeling deflated and let down, I called Gillian. The unexpected announcement rather put the mockers on my planned knees-up.

"Fancy a night in instead?"

I took my usual solitary course past the alehouses of the town, and picked up chips and gravy on my way to the Gilbert residence. We spent the night sitting on the kitchen floor listening to the radio.

Not the night to remember we'd been expecting.

So, by the end of 1978, as I recall, Ian was married, had his house in Barton Street and was going to be a father; Bernard had just married Sue and they sorted out a flat in Peel Green; Hooky had moved into a place in Moston with Iris; and Rob had a flat in Chorlton with his girlfriend Lesley, making me some sort of mummy's boy stuck at home with my parents, living the shy bachelor life. A spoilt cuckoo.

I would often get home just as my father was getting up to work and struggle to get to sleep over the strains of Ella Fitzgerald and Duke Ellington. I would fitfully sleep till lunchtime and then, bleary-eyed and sulky, bid farewell to my mother who would bemoan the state I left my room in. Then I'd fill up the Cortina and head off to Manchester for some band-related business or other. I very rarely watched TV and my music consumption was almost entirely Joy Division-related, apart from the odd occasion when I could coax the Ford radio to produce something more than static.

One night, I was driving home from rehearsals with Ian and, just at the top of Kingsway, he spotted a couple of girls hitch-hiking.

'Pull over, Steve! Let's give them a lift.'

'Er, OK,' and I did a rather abrupt stop.

The girls wanted a lift to Altrincham, technically in the wrong direction, but Ian insisted. Ushering them into the back seat, Ian launched into copping mode while I tried to figure out how to get to Altrincham and still get home before dawn.

A few weeks later, on the way to another Sunday rehearsal, Ian seemed a bit more lethargic than normal. When pressed for the cause he eventually spilled that he had spent the night with one of the afore-mentioned lady hitchers and said not to mention it again. How he'd managed to cover that one with Debbie, I didn't want to know. I believe this made him a bit of a dark horse in northern man mythology. A normal life was never going to work for Ian.

* * *

Hooky was always the first to blow, leaping off the stage wielding his bass like a war axe to deal with some gobber who got a bit threatening. Always wearing his heart on his sleeve and whatnot, you knew what you'd get from him. It was almost always about class. Or what he thought was class – he had a shoulder-borne chip. Like *The Frost Report* sketch with the Two Ronnies and Cleese, he was lower class and I was middle class, and that apparently made me less of something in his eyes. It was something I'd never given much thought to – where you came from was, to me, unimportant; it was who you were that counted. That someone might think I was a spoilt little rich kid hurt, I admit.

Hooky was, and is, adversarial. 'I am a punk,' he would say as though being a punk gave him a right to do what he wanted and fuck you – which I guess to him it did. These things are always open to interpretation.

He is also very charming.

Driving to gigs, he always led. If he found the Jag to be behind someone he knew at traffic lights, he would delight in nudging them forward across the lights, into oncoming traffic. John Peel was a famous celeb victim.

Or pulling up alongside, he would chuck empty cans at my car, and Ian would return fire. The Cortina always had a healthy stock of ammunition, with empty cans rattling about in the footwell. This would quickly degenerate into a mobile battle like some modern chariot race or dual carriageway naval battle, as innocent bystanders were splattered with sticky residue from unfinished fizzy drinks of days gone by.

Bernard, slightly more reserved and analytical, was usually the calmest, most thoughtful, and least likely to do the heavy lifting.

Maybe I was a bit too passive and malleable. I put it down to the books on Buddhism and science fiction I was reading. I really was keen on the death of the ego and all that reality-is-illusory line. It was tied up with some of the rants that Timothy Leary did in *Politics of Ecstasy* (turn on, tune in, drop out), and would eventually get me into Robert Anton Wilson and Bob Shea's epic trilogy *Illuminatus!* and then later, as I got slack, the Church of Bob Scientology piss-take.

I'm not trying to criticise anyone here. It was the fact that we were all different that made the band what it was. I was a wimp. But a wimp with wheels.

21

UNKNOWN PLEASURES

Buoyed up by the success of *A Factory Sample* and the gigs we'd been doing, it was time to move on to an album. Nobody had lost any money on *A Factory Sample* so, for Tony and Alan, an album could potentially be an earner for Factory. We'd explored other options, even done some demos with Marin Rushent for Genetic. But nothing ever came close to Factory's appeal financially and artistically.

It was that impetus thing again: the desire to keep moving on to the next thing, bigger and better, to climb higher, sometimes even before the paint was dry on the last thing.

In April 1979, Martin was camped out at Strawberry in Stockport, working on John Cooper Clarke's first album for CBS. A scheme was cooked up whereby we would go in when JCC was elsewhere, weekends usually, which, as we all still had day jobs, suited us to a T.

Now, who footed the bill for this is one of life's greatest mysteries. It is an accounting grey area. Was it Factory? Was it CBS? Maybe six of one and half a dozen of the other. For now, we innocently revelled in the simple wonder of the creative accounting that usually took place on the back of Tony's hand, usually inked in red Pentel. It worked for us. If we just didn't think about it too hard.

Recording at Strawberry suited Martin, too, of course. He was set up with his gear already and was working with Chris Nagle, the engineer. Martin and Chris would be a double act with Chris as Martin's straight man, holding court behind the red Helios desk.

'Look, Steve, it's got a cigarette lighter. You just push this . . .'

'No, it doesn't work any more, Martin,' said Chris. 'I think you broke it.'

'Oh yeah.'

Strawberry was one of the most modern and well-equipped recording studios at the time. In the north-west, it was probably the only modern studio. 10cc's 'I'm Not in Love' is one of the finest examples of a '70s band using studio technology to create a unique-sounding record. Now it sounds a little ordinary but in the 1970s it was a 'Wow! How have they done that?' record. The way 10cc used multitracked vocals and tape loops on 'I'm Not In Love' pre-dated sampling, and it was precisely that kind of pains-taking sonic exploration through technology that Martin loved. That such things could have taken place in Stockport, of all places, seemed bizarre.

Strawberry hadn't changed that much since my earlier brief visit. It had all the signs of a successful recording studio. Gold and silver discs lined the walls, proof of the place's hit-making potential. The smell of freshly brewed cona, proof of work in progress. In the control room with its crazy-paving stone-lined walls, Martin fiddled with switches on the desk while Chris loaded reels of tape on the twenty-four-track Studer. Through the glass the live room, the Steinway grand just visible on the left. At the far end adjacent to the large lift that hinted at the building's previous occupation, the walls were covered in mirrors like a ballet school.

'Maximum reflections,' explained Martin. 'Stick the drums there for now.'

There was more gear than I remembered from my earlier brief visit. An Ursa Major space station that sounded interesting and an Eventide 910 harmoniser. At last the Low snare-drum sound would be mine! Martin had other ideas and copying Tony Visconti was not one of them.

Like being given the keys to the Tardis, Martin and Chris would explore exactly what the studio was capable of. They were using it more as a musical instrument than a recording facility or, to put it another way, Martin was fucking about a lot. But most of this fucking about was intriguing and educational, especially Martin's use of the AMS DMX 15-80. By this point, I had a vague idea of what the AMS did. On the face of it, it sounds quite simple – it recorded the input sound onto some memory chips, waited a bit (the delay time), then played it back, giving echo and repeat-type effects. Combined with this, the output sound could also be changed in pitch by using a keypad to speed up or slow down the playback rate. This could give you phasing, flanging and chorus-type effects. Its show-stopping party trick was its ability to record a snippet of sound and play it back at the push of a button. We used this on drums to replace/repair out-of-time hits or just to change the sound completely. We tried recording a short guitar phrase from 'Disorder' into it with the intention of doing a similar repair job. But the process transformed the sound into something so completely different and unexpected that it became a part in itself.

Not all of them would end up on the album, but songwise we had 'Shadowplay', a reworked 'Interzone', 'Exercise One', 'Insight', 'Wilderness', 'Walked in Line', 'Disorder', 'Day of the Lords' and 'The Kill' (version two) finished and ready to go. 'The Only Mistake' was about half done and 'New Dawn Fades' probably just needed the lyrics. 'Candidate' and 'Autosuggestion' were written in the studio out of jams between me and Hooky while Martin checked the sound of the drums and bass. Getting the sound right could take a while.

The song that became 'I Remember Nothing' was up until then known as 'the synthesiser one' (it was called 'The Visitors' for about five minutes). It was pretty loose and was something that we usually did at the end of the set with Bernard playing the Transcendent. Live, it either worked really well or not at all, depending on how well the synth was behaving and the direction Ian's improvised words took us. I wasn't a big fan of it at that point. I felt that it meandered a bit too much and didn't go anywhere – it really needed another element from somewhere. It got much better once we convinced Ian into having a go at playing guitar. Even then the song still felt a bit empty somehow. Of course, that is what is great about it. I just hadn't realised that yet.

Even though he had no idea what it did, Rob liked the idea of the synthesiser. He thought 'I Remember Nothing' was epic live (it was his idea that we introduce the synth song at the end of the set). Ian also liked the idea of being experimental. He found it appealing that it might lead us into something like Throbbing Gristle territory.

Ian was a reluctant guitarist. He took a bit of coaxing and encouragement to play his Vox Phantom. This was a white rhomboid-shaped guitar that would have looked at home in a 1960s beat group, perhaps played by a mop-top at a freakout framed by go-go dancers. It oozed cool from a retro version of the future, but it was also fiendishly complicated. This was not good, for Ian was not technical in the slightest. He was easily bamboozled by anything even slightly complicated and the Phantom was a bit more than that. It augmented the basics with built-in effects such as fuzz and repeat, plus a tuning tone, all controlled by six buttons and five knobs. As the lettering on most of these buttons and switches had worn off, it was a case of trial and error to find out which switch did what. Push the wrong button and the guitar would emit random squawks and wails. Ian would randomly push buttons and turn knobs until he hit on the combination that quelled the screeching. In time, Ian improved as a guitarist but he never lost his distrust of the Phantom, which we called the Fred Flintstone.

Bernard gets this story mixed up, but Gillian ended up playing guitar on 'I Remember Nothing' at a gig at Eric's in Liverpool. Rob had been pissing about trying to open a bottle and in the process managed somehow to injure Ian's hand. As 'I Remember Nothing' was the last song of the set and the only one that Ian played guitar on while Bernard did the synth, Gillian, in Liverpool on a geography trip, was hastily drafted in for just that one song.

I could never really appreciate what effect Ian might have on the audience. I only ever saw the back of him. He moved about a lot, I could tell that, which compensated for the way Bernard and Hooky stood quite still, just concentrating on what they were playing. At the back, I would be frantically banging away but hiding behind the cymbals and doing my best to be invisible.

We also had 'Transmission' by then, but we had already decided it was a potential single (hit or otherwise) and therefore shouldn't be considered part of the album at all. So we wouldn't record it. Considered from a purely commercial perspective this might seem naive, stupid or puzzling. All I can say is that it made sense to us back then.

The difference between a single and an album was important to me. I did not like the idea that a single was just a marketing tool for the LP it featured on. It felt like you were getting people to fork out twice for the same thing.

Making *Unknown Pleasures* exposed me to many of Martin's unorthodox recording methods. It sometimes felt like we were taking part in a series of experiments in sound recording, most of which we willingly participated in. The one that affected me the most was obviously his approach to the recording of drums. In particular, the deconstruction of the drum kit.

Recorded drum sound is something that has over time evolved and changed along with advances in studio technology. In the seventies, the typical drum sound was one that was muffled and very dry – bass drums were stuffed with old pillows and cushions. (My mum was very worried when all her towels and soft furnishings started vanishing.) Toms were covered with tape and toilet paper to deaden them, and snare drums were draped with tea towels to remove any unwanted overtones. All this was accomplished by a lengthy process of trial and error seen by the rest of the band as time wasting.

I went along with all this as I found it interesting and also because I wanted the drums to sound as good as possible. Obviously. My slightly biased reasoning for this being that the drums are the foundations of the sound of a record. If the kit doesn't sound good, then it's going to be difficult to get the rest of the recording sounding great.

I would sit at the kit in the stone-and-mirror walled end of the recording studio and pound my drums for hours on end as an infinite number of reflected Steves did the same on either side of me. One of the most disorientating things about recording studios is the lack of windows, so the sense of time passing gets suspended. I would become totally engrossed in what we were doing. This would be interrupted occasionally by Rob bringing in a joint or by Martin and Chris coming in to look at a microphone and swap it for another fancier-looking one. Then sticking more towels on top of the previous towels with ever thicker layers of gaffer tape. I felt like I was being eroded or smothered in padding. Martin would sigh then chuckle to himself enigmatically before retreating to the mixing desk.

Having finally reduced the sound of each drum to something approaching a dull thud or a short lifeless thwack, which passed for a 'technically good' drum sound for 1970s engineers, I thought we were ready to do some actual playing. But Martin, being an innovative kind of guy, then decided to take the thing one stage further. He thought he would invent the drum sound of the 1980s.

The problem was that if I hit the snare drum, it would appear on all the other drum microphones as well; if I hit a tom-tom, that would also appear on all the other mics as well. This is called spill and there are a number of ways of minimising it using studio tools. The sound Martin was after was one devoid of any spill at all. Perfectly clean.

Martin's solution to this problem was to record each drum individually.

The drum kit I'd just spent ages setting up was gradually removed piece by piece until only one remained. Feeling naked and exposed I would again play away for hours as Chris moved, fiddled and added yet more microphones to the forest pointing at my solitary snare. My inner Keith Moon was mortified.

Take a regular, minimal sort of drum pattern, the simplest beat you can think of – boom-crack, tsh, boom-crack, tsh sort of thing – that would be a combination of three sounds, the bass drum (boom), the snare drum (crack) and the hi-hat (tsh), all being played at the same time ambidextrously. This is one of the first things you learn as a drummer but now I would have to forget all that, for Martin's solution entailed playing each part separately. For example, I would have to record the whole song just playing the bass drum and nothing else, then the snare drum and nothing else, until I had built up the part from all its individual pieces. This took considerably longer than the more 'conventional' method of recording and was ten times more difficult and confusing. After a few spliffs I thought I'd got the hang of it, but I ended up covered in bruises where I had been bashing my leg as a noiseless snare or tom substitute. At times I struggled to see just what Martin was trying to achieve apart from making my life a misery.

The other consequence was frustration and boredom for Rob and the band.

'Has he not finished those fucking drums yet? Come on, Steve, get a move on' was heard more than once as our weary manager stuck his head into the control room for a progress report.

'Fuck off, Gretton!' was the usual Hannett retort.

Imagine all this combined with Martin's oblique and zen-like method of coaxing a performance. He actually said things like 'play faster but slower' and 'louder but quieter'.

Not all the songs were done this way, thank God. 'Candidate', 'Autosuggestion', 'New Dawn Fades' and 'Day of the Lords' were done in the more conventional manner, by recording the backing track of us all playing together while Ian did a guide vocal. Then overdubbing onto that.

I was not the only one to suffer at the hands of Martin. Bernard was very unhappy with most of the guitar sounds Martin got. Instead of the powerful full live sound of Bernard's amped-up guitar, Martin's treatment left it thin, weak and tinny. Horrible was the verdict at the time.

Martin, being a bass player and up-to-the-minute gear fan, would give Hooky his opinion on what he should be using instead of his Marshall amp – 'Get an Alembic preamp,' was Hannett's advice, 'and a Crown DC-300 power amp too.'

Historically the way things worked in the studio was based around the dividing line of the control-room window, behind which those in charge lurked: the producer, the engineer and the man from the record company, should he deign to turn up. This was mission control. Musicians were admitted by invitation only with a strict 'look but don't touch' caveat.

The musicians were restricted to the studio area itself, where they would set up their equipment. Microphones would be placed by the engineer and producer, who would then retreat to the control-room bunker. From where, they would observe through the pillbox-slit glass window and communicate through headphones and the all-powerful red light above the door – signifying, like the factory hooter, that work should commence.

When we were recording with Martin, though, most of the time I was the only one actually set up in the studio. Bernard and Hooky both played from behind the glass in the control room.

There was I, stoned and alone, doing my best to interpret Martin's cryptic commands.

Being a part of his experimentation led us to become more aware of the creative possibilities of the recording studio. As I said, we were usually willing guinea pigs in Martin's experiments – the more outlandish the better. We were wide open to trying new things. Smashing bottles, recording lifts, you name it. We gleefully joined in with a pioneer spirit. It was fun and educational.

Bear in mind, though, that one man's sonic experiment can be another man's fucking about. For now, we liked being leftfield and off the wall.

Were we happy with *Unknown Pleasures* when it was finished? No, generally speaking, were we fuck.

When you hear a recording of your spoken voice for the first time, you recoil: that is not how I sound or how I want to sound. Our reaction to the mix of *Unknown Pleasures* may have been similar, but the general feeling was that Martin had somehow emasculated the sound. To some extent, the 'Well, it's not how I would have done it' complaint really meant, 'My bit's not loud enough.' The rawness of the live versions had evaporated and only their ghost remained. Ian and myself could be a bit leftfield and cerebral but Bernard and Hooky always liked our sound to be raw. But we'd run out of time and that was that.

The main complaint was that it didn't sound like us, it sounded like Martin: Martin was acting as an interpreter and he spoke hi-fi, not passion.

With the benefit of hindsight, though, I think we were being a little overcritical. But hey, musicians tend to be like that: never happy. I thought it sounded great, well the drums definitely did – I'd spent long enough recording them, after all. But, at the time, I did understand Bernard and Hooky's misgivings. Today it's hard to hear what all the fuss was about. *Unknown Pleasures* is a classic – after forty years it still sounds tremendous.

Joy Division comes across as being deep in thought. Something we never really were – well, Ian possibly, but never actually *that* deep. It is a peculiar-sounding record. Not really like anything else at that time. But Martin wasn't like any other producer.

We wanted to be unusual, unlike all the other bands, and that's what we got.

We had been overambitious with what we could do in the time available and had ended up recording six more tracks than could physically fit on a vinyl LP. So it was shortlist time again. Between us all, Martin included, we came up with the track list for the final album. Martin got involved on the sequencing of the tracks, which he explained should have complementary keys. I guess he knew more than us about that. 'Exercise One', 'The Only Mistake', 'Autosuggestion', 'Walked In Line', 'The Kill' and 'From Safety to Where' were removed for use elsewhere.

Potential album titles included 'Symptoms of Collapse', 'Bureau Of Change' and 'The Aura'. In the end, the name was chosen democratically: 'Unknown Pleasures' got three votes and 'Convulsive (Compulsive) Therapy' got one. No idea who voted for that one. Not quite unanimously, *Unknown Pleasures* it was!

If you're looking for cosmic coincidences, while we were making *Unknown Pleasures* Ian became a father. His daughter was born in mid-April 1979. I guess that made him a grown-up – maybe not, but more responsible. He had somebody else to think about and care for. We all said 'Aaaah' when we were introduced to Natalie for the first time. Who doesn't love a newborn baby?

Not very cosmic, you might say, or even much of a coincidence come to that.

OK then, how about this. On my sister Amanda's seventh birthday, Jocelyn Bell, an astrophysicist, was doing whatever astrophysicists do for a living – using lovely Radiophonic Workshop-type gear I would imagine – and discovered a very regular signal somewhere in the constellation of Vulpecula. So regular that it seemed to be a cosmic lighthouse or an alien signal of some sort. It was discovered by looking at a very long line of data traces, which, when laid on top of one another, produced a spooky pattern of wavy lines. These were the first recorded radio emissions of a pulsar – the first time anyone had ever found one. Now that surely is cosmic.

The pulsar was called CP1919. An image of its wavy pulse line was found by Bernard in a scientific journal in Manchester Library, sparking the idea for the cover of *Unknown Pleasures*.

I liked pulsars – I thought they might be celestial rhythm machines – and I liked the CP1919 image a lot.

'This'll look great on a T-shirt,' I said.

The others winced. Band T-shirts are shit. We're never doing T-shirts. EVER.

Principles again. It does look good on a T-shirt though, doesn't it? I bet you've got one.

The inner sleeve's photo of the hand through the door was Rob's idea, and the 'Inside Outside' naming was me.

Peter Saville took all this and turned it into a sleeve that is timelessly perfect in its mysterious textured blackness.

Unknown Pleasures was given fantastic reviews almost everywhere. It seemed as if Factory could do no wrong, and the music press suddenly became interested in us.

Despite the fact that I avidly read the music press and had done a tiny bit of writing myself, I did harbour a sneaking suspicion that most of its contributors were pretentious dickheads at heart. But you've got to make a living somehow. And anyway, the feeling was probably mutual.

If there was one person whose opinion on music was generally respected it was John Peel. He was essential listening and I very rarely missed his Radio 1 show. John was the absolute antithesis of a pretentious dickhead. He played tracks from *Unknown Pleasures* regularly and spoke of it enthusiastically. We'd done a session for him in January which had featured some tracks from the album. These serve to give a hint of what *Unknown Pleasures* would have sounded like without Martin's production. They were fun things to do – Peel sessions. No struggling to get a sound. No messing about. Basically do each song live, maybe the odd overdub, then back in time for tea. Getting a session on the Peel show was a major stepping stone for many unsigned bands.

His show was always entertaining and educational. John always seemed to play music that he genuinely enjoyed and that enthusiasm was genuinely infectious. It encouraged an open mind and exposed me to a lot of great music that I would never otherwise have discovered. His opinion was something that mattered to me and getting played on the Peel show was the first sign that we were getting somewhere.

22

NOT NECESSARILY COMMERCIAL

We were all inarticulate. I certainly was. We couldn't verbalise what it was we felt or wanted. We especially couldn't have explained why we felt the way we did. We definitely never spoke about these things to each other. Writing and performing becomes a kind of therapy. It, whatever it was, got put in the songs. We never thought about it or analysed why we liked our music. We were instinctive illiterates but we knew we were onto something.

I became even more inarticulate when we were questioned as a group. Rob usually took up the slack, goading us into participation or silence depending upon the nature of the questioning. Ian and Bernard came across as the more artistic types, while Hooky and I frequently seemed more like mechanics or builders.

We didn't like the media nosing about in our business. We were a gang of misfits.

Having recorded and released our first LP, tradition dictated that to expand our horizons, a single was required to complement it. Another word for this would be promotion but that was not part of our vocabulary. Promo was a dirty word.

Rob, though, was adamant that we keep 'Transmission' in reserve for just this purpose. We agreed it was the most commercial and radio friendly of all our songs, in that it mentioned the wireless in the lyrics, I suppose. I'm still not sure exactly what 'commercial' means here. It had a chorus and it was catchy. Everything you need for a hit single. It also had that rare effect of eliciting goose bumps when it hit the chorus – maybe that was it.

What to put on the B side was slightly trickier. A major label trick would have been to put a track off the album on there, but our principles on standalone singles wouldn't allow this: it had to be something unique. I don't think we had a particular soft spot for 'Novelty' – it was an old song harking back to the days of Warsaw – but in the spirit of want not, waste not . . . 'Novelty' it would be.

Late July 1979 saw us back in Strawberry, on the night shift this time. After the album sessions, we pretty much knew what to expect from Martin. We were wise to his ways. This time we decided we would keep badgering him in turn until we got our way.

Should be simple. Probably get home for bedtime.

During the recording of 'Transmission', we got the idea for a fast Morse code kind of riff, and finally my years of plonking about tunelessly on the dining-room piano paid off. This was a piano part for a drummer. A line of whizz later and I was battering away at the keys of the Strawberry Steinway (which featured on many a hit) like it was a hi-hat. There was no melody – just one note, speed and brute force. I was now technically a multi-instrumentalist. Honest I was! Listen carefully to the last chorus.

The stumbling block on this session turned out to be the tom fills (overdubbed of course) on 'Novelty', for they took an eternity.

Ian, Rob, Hooky and Bernard, engaged in a marathon pool tournament downstairs in the Strawberry kitchen/TV/recreation area, were asking themselves:

'What are them potheads up to now? You go and have a look.'

'Best of three?'

The loser of a game would have to venture upstairs and report back.

'Still doing the toms, Rob.'

'We'll be here all night at this fuckin' rate.'

Perhaps the drugs didn't help shorten the process, but Martin was after something rare and elusive. Explaining what that thing might be was not his style. His approach went something like this . . .

'I know what it is I'm after and I'll let you know what it is when I hear it.'

Which was very helpful.

One strategy for dealing with this would be for someone to venture into the control room and say something like, 'Fucking hell, Martin, that sounds great! Don't go over that take. That's the one!'

Very occasionally it might work but Martin was singularly bloody-minded and could be very difficult to sway. Working with him was always an education, but at times it could feel more like a war of attrition.

'Transmission' was the first time we were unanimously unhappy with Martin's mix. Ian was especially displeased and for once Martin seemed to take our views onboard. I don't think he was satisfied with it either and he did a remix. This time with supervision.

I wasn't totally happy with what Martin did on 'Transmission'. His method of recording each drum separately gave him the ability to manipulate the sound easily, to the extent that he could change the pattern to something I wouldn't naturally have played. Sometimes it just felt or sounded wrong to me (I bet no one else has ever noticed or cared). But the piano bashing kind of made up for it.

Despite this I got on well with Martin and I respected his judgement and ability. He liked Todd Rundgren's stuff, admired the production on Love's *Forever Changes* and being a fan of electronic music generally meant that, to me, he was an OK guy at heart. He was scientific and very well informed about what was happening in the world of technology, particularly in regard to how it might be useful for the jobbing musician/producer in making innovative and different-sounding music. In many ways Martin reminded me of two of my musical heroes: Joe Meek and Conny Plank.

One weekend, Martin invited me down to Strawberry to do some drums on John Cooper Clarke's next single, 'Gimmix'. I'd become used to working with him and Chris Nagle, and expected the process would be pretty similar. But playing without the rest of Joy Division felt like being a fish out of water. Drumming along to something that wasn't the product of the four of us felt odd, a bit alien somehow. Instead of someone nipping out for chips at lunchtime, Suzanne, Martin's partner, arrived with a buffet selection of wine and cheese. It was far more civilised than I was used to and that made me feel even more uncomfortable.

It was the usual drumming in sections/one drum at a time routine that we'd been doing with Joy Division but Martin's dub-style bass playing took some getting used to. It turned out OK, but it was a bit heavy going. I didn't really enjoy the experience at all, but I learned one thing: I would never be a session drummer. My session fee (Musicians' Union rates) went straight to Rob and into the band kitty. But I came away from the experience with a much greater appreciation of what I had with Hooky, Ian and Bernard.

To say *Unknown Pleasures* was a success is a bit of an understatement. It was released on Factory in June 1979 and, like some indie *Dark Side of the Moon*, it took up residence in the Independent chart and stubbornly refused to budge. (Look how seriously the biz were taking this indie thing – its own chart. You can tell you've made it when you get your very own chart.) 'Transmission', released in October, in its turn helped keep the album from being displaced from the Indie top ten. As a bite-size introduction to Joy Division it was perfect.

These were the days when indie actually meant something. The chart was for independent labels only – technically, anyone not distributed by the majors, though stealth and guile were already seeing them turn up in disguise. 'Independent-sounding' labels owned by a major but not distributed by it – cake and eat it anyone?

The success of *Unknown Pleasures* was of course good news for Tony and Alan. Factory was soon the coolest label on the independent block. It had class, style and Tony's unshakeable self-confidence.

Fast forward to October 1979 and we were back in Cargo in Rochdale to record 'Atmosphere' and 'Dead Souls' – our two newest songs. If the Factory Sampler had been the bridge between *An Ideal for Living* and *Unknown Pleasures* then 'Atmosphere' did a similar job leading up to *Closer*.

While we were in Cargo, we decided to record the old fave 'Ice Age' as well, for possible inclusion on a Futurama festival tie-in compilation album. One thing these three songs had in common was they all featured lots of drums. Yippee, great for me! Hours of drum sound-checking with Martin.

Back in a 16-track studio instead of Strawberry's 24-track meant fewer studio compilications than on *Unknown Pleasures*. Cargo more than made up for this with its fantastic-sounding tape machine – a Valve 2-inch 16-track. A big, punchy sound, especially on drums. The songs were the most accomplished and sophisticated yet. 'Atmosphere', the most keyboard-based song to date, was also the most spine-tinglingly beautiful.

The three tracks were recorded more conventionally than most of *Unknown Pleasures* with all of us playing together in a room, as opposed to the bits-and-pieces approach. Most likely to save time more than any other reason. It was never going to be that easy, was it?

Martin's latest painful innovation was to try to get me to play to a click from an old-fashioned piano-lesson metronome. This worked fine when I was playing on my own, but by the time everyone else came in, the click became inaudible no matter how much Hannett cranked up the volume. It was swamped by the bass, and it became impossible to keep time to. The click idea soon got dumped – around take three, I think. To compensate for this, Martin came up with an experiment using the AMS: a cascading delay, pitch-shift effect. A very short metallic sound was processed, its pitch getting shifted down a semitone, slightly delayed, then fed back in again, and the whole process repeated itself over and over again. Until the signal decayed into silence.

I had the chime off a broken tambourine perched on a scissor blade held very close to a microphone: softly pinging the chime produced the shimmering icy bell effect for the chorus on 'Atmosphere'. I've seen 'the chimes used by Joy Division on their track "Atmosphere"' for sale on eBay a few times and more lately in musical car-boot sales. It's hilarious. It would have been so much simpler to use good old-fashioned metal and wood, but that was no fun for Martin. Much more satisfying to get the ham-fisted drummer to delicately ping a precariously balanced tiny chime for a few hours and let digital technology do the rest.

Another trainspotter fact about the writing of 'Atmosphere': it was one of those 'we've got a new (well new to us) bit of gear, let's write something with it' songs. In the case of 'Atmosphere', this was another keyboard: it was a Woolworth's Winfield brown Bakelite plastic reed organ. It featured chord buttons: press a button to play a chord. Beautifully simple. It had a lovely mournful tone that gave the mood of the track. On the record, it's the thing that does the melody line. We used to do the whole song with it live, until it got dropped and shattered into a thousand pieces. The fragility of Bakelite. Strangely, despite scouring eBay and musical flea markets, I've never been able to find another one exactly the same. Its finest hour was on a very early version of 'Atmosphere' when the song was still called 'Chance'.

Eventually, the Woolie's organ was permanently replaced by the ARP Omni-2 synth. This would feature on several of the next batch of songs we wrote that ended up on *Closer*; 'Heart and Soul', 'Isolation' and 'Decades', plus 'Love Will Tear Us Apart'. Bernard even tried coaxing Ian into playing the Omni on one of these. But as ever Ian was reluctant, claiming the synth never worked whenever he went near it.

In more musical experimentalism, Hooky bought a six-string bass. On the strength that it was two strings better than a regular bass, I guess. Hooky used this to play increasingly more melodic parts instead of the traditional rhythmic bass riff, the drums taking up any slack in the rhythm department.

Infact, Joy Division have just recorded a single for the French "Sordide Sentimentale"lable. It features Bernards synthesizer on a very moody song called "Atmosphere". According to their manager and hairdresser, Rob Gretton ("It's going into the realms of stupidity, in my opinion!"- Stephen Morris) It's probably one of the best things they've put on vinyl.
Rob has hopes of getting the band into the studio soon to cut the second album, but before that, they have dates in Holland, Belgium Germany and tentively, America. People are beginning to take notice.
The Ayatollah of Factory Records, Tony "Whizz-Kid" Wilson, seems keen to get them on a British College Tour. He thinks the intellectuals will love them. This may not be for sometime though, since they have just completedan exhausting British tour as special guests of the Buzzcocks. Audience reactions were mixed, but never hostile. On the last night of the tour, they perprtrated an act which showed them to be rather less solemn and intense than others might have us believe. I trust that the Buzzcocks found the White Mice good company on the return treck to manchester!
The band have suffered from too much Hot and Cold publicity in the past. It's time that they were acknowledged as being in the vanguard of British new age bands.
Perhaps for the commercially-minded hypocrites of the "Pop" press, Joy Division are indeed emotionally a scapegoat.

1979 fanzine. A scapegoat?

The tracks we recorded at Cargo were a more accurate representation of how the songs sounded live. We were all happy and the production moans were non-existent. Almost ... as time went on I learned that the chances of everybody being universally happy about something in a band were pretty much zero. Compromise meant give and take; it all depended on how much you were prepared to give to keep the wagon rolling.

That these tracks were recorded almost for the hell of it and not with any specific release in mind says something about the creative freedom we had with Factory. I say 'almost for the hell of it', though

I do suspect there was an inkling that 'Atmosphere' would make a great follow-up to 'Transmission'. Just the vaguest of inklings, mind.

'Atmosphere' and 'Dead Souls' were released in March 1980 by Jean-Pierre Turmel's French label Sordide Sentimental rather than Factory. Our non-deal with Factory meant that we were free to do this. Ian was keen on Sordide Sentimental, who did what amounted to limited-edition art pieces rather than commercial releases. He'd come across them through a Throbbing Gristle single, which Jean-Pierre had released six months earlier.

By the end of the seventies, the concept of the extended 12-inch single mix was becoming a popular item. The first 12-inch single I'd come across had been in 1976. Oddly it was a version of 'Substitute' by the Who, of all things. It was no longer than the 7-inch but it was a lot louder and punchier-sounding. The extra groove thickness saw to that. But it was in disco that the 12-inch found its natural habitat, Donna Summer's extended 'I Feel Love' being the prime example.

I think it was the 12-inch of Blondie's 'Heart of Glass' that was responsible for the idea that we should try and do an extended version of a track. Maybe it was just to try and beef up the sound of something that we felt sounded particularly weedy on *Unknown Pleasures* or, more likely, because it was something that Rob liked the idea of doing. Either way, we ended up reworking 'She's Lost Control' with the idea that it should be longer, louder and more percussive.

Rather than take what had already been recorded and add to it, we started again from scratch. This began with building the toughest drum sound I could come up with using real drums augmented by the Synare 3 and the SDS4 (Simmons Drum Synthesiser 4). I knew by now what to expect from Martin and could play the drum parts in sections with a lot more confidence and conviction than I had on *Unknown Pleasures*. All was going swimmingly when an aerosol of tape-head cleaner caught Martin's eye. A couple of playful squirts and a manic Hannett cackle later convinced the producer he had found the missing percussive element that the track was crying out for.

Let the drummer torture commence. There had to be some, didn't there? I was not getting away with it that easily. Martin's idea was to augment the white noise chi-chi parts with the aerosol squirts.

'S'gonna add a bit more top-end fizz,' he said enthusiastically.

Chris set up a mic in the small wood-and-glass vocal booth and shut me in there.

'Give us a few squirts for level' was the slightly surreal request I heard in my headphones.

I commenced to squirt the aerosol of Isopropyl Alcohol in time with the track. I don't know what unnatural spirit of optimism led me to believe this might be a quick job. It was probably that same gung-ho spirit that had led me to neglect the safety warnings that the can carried.

There were two main ones: 'Always use in a well-ventilated area' and 'DANGER HIGHLY INFLAMMABLE'.

The small stylised rendering of a blaze was a bit of a giveaway. But in my keenness to get on I was oblivious to even this.

Instead I chi-chi'ed away like a squirting fool as my completely unventilated confined space began to fill with the ever-so-slightly-toxic fumes. I put the buzzy headache and blurred vision down to some unforeseen side effects of the last joint, like you do. But by the end of take four and aerosol number two, things were looking distinctly weird. But we had got to the end.

Thank fuck for that, I thought, taking off the headphones and pull-ing out a reinvigorating cigarette and . . .

Luckily Rob had pinched my lighter and was too lazy to come into the booth to give it back. It was only as I stepped out into the fresh blast of air-conditioned chill that I realised that my tiny room was now a highly explosive, haze-filled chamber. One match and ka-boom, another exploding drummer like something straight out of *Spinal Tap*.

This session was also part of the quest for the perfect recording of 'Love Will Tear Us Apart'. The song was nearly six months old, and this was our third go at recording it. One John Peel session and one session in Pennine, which Martin didn't feel was an adequately-equipped studio for the job. Third time lucky you might think. But no . . . as was becoming traditional, Martin liked to mess with singles and their rhythm tracks. This one would continue until the end of the month: at the time, the longest we'd spent on one track.

23

MUSIC ON THE MOVE

One of the downsides of the job multi-tasking was that I found I had less and less time to actually listen to music. When I did, it was usually a crackly late-night John Peel show on the Cortina's ailing radio. What I needed was some proper In-Car Entertainment. Hilary, one of the girls at work, was getting rid of her lovely beige Ford Capri and though there was no way I could afford the motor, I made her an offer on her Capri's Motorola cassette player and speakers. This was snazzily mounted on the Capri's transmission tunnel between the two front seats. I assumed that it would fit perfectly into the Cortina. They're both Fords aren't they? I was over-optimistic. Yet again.

After a bit of struggling, first of all with some gaffer tape, scissors and screws, I finally managed to instal this not quite hi-fi into my vehicle: I managed to hold it in place with some badly knotted fishing line, which was fine so long as I kept my elbow on the cassette player. To achieve this, I cornered gently and didn't change gear too often. A small price to pay on top of the £12 I'd managed to haggle Hilary down to.

Music on the move, you can't beat it. I copied my current fave albums onto tape and hit the road.

Ian was impressed – he was easily impressed by technology. Once I had explained that it was now his job to keep his elbow firmly pressed on the unit when cornering or shifting gear, we were off.

The rest of Joy Division for some reason found my new music system hilarious. Maybe it was the underwhelmingly quiet, muffly sound that the Motorola produced.

'I've not figured out how to turn the Dolby off' was my excuse.

They also found my selection of cassettes tortuous listening. I know Amon Düül 2 are a bit of an acquired taste and the Doors live at the Matrix bootleg had a bit of an iffy sound, but come on, it was classic stuff. Despite this, my suggestion that we should have some music on to speed our journey generally produced howls of derision from the back-seat drivers. Cassettes were frequently flung out of the window in disgust.

Philistines, I thought.

The unit only caught fire once, just off the Bayswater Road in London. A cloud of acrid smoke poured out of the windows, and was eventually extinguished with a handy tin of Coca-Cola.

The Motorola's precarious existence came to an abrupt and mysterious end on the night of 3 October 1979. A night in Leeds that's best forgotten. It wasn't our gig at the university that was bad. No, that was a fine performance. But what transpired in the show's aftermath was an unspeakably shameful study in depravity. So I'm not going speak of it. Just the thought of it makes me shudder. Just forget I mentioned it.

Well, since you insist.

The night in question ended with Me, Bernard, Ian, Twinny and Dave finishing off the last of the pale ale in some poor unfortunate's hotel room. With nothing else to entertain us a game of forfeits was suggested. It was probably a mistake to allow Ian and Bernard to define exactly what these forfeits should be. Suffice to say they were for the the most part scatological in nature. The top prize being the taking of a dump out of the hotel window. I'm not entirely sure what happened after that but things certainly went downhill. The next morning I awoke with a sore head and several gaps in my memory to find that the Cortina, which had been parked outside, was covered in . . . er, footprints and my prized hi-fi had disappeared – see I said it was mysterious. It's fair to say the night ended as a blur but no one ever owned up to the theft. I still have my suspicions.

Playing gigs usually meant skiving off work, and picking up Ian, Rob and Bernard, then meeting up with Hooky and the Transit before actually hitting the road to the night's venue in a Hooky-led convoy. This was all pretty exciting, setting off on a lad's trip out to new and uncharted territory. Most of the venues weren't that great but the gigs themselves were always exciting and cathartic. We would feed off each other's playing and energy. After the euphoria of the gig would be the comedown of packing up the gear and loading up the van. It was Hooky, Terry, our roadie Twinny and me that usually did that. Then autopiloting the car back down between the strobing orange lights and white lines of the motorway, struggling to stay awake while, despite my lousy driving, my passengers snoozed. The odd line of speed helped keep my eyes on the road but it could be unpredictable and jittery.

Then dropping everyone off home in reverse order before finally hitting the pillow in Macclesfield for an hour or two, then up and back to work. The up of the music always beat the down of the ferrying around though – every time. Doing one-offs here and there was the only way we could play and keep the day jobs going at the same time.

The long drive back up the M1/M6 after a gig in London was always the hardest slog. There always seemed to be some unexpected hazard lurking. The drive home from the Nashville Room in west London on 13 August 1979 was (after Ian's seizure returning from the Hope and Anchor) the most potentially catastrophic.

Coming out of a long section of roadworks on the M1, an articulated lorry bulldozed into the back of Hooky's Transit, pushing it into a spin and ripping open the rear doors in the process. Gear and drums poured out in slow motion, bouncing over the central crash barrier, before rolling off down the opposite carriageway.

I could never watch *Hell Drivers* in the same way again.

TW: WHAT'S HE DRIVING?! WHAT'S THAT?!

IC: Only cost him forty quid.

TW: Ha ha ha ha ha.

BS: The thing was, he sold it originally to the lad that he bought it off for three hundred and forty . . .

IC: And bought it back off him for forty.

TW: OUTRAGEOUS!!

RG: I didn't know it was him, then.

TW: It's incredible.

BS: But he wrote the van off. Did he not tell you?

TW: I've heard about the van, you know, after that gig at the Nashville, lorry went right through them.

MH: Really? When was this?

IC: Driving back up the M6 and this artic just ploughed into the back of the van.

MH: Yeah, so what happened to you?

BS: I was all right, I was in the car . . . ha ha.

RG: We were in the car behind, we were watching it.

Another trip to London, another disaster . . . Ever get the feeling someone's trying to tell you something? That Twinny (who normally slept with the gear in the back) was not killed was a miracle. The van was a write-off as was most of my drum kit. It could very easily have been a lot worse.

It was a very tight squeeze, sardine-packing everyone in the Cortina for the rest of the journey home.

*   *   *

The ramifications of this were that we were now vanless, a bit low on gear generally and I was totally drumless. The kit that I'd proudly built up and collected over the years was no more. There would be a long battle with the insurance company before we could expect to get any money from them . . . if we ever would.

Somehow I managed to persuade a bank to lend me some money. They were reluctant but by talking up my future financial prospects they agreed to a loan of £1200. A king's ransom!

With this, I bought myself a brand new black Rogers kit (I wasn't bothered who made the drums, so long as they were all black) from the London Drum Centre in Portobello Road. For the first time, all my drums were the same colour. They made their TV debut on *Something Else* on BBC2, 15 September 1979. It's imprinted on my mind, like remembering where you were when Kennedy was shot, only slightly more positive.

Rob persuaded me that some of the leftover cash would be best spent on flight cases. Nothing signifies a professional road-hardened rock-and-roll band more than a selection of heavy-duty trunks on wheels with the band's name stencilled prominently on the side. This was the first sign of what is known in the trade as THE BIG TIME.

That one of these cases would occasionally be pressed into service as a makeshift bobsleigh shows just how seriously we took these things. Our first proper flight case was a large blue chest on four sturdy wheels, its ample interior lined with a thick layer of protective foam. One particularly unproductive Sunday afternoon, we came up with the idea of converting it into a go-kart, presumably for a bet or dare. Ian got in the case wearing Bernard's gloves and crash helmet. This wasn't for protection from a crash: it was because he claimed to have a severe allergy to foam. We would lock him in the case like Harry Houdini while Terry and Hooky pushed it at speed down the steep staircase at T. J.'s rehearsal rooms. It was a Poundland version of Evel Knievel jumping the Grand Canyon. These were the lengths we would have to go to to get inspiration for some of our most sombre and profound works.

An undeniable fact of life and potential source of hazard and pleasure for any band is that sooner or later you will have to tour. Wave goodbye to one-off gigs and, for richer or poorer, hit the road for a lengthy spell of joined-up gigs.

It's widely documented that what can occur on these excursions can be somewhat bacchanalian in nature, and there are certain rites and traditions that must be observed. As a keen student of rock-and-roll behaviour, I had paid close attention to the lurid accounts put forward by Frank Zappa in the film *200 Motels* and album *Fillmore East – June 1971* describing the life of a band on the road. The touring exploits of the Who and Led Zeppelin were legendary. Hotel room wrecking, hotel towel stealing, hotel TV set destruction. Why did hotels even allow bands through the front door? They must have known what they were letting themselves in for.

These were the 1970s, remember that. In many respects, a completely different world to the one you're living in now. In others, exactly the same. Unfortunately.

TW: So what's the news? Any news?

RG: No, nothing I can think of . . . Oh, someone told me we might be going on Buzzcocks' tour with them.

TW: Oh yeah?

RG: Oh yeah! Not Pere Ubu!

TW: Pere Ubu cancelled out, have they? Cancelled out?

RG: Don't know. Well, they were still talking about it yesterday . . .

IC: Aren't Pere Ubu supposed to be doing?

TW: Buzzcocks' tour . . . mmm . . . You fancy Buzzcocks' tour?

RG: Don't know. It's the money involved . . . apparently. I

phoned Genetic up and asked them whether they had to put
any money into the tour. Which is bad news if you've got to
pay on to . . .

TW: That is bad news – to buy on to a Buzzcocks tour. I know.
That is one thing I used to get really angry with Magazine
about, the fact that on all their tours they used to put out, they
used to always have . . . they had Simple Minds and the Zones
on two tours . . . I mean, real Arista buy-ins, you know, and
Buzzcocks never used to do that. They used to put the Gang
of Four on, they used to do people like that, no buying on.

RG: I mean, I can't see why we should . . .

TW: Why you should . . .?

RG: Pay.

TW: Because other bands pay.

RG: Yeah, but we'd be pulling people where . . .

TW: Other bands wouldn't.

BS: But why should other bands pay?

RG: Because, a lot of them, it's a way . . . it's a quick route to
building an audience.

TW: Probably at some point back in about 1967, some record
company had a band they wanted to get somewhere that
were getting nowhere and they said, "Hey, can we go on your
tour?' and the guy said, 'No you're not good enough,' and
they said, 'I'll give you three thousand towards the costs,'
and the guy said, 'Yeah,' and the principle was established
and it's now the established thing.

The doorway to hideous excess creaked open a crack and we shoul-
dered our way through.

Richard Boon and Buzzcocks were very good to us, much better
than we were to them as it turned out. We got the support slot on
their UK tour promoting *A Different Kind of Tension*, Buzzcocks'

'difficult third album' and we gleefully ran amok in the metaphorical sweetshop.

There was never any question of buying on. We were there because Buzzcocks wanted us to be there.

We'd had a small taste of playing larger rock-circuit venues when we'd done a few gigs supporting John Cooper Clarke earlier in 1979. But this was a full tour. To do this would mean either an extended absence from the day job – potentially resulting in the sack – or take the plunge and say goodbye to life in the office. Which was what I did. I had a leaving do, a slice of cake, and was presented with a light-blue two-tone shirt instead of a gold clock. I did get to keep the car. It had become so unsafe and rancid that no one else wanted it.

We were now a full-time band though not necessarily what you would call professional in outlook. I know it's a hard line to swallow considering the sincere reverence with which Joy Division is held but, honestly, we were all fun seekers at heart.

The tour itself was a riot in nearly every sense of the word. The litany of carnage was fairly comprehensive. Breaking into hotel bars for extra late-night alcohol, the bizarre game of Forfeits that I still shudder to recollect, Bernard wearing beer-can shoes for a bet, the mysterious and to this day still unexplained disappearance of my much loved in-car entertainment system, someone generally sabotaging the car, piss-drinking bets, hurling eggs at Buzzcocks from a circling Ford, a plague of white mice and maggots, and, of course, drugs and booze.

Buzzcocks were great but I think I can say, in all modesty, we were totally brilliant (nearly) every night.

We were playing a mixture of *Unknown Pleasures* stuff as well as new songs that would end up on the next album. 'Twenty Four Hours' and 'Colony' went down particularly well, as did 'Love Will Tear Us Apart'.

Halfway through this tour (on 15–16 October 1979), Buzzcocks had a few days off but we obviously did not see the point of a day off, so we made our first trip abroad, to Brussels.

A few weeks earlier, after a gig in London, I think it was our second gig at the Nashville, a girl had approached Rob asking to do an interview with the band for a fanzine. Nothing unusual about that. That she was from Belgium was a little bit novel though. We were spending the nights after gigs in London at the Walthamstow house that Dave Pils, our drum roadie, shared with Jasmine Hooper, who ran the local youth club. It was there that we agreed to do the interview after the gig. The journalist's name was Annik Honoré.

Bernard and Ian had by this time become 'copping partners', the main question of the night being who would end up with Annik.

During the Buzzcocks tour one of the pair would sheepishly ask me if I could lend them the keys to the car on the pretext that they could get some, cough, 'badges' to hand out to fans. I didn't delve or point out that Rob had all the badges in his briefcase. Just blithely handed over the keys. The sexual potential of gigs seemingly increased in relation to the distance they were from Manchester. It also seemed to be linked to the widely held never-on-your-own-doorstep philosophy. Like much in life, there is a hierarchy that exists in bands. It may not have been there at the inception, but believe me it will develop like algae on a pond. As a rule of thumb, I have found this usually equates to the individual band member in question's proximity to the audience.

The hierarchy would be 1 – singer, 2 – guitarist, 3 – bass player, 4 – keyboard player (if any), and then a close tie between the drummer and the more visible members of the road crew. This hierarchy is perhaps driven by primal survival traits or the appearance of who looks the cleverest, but I'm sticking with the idea that sexual allure was relative simply to proximity to the audience.

Despite my fervent refusal to be educated as a teenager, there was one area of study that I did find fascinating. It was the widely regarded waste-of-time subject (now discarded) called Classical Studies. The Latin bit was pretty useless (it did come in handy when talking to Tony, who would come out with the odd Latin quote), but the Greek myths I thought extraordinarily interesting. They actually made sense, seemed symbolic of the way the world actually worked. I was fascinated with the *Odyssey* and the *Iliad*, and read and reread bits at home. It was the Trojan War that especially got to me. Specifically how that conflict began in the first place: a war over a woman or a war that originated with the disputed result of a beauty contest of the goddesses. The judgement of Paris lay at the root of it all. A cultural dilemma.

Annik was a well-educated woman. She worked at the Belgian Embassy in London and belonged to a world that, to a lad from Macc, seemed exotic and rare. She was cultured and intelligent. She and a friend were organising some events in Brussels and wondered if Joy Division would be interested in taking part.

A trip abroad? Why yes, of course. Travel broadens the mind. And we were an aspiring international band.

Annik appealed to Ian's intellectual streak. His artistic side. It is a pivotal event that occurs time and again in the history of nearly every band. The transition from lovable knock-about pop mop-tops to serious artists. It is closely related to that tragic condition more commonly known as taking yourself too seriously. It's a very, very fine line. But there's usually a golden apple in there somewhere.

We would be seeing more of Annik. That was a safe bet.

All that lay ahead. For now, the Belgium show filled a gap in the gig calendar. A trip to Brussels with Cabaret Voltaire.

We'd done many gigs with the Cabs and got on with them really well. Musically we seemed to complement each other. A night at Plan K, a disused sugar refinery on the appropriately named Rue de Manchester in Brussels, was agreed for 16 October 1979. A trip over the choppy sea to the heart of Belgium. Here, we would enter yet another stage of band development: the upstairs-downstairs (us-and-them) problem. Hierarchies again.

Over the years of my involvement with musicians I have often wondered if there wasn't something subconsciously or unconsciously at work. Some invisible force that influenced their behaviour and some-how shaped their personalities. A system or process that worked along similar lines to that of the astrological system of zodiac signs that infal-libly inform and influence the daily lives of the fanciful true believers.

There did seem to be certain personality traits that each member of the rock combo had in common with others of their ilk. But had these behaviours, which had been present since birth, somehow influenced the individual's choice of instrument and musical role? Or was it the other way round? Had the music in some way evolved their behaviour in some way?

Was it predetermined, some quirk of fate or just dumb luck that led bands and their members along such similar parallel paths? Is it the action of malign market forces or a shared stupidity? An undiscovered quantum force? It turns out there is a psychological concept of situationism – not to be confused with the politics/art of the similar-sounding Situationists – that investigates these processes.

Let's take the stereotypes of the Attractive One, the Moody One, the Mysterious One and the Wacky One. I reckon that roughly corresponds to the Fab Four and a fair quantity of other four-piece pop funsters including, to some slight degree, Joy Division.

Two rooms were booked at the YMCA in Brussels (we were still living the high life of rock superstars): a large brightly lit downstairs dorm sleeping six with all the charm of an intensive care ward, yet none of the facilities, and a much cosier upper room, more hotel-like, sleeping four. The more artistic members of the party – Cabaret Voltaire and Ian – took the upper berth; the louts – the rest of us – made do with the lower. A fine line and a slippery slope. A band somehow stops being a single unit. Distinctions and privileges begin to eat away.

The Plan K had something for all of us. Brion Gysin and William Burroughs set up their *Dreammachine* art object and were reading from their book *The Third Mind* in part of the venue. Ian famously asked Burroughs if he had any free copies of the book – in English – and got a predictable response. There was a pop-up cinema that attempted to show Jagger's movie *Performance*, but the projector kept stalling, and writer Kathy Acker was there somewhere – all very arty and 'interesting', but for those of less cerebral interests there were always the crates of Belgium's famous Duval beer, a novelty in which we predictably overindulged.

The Plan K was a great venue and a typically European art endeavour. Repurposing an otherwise decaying building and giving it a new life. Dark and cavernous, it was the sort of place I imagined hearing Krautrock bands such as Neu! or Cluster, so I was glad to play there. It was the polar opposite atmospherically to the traditional rock-circuit gigs we were doing on the Buzzcocks tour; these being for the most part either fading variety theatres or hastily camouflaged university recreation halls.

Two days later, we were back on the second leg of the Buzzcocks tour, charging from gig to gig in the slowly rotting car, our heads still spinning from the night before. Getting to that night's venue as the light began to fade, just in time to soundcheck. Since our previous London gig, we now entrusted the entire setting-up of our gear to Twinny and Dave Pils, our road crew. (After flight cases, having road-ies put the gear up for you is the hallmark of a truly dedicated combo.) Terry Mason had by now been permanently promoted to the front-of-house mixing desk, aided and abetted by Rob.

At first, I distrusted Twinny and Dave with my gear. I was used to setting up myself and letting someone else do the work seemed alien and to me unnecessary. I'd been denied Meccano as a child and saw this as my way of compensating. But it's one of the prime rules of rock so, with some misgivings, I bit my lip and reluctantly left them to it.

Drums are funny things in that they react to their environment in peculiar ways. I've found they need coaxing and tweaking and, failing that, hitting very hard, just to sound the same as they did the night before. It is a bit of a black art. I wasn't sure Dave and Twinny understood.

The daily drinking started around four. Usually pale ale. It was generally assumed that support bands who didn't have a rider were secretly craving India pale ale, preferably with an expired best-before date. An odd thing about the seventies was the popularity of home-brewed beer. A precursor to the boutique beer boom of today perhaps. Most of my friends had a white plastic bucket full of the stuff hiding in a cupboard at home. They would pass off its disgusting flavour as the authentic taste of real ale. None of us liked pale ale, but we drank it anyway. It was free. A bottle of pale ale, a bluey and a spliff, and I was set for the night.

It was winter, cold and dark. When I remember Joy Division gigs, it is always wet, freezing and poorly lit.

Ian's appreciation of Throbbing Gristle had grown into an exchange of letters with Genesis P-Orridge, and he still admired that band's uncompromising leftfield art noise approach. Something that he didn't talk about much with the rest of the band. I didn't blame him. It would inevitably result in a round of band piss-taking.

One night later on in the Buzzcocks tour, I think it was Guildford . . . 'Er, Rob, any chance you can put Throbbing Gristle on the guest list for tonight, please?'

Bored and feeling marooned in the fluorescent strip-lit dressing room before the gig, I rummaged through my bag and found an old bright red Frank Zappa T-shirt with hippie-style flared sleeves.

'What the fuck is that?'

I was not renowned for my fashion sense and even I knew this was a bit crap, but it was my last clean shirt.

'Fucking hell, Steve, yer not thinking of wearing that are you?' said Rob.

'Er, well actually . . .'

'Tenner!' said Bernard. 'I'll wear it for a tenner.'

'Fiver,' said Rob, always a betting man.

The idea of Bernard dressed in a vividly coloured hippie shirt amused us all, but Ian was absent from this bit of wardrobe-related bargaining. The bargaining continued getting progressively more outrageous until a compromise was reached. Bernard would go on wearing the shirt *and* a pair of crushed-up beer cans attached to his feet with string.

It's amazing the things that boredom transforms into the height of hilarity. Rob, Hooky and me were falling about in hysterics trying to devise a successful way of attaching the cans to Bernard's feet.

The door opened.

'The band are just in here, Genesis, would you like . . .'

'All right, Ian. Bernard's going on dressed like this for a tenner, what do you think?'

Ian did not see the funny side at all. Throbbing Gristle were not the sort of band who wore stupid T-shirts and had beer cans for shoes. Our antics embarrassed him in front of his new friend.

Of course Bernard welched on the bet, but Ian was still not amused.

In terms of his health, Ian, for the most part, coped with the tour pretty well but as it wore on the daily repetition of late nights and long drives took its toll. It was the same for all of us: the stag-party gang mentality will get you quite a long way in your twenties. These days, when I look back at the list of dates we did and the short amount of time we did them in, I am agog at the seeming logistic impossibilities of it all. I wonder, *How did we do all that?* I couldn't do it now. But time always takes its toll and towards the end of the tour Ian was having some terrible seizures. Bournemouth was particularly bad, ending in a trip to hospital. Before the onset of these, his mood would darken. He would become childishly argu-mentative and generally uncharacteristically unpleasant towards everyone. It's easy to think we should have spotted the signs in hind-sight, but in the there and then, it all just seemed part of tour fatigue. *Just keep going and it'll get better*, I thought, ever the unconvincing optimist.

The world of four lads on the road was only thinly connected to the 'real' world of home by payphones.

'Got to go, love, no more ch . . . beep, beep beep.'

This musical road movie was interrupted by the arrival of the Wives and Girlfriends for the two Buzzcocks' shows we did back in Manchester at the end of October.

When two worlds collide, it's rarely good. Playing in the vicinity of Manchester was an invitation to over-complication: never on your own doorstep, lad, not when it comes to sexual shenanigans.

A West End and BBC TV staple of the fifties and sixties was the series of Whitehall farces produced by the late great Brian Rix. Farces often start with a little lie, a little bit of deception, which snowballs into a convoluted tale of misadventure and misunderstanding, with the central character's fortunes consequently placed in increasing jeopardy, all to hilarious effect. Should there ever be a need to reboot the Whitehall farce, the band on tour playing a home gig would provide an excellent alternative situation.

For there in one corner of the Apollo dressing room was Debbie, and just over there in the other was Annik ...

This was the Saturday night, and the tiny dressing room was packed with the ever-expanding throng of well-wishers who provided just enough cover to prevent the two sides of Ian's life from colliding. I stood guard at the dressing-room door with Gillian and Julie trying to deter entry by offering prospective entrants free rides in a Tesco's shopping trolley I had recently commandeered. The gig itself had been a bit of a weird one; the stage at the Apollo felt enormous and I think we all felt disconnected from each other. That and the pressure that always accompanied the home town show made it all a bit nervy.

The second night was a more subdued affair: my birthday and by curious coincidence Bernard and Sue's first wedding anniversary. In what was now becoming some crap tradition I celebrated with Gillian in the Kentucky Fried Chicken on the way home. A 'Bargain Bucket' marking a step up from chips and gravy.

'I thought you were going to have a proper party this year.'

'Next year, definitely,' I promised and almost kept my word.

The Buzzcocks tour ended in November with two nights at London's Rainbow Theatre that culminated in an orgy of band japery involving mice, maggots and egg throwing. Several of these eggs fractured in the car, which was being used as a launch vehicle for our egg assault on Buzzcocks. The aroma of rotting, ground-in egg yolk lingered on . . . or it could have been the result of an earlier amyl nitrate spill-age, another story that's probably best forgotten.

By the end of the tour my trusty drum synth was beginning to give up the ghost. A couple of its knobs were hanging off and it was getting a bit crackly and unreliable. It had never really been the same after spending the night outside in the car park of the Bournemouth Winter Gardens. It began acting up shortly after that, possibly in protest.

It got replaced by the SDS4 that I used on the 12-inch reworking of 'She's Lost Control'. This was a two-channel drum synth, in some respects not as versatile as the Synare, but the range of frequencies, from below the range of human hearing to so high only bats could hear, was amazing. It did everything I needed. And didn't run off batteries.

If the Buzzcocks tour was us running amok in a sweetshop, Joy Division's European tour in January 1980 was a slog. Like Scott's visit to the Antarctic, it was cold and troubled.

The decade had not got off to the best of starts with a Factory New Year party-cum-gig at some place on Oldham Street that Tony had papered with old Durutti Column posters. It descended into a boozy chaos that, despite the odd fight and drunken fumbles, still felt like a non-event.

Surely this was going to be our decade, the one when it all came good.

'Joy Division – dance music for the eighties' was Martin Hannett's prediction.

Around the end of 1979, we had switched rehearsal rooms from T. J. Davidson's to a place that I think Hooky had found in Lower Broughton. It was adjacent to Pinky's Roller Disco and, as estate agents are prone to saying, 'afforded good views' of the swimmers in Broughton swimming baths across the street. This first-floor room we shared with A Certain Ratio.

We took the less gloomy half of the room nearest the greasy window, through which sunlight, never mind good views, struggled to penetrate. Fellow Factory workers, A Certain Ratio, managed by Tony and Alan, had the dingy bit to the rear. Downstairs, two ladies worked industriously on sewing machines manufacturing garments of some sort. On the floor above, other bands occasionally practised and, when they did, bits of the ceiling would fall down upon my head. By anybody standards of health and safety, it was a shithole. Even the mice looked disgruntled. It had an atmosphere of a building waiting to collapse, and made T. J.'s mill seem like a palace. On the plus side, our room was adjacent to the toilet. A big step up for us.

Starting off the new year with a trip to Europe in the depths of winter seemed like just the thing to escape this and further broaden the mind. Since *Unknown Pleasures*, things had been accelerating and the days of struggling to find a gig were long gone. There was always the next thing to move on to. Before we set off for our trip to Europe, Rob decided we needed smartening up. Apparently hairdressing was one of his many undiscovered talents and Rob took to administering 'tour haircuts' with a huge pair of rusty parcel scissors. Suffice to say our manager was no Mr Teasy-Weasy and we all ended up looking like we had recently escaped from some Siberian gulag. Only Ian was spared the shearing.

We were off into the wider world, this time in a minibus and a van, just like a proper rock band on the road. We shared the driving, though driving on the wrong side of the road didn't come naturally to me. It was Terry and Hooky who did the most mileage. It was gruelling – there was too much quality dope in Holland and it left me knackered. We hadn't been eating much either; the food we had was usually at the gigs and this was generally lentil casserole or stew involving beans of some sort. Holland, it turned out, was flat and vegetarian. The venues were mostly hippie-run large bars with a large live room for bands or a subsidised community arts place. There was nothing like this at home. We would unload our gear and the rattly PA we'd brought with us, set ourselves up, soundcheck, and then try and find some food that used to have a pulse, rather than being pulse based.

Then we'd do – for us – a long set of about fifteen or sixteen songs. Up until then our sets averaged ten songs at the most, but as this was our first headline tour, Rob wanted us to play a bit longer. I could see the point: if you were supposed to be a headline band then you couldn't really get away with forty-minute sets. We had enough songs, so why not play them? I don't think everyone agreed with this departure from the spirit of punk, but we compromised.

Amsterdam, January 1980.

We were sitting post-gig in the dressing room at the Paradiso in Amsterdam. Hooky and I were casually throwing small brown empty beer bottles onto the concrete floor. One after another, they smashed and tinkled. We laughed at the sound they made as they shattered. I'd been in the dope shop and had some Turkish hash and a couple of cookies. I was pretty spaced. It was Amsterdam, after all. We done the red-light district the night before. It had been a long day – no support band so we'd played two sets. Never let it be said that Joy Division weren't value for money.

Taking turns, we glugged down the tiny beers and hurled the empties as far as we could. It was a contest, but what the object was probably didn't matter. We were both pissed and pissed off.

'Fucking Dutch arty wankers!'

It wasn't the gig that annoyed – the gig had been great – it was the Dutch fan who appeared some time during the day and attached himself to Ian like a limpet.

'You are a big fan of Faulkner, yes?' It was less a question, more an instruction.

'Er, I've heard of him, of course,' Ian replied, not wishing to offend.

This delighted the Dutchman. 'I knew it, I knew it! I could tell from your words you are a fan of Faulkner. I have a gift for you,' he went on, and produced a dark T-shirt bearing the title of one of William Faulkner's better-known books.

'*The Sound and the Fury* – that is you! You are the sound and the fury, like him you are ...' By now the Dutchman's head was firmly stuck up Ian's arse. 'You are the great artist ...' etc., etc. He was convinced Ian was speaking directly to him through his lyrics, that Ian knew his innermost thoughts, they were kindred spirits. He would not let it go. Not even Rob's 'Oi you wanker, fuck off!' could deter him from his goal of ingratiation.

'This man is a genius and I have a gift for him. You must wear this shirt tonight for you are indeed the sound and the fury!'

'Like fuck he will! Fuck off, twatto.'

Ian's sycophantic new best pal was having none of it.

It was a recurring theme that people assume you are what you write about, what you sound like. That the impression your sound creates is a true reflection of your inner selves. This was, naturally enough, the assumption that most journalists had when they came to interview us. I say this because the Dutchman had most likely used the 'I'm a journalist here to interview the band' ruse to gain admission in the first place.

I could understand that – hadn't I done a similar thing myself with the *Record Mirror* job? If you can't be in a band, then write about being in a band – mythologise. Maybe that's what I'm doing now.

Things worked better when we allowed journalists time to hang around with us for a day and they realised we were, for most of the time, idiots.

Interviewers always had preconceptions, they arrived with them and more often than not they could not be dissuaded. That the rest of us might be clueless they could accept, but not the main man, not Ian.

Ian enjoyed the flattery. Let's face it, who doesn't like to hear themselves bigged up at some time or other? He defended the Dutchman, calling us bastards for taking against him so. The Dutchman smiled. He had won. He was vindicated. He'd known it from the start: he was in the presence of greatness.

Ian waltzed off with his new best chum and of course wore the shirt for the second set, most likely just to annoy Rob more than to display his literary prowess.

'Have you ever actually read anything by William Faulkner?' I asked Ian after the gig.

'No,' he replied, 'but I'll read some when I get home. That bloke made him sound really interesting.'

We both laughed and vented our collective spleen by breaking glass on the dressing room floor.

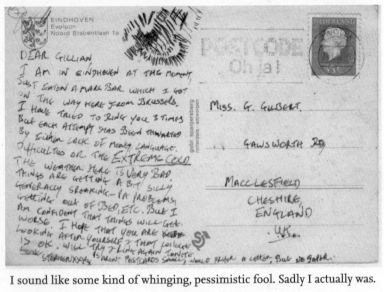

I sound like some kind of whinging, pessimistic fool. Sadly I actually was.

In an attempt to alleviate chemically the cold, hunger and tiredness, I tried to get hold of some speed, but all I could find was cocaine and that didn't interest me that much – too expensive. I had the odd line, of course, but it seemed like a lot of money for a numb nose and very little else. I couldn't see what was supposed to be so great about it. I asked every likely-looking individual but amphetamine sulphate was not popular in Holland. Dope yes, speed no. Rob had asked around. Terry, also pretty knackered, had asked around, but we'd all drawn a blank.

Things were about to change. When we got to Cologne (home of Can), Dave Pils appeared beaming shortly before we were supposed to go on at the Basement Club located underneath an old church. (I should point out that Dave Pils touched nothing stronger than lager, obviously.)

'Hey, Steve, I've gotcha some speed,' he said holding out his palm in which rested a tiny bright-red five-pointed star.

'What the fuck's that?' for it did look very unusual

'It's speed. I got it off a geezer at the door. He said its German speed.'

That was all the explanation I needed. I downed the tiny pill and immediately enquired, 'Do you reckon he's got any more?' as I thought one pill that size wouldn't do too much.

We always tried to play a different set every night. Generally the four of us and Rob would work out a set just before we were supposed to go on stage. By then we knew the songs inside out so it wasn't a problem which order we played them in. However, I didn't particularly look forward to the nights when 'Disorder' and 'Transmission' where played consecutively. Playing either of the two songs was tiring enough, but both played in quick succession was like running a one-minute mile. I'd feel like I was about to have a heart attack. I never did, obviously, but once you get an idea in your head that something is going to be difficult it becomes magnified. A worry, something to dread. That the hastily scribbled set in Cologne had these two songs next to each other might be pushing my overtired soul a bit, I thought. Some chemical assistance was required, sharpish. My need for speed had been urgent.

This was going to be another long set. Fifteen songs, over an hour, a marathon in those days. Ian never complained. He could see there was a point.

It was a great gig apart from an un-together ramshackle (and far too fast) version of 'She's Lost Control' in which everybody seemed to get lost (especially the drummer). The sound on stage was particularly bad. There were howls of feedback and complaints from Hooky and Ian to Terry, who was doing the mix.

'Turn the vocals up, Terry. Can't hear a thing.'

We did a high-energy, intense set. As usual, I did a lot of sweating but I wasn't feeling particularly chemically enlivened by the time we came off.

'Any more luck with the speed, Dave?' I asked, thinking of the next night and the next. 'This stuff's shit.' But no, he'd drawn a blank.

'Fucking German drugs are shit. You must need loads to do anything.'

Our accommodation for this tour had been hit and miss. Previously, in Antwerp, the promoter Raf first had us staying in a semi-derelict student hotel. It was only when we complained about the rats and the broken glass (not ours, honest) that he admitted it wasn't the sort of place he would stay in himself, and so we began a late-night tour of the city looking for a bed. Our search ended with a stay in a cosy brothel (the Boomerang – I've never been back). I bunked up with Bernard – well, I slept on the floor. I thought this safest.

'It's a good place this innit, Bernard? Not many hotels have this fancy UV lighting,' I said naively, checking for dandruff, 'or speakers under the bed, that's a nice touch.'

Trips to the toilet along the hall were . . . interesting.

Annik, a semi-permanent fixture on this tour, was disgusted at our eventual choice of lodgings. She would not countenance staying there and ended up being taken, along with a sheepish Ian, to the house of one of the promoter's friends.

'See you in the morning, you fucking lightweight.'

Rob tried to negotiate a nightly discount price with the lady in charge. The normal rate was by the hour.

That night in Cologne, two friends of the promoter were putting us up for the night. It was on the way to the digs where myself, Hooky and Bernard would be sleeping that I began to notice that something was slightly amiss. Out of nicotine, I'd persuaded our driver to stop at a cigarette machine, Ian and Rob having made off with the last of the fags and I always needed more.

Getting out of the van into the cold night air was an oddly slow-motion action. As I rummaged through my lint-lined pockets in search of what looked like German coinage, the glass-and-tin mechanical cigarette dispenser seemed to emit a strange blue glow that shimmered and vibrated gently under the Cologne streetlights. I found inserting the coins into the vending machine's slot produced a curiously melodic tinkle accompanied by a throbbing sensation in my temples and behind my eyeballs. I began to feel very weird. The sort of feeling you get just before you come down with a bad dose of flu, but a lot more heightened and colourful.

Our lodgings looked like a construction site. There seemed to be some odd structural renovation going on.

To break the ice, I tried asking one of our hosts why speed was so hard to come by in this country, and explained what I had recently ineffectually ingested, 'A little red speed star.'

He reminded me a lot of my old hippie friends, Dizz and Hobbo. He looked like he had more than a passing acquaintance with German drug culture. The joint he was rolling was a bit of a giveaway.

I took the spliff and began to notice that my new friend had an uncanny resemblance to the friendly gnome, Big Ears, Noddy's pal from the children's books by Enid Blyton. His ears were definitely getting bigger. Was his hair vibrating too?

It began to dawn on me what might be going on. Uh-oh.

'Oh ja, Red Star,' he said.

'Ja, Red Star speed,' I replied.

'Nein, das ist kein Speed. Ist . . .' Things in the room became a lot clearer and brighter. Vivid. 'Acid fünf.'

'Yes, it's usually quite fun, acid.' By now I was pleasantly confused by our conversation.

'Fünf!' he said, holding up his splayed hand, the internationally understood sign for five. Each finger left a vapour trail in its wake.

Now my German, what little I could recall from school, was not exactly the best in the world and my somewhat fuzzy mental state was not helping things. But somehow I managed to get the message that what I had swallowed was in fact five tabs of acid. Five microdots, all in one go, each point of the star being one hit.

Was I meant to have shared it with the rest of the band?

What a fucking dickhead. I'd spiked myself. This news amused Bernard and Hooky no end. Of all the people in all the world I would never pick to share a trip with, top of the list would be Bernard and Hooky.

'Oh fuck, this is going to be interesting.' For the last few years I'd avoided LSD or it had avoided me, so I was a little rusty. But I knew from previous experience that there was no predicting exactly how long a lysergic expedition would last. It could be a long time. A very long time. I tried to imagine that multiplied by the magic number five. It came out a squiggly zillion. I lit another awful-tasting, badly rolled joint in an attempt to calm my bubbling mental cauldron, and took another look at my surroundings, by now ablaze with electric-blue flickering vapour trails.

I began asking my German friend about indigenous German music (I tried to avoid using the term Krautrock). But despite looking the part, he had never heard of Amon Düül, Faust, Neu! or Cluster. He had maybe vaguely heard of Can, but that was about it. I was disappointed in our man from Cologne. I expected more than a very slight acquaintance with Holger Czukay.

He'd never heard 'German Overalls' by Peter Hammill either, the lyrics of which tell the possibly autobiographical tale of a band on tour in Germany undergoing some form of severe psychological and possibly psychedelic breakdown. I know it's depressing but I loved that song and the words were echoing around my head now with particular resonance.

I was sat at a table opposite my new German Gnome friend in a room with an unnaturally high ceiling. What had once been two storeys had been converted to one and a half. Half the upper floor had been removed, leaving only an elevated platform where the upper floor had once been. There was no way of accessing this mezzanine area except by means of a tall, spindly ladder propped against the wall.

I have mentioned my fear of heights, but did I mention ladders, particularly when tripping, as another phobia?

To make matters worse, or just plain weirder, Bernard and Hooky had started stripping off – this was the warmest place we'd been in all week – and were semi-nude as they gleefully chased each other around the room. To my dizzle-dazzle eyes, they looked exactly like Tweedle Dee and Tweedle Dum after falling down the rabbit hole of a Lindsay Anderson movie. This was not how I imagined the night ending up. Not in my worst nightmares. This was turning into one of them.

I tried asking our host if he had any orange juice. I remembered the old Tim Leary tale that the drinking of copious amounts of orange juice will help straighten out a bad trip. It is bollocks, by the way. He never mentioned orange cordial, anyway, and that was all my friend could find.

My bandmates reacted to my situation with a mix of hilarity and horror. Mostly hilarity. They must never have seen anyone on acid before and I began to feel like a zoo exhibit. Bernard was curious as to what might happen to someone who had taken five times the recommended dose of a powerful psychedelic drug – curious but not that concerned. Hooky was afraid in case I turned into a homicidal maniac or tried to peel my face off. Either way, to them it was a bit of a laugh.

I didn't particularly like their attitude to my plight but there was fuck all I could do about it. In fact, knowing their enjoyment of practical jokes, I began to feel ever so slightly paranoid about the whole affair.

Not good.

This unease intensified greatly when it was decided by Bernard that I should be 'sleeping' in the upper area of the room and should climb high up the spindly ladder to the heavens. I started to clamber up.

'Go on, Steve. It's not that high. You'll be all right. Won't he, Hooky?'

Hooky, from above, reassured me, 'Yeah, come on, nearly there,'

It was very hard to concentrate, even harder to move upwards. I'd heard of folk – mostly old wives – believing they could fly while undergoing an LSD experience, but not me. I still maintained my belief in the inexorability of gravity despite the electric storm raging in my brain.

My lack of faith in the trickster bastards proved justified for, upon reaching the summit and apparent safety, Bernard snatched the ladder away and gleefully ran off with it, leaving me trapped on the elevated platform for the rest of the night. With only Hooky and five tabs worth of hallucinations for company.

Fucking bastards, I thought, for Hooky must have been in on the jape. 'I'm going to fucking kill the pair of you!' I was not joking.

'Fucking go to sleep will you?' cried Bernard from below.

'Put the ladder back. What if I want a piss?' I tried to plead.

'Use a bottle. I'm not having you keeping me up all night,' said the ever-compassionate guitarist.

'Just go to sleep,' was Hooky's well-meant advice.

Easier said than done. I hoped that an overdose of LSD was unlikely to be fatal, but all the same, I didn't want to find out on a Tuesday night in the middle of Germany. My mind and my body began to separate.

I'd taken acid in some unusual places in my time, including one summer night spent in a cave on Alderley Edge. It was a Crowley-inspired experiment trying to summon some demon or other – don't ask. It was a foolish and crazy idea. I had in my younger days been given a good kicking by a band of angry young farmers while tripping, and that was a bundle of laughs compared to this. This elevated perch took the biscuit. The crème de la crème of nightmare scenarios.

It was my companions for the night as much as the precarious locality that made this one excruciatingly unpleasant hallucination. I began to feel annoyed first with everyone else and finally with myself. As the flashing technicolour hours wore on, I began to succumb to some sort of paranoid psychotic breakdown involving dark and murderous thoughts. That took days to wear off – if they ever entirely did. I do wonder sometimes.

To this day I still cannot completely forgive them. I spent the rest of the tour psychotically staring out of the minibus window planning the best way to extract my murderous revenge.

After a while, Rob did begin to get worried about my welfare but by then it was too late. I was as back to normal as I was going to get for a while.

The following night's gig in Rotterdam is one that I still have recurring dreams about. The fact that there was no stage gave the thing an odd feeling – we were level with the audience – and then, when we came out for the first song and I sat behind my drum kit, I knew at once that something else was wrong. It took me a while to work out exactly what it was: half of the drum kit was missing.

Dave had forgotten to set up my hi-hat and cymbals. I managed to attract his attention and, as the set wore on, Dave would scurry on and add another item until, by the third or fourth song, all was present and correct. I'm sure it all looked like part of the act, but to my still befuddled brain it was incomprehensible.

Two days and one Mars bar later, I was getting better but they were two of the longest days of my life.

Listening to the recordings of these gigs today, it's surprising that, despite the fact that we were all tired and I was extremely spaced, we were really tight and powerful. Even the Cologne gig, starting with 'Atmosphere' and ending with 'Atrocity Exhibition' is still electrifying. We had become by this time an incredible live band, unbeatable. It was hard to tell when we were doing it just how good we actually sounded. I can be immodest now because it's so long ago – it's another person, another time.

My reckless attitude to drugs, though, had once again got me in trouble. After the fistful of barbs incident of my younger days, you'd have thought I would have learned, if not a lesson, then at least something like caution. But no, I would still blithely swallow anything. I thought myself invincible, but now I know I was just lucky.

It would take me nearly thirty years to figure that one out.

Mars Attacks Eindhoven.

24

CLOSER

Closer as in 'nearer to' or Closer as in 'shut off from'?

It's the former, I think.

The way we went about making Joy Division's second album in March 1980 was a development and departure from the way we'd previously worked in the studio.

We wouldn't be recording at Stockport for a start. This time we were off down south to Pink Floyd's Britannia Row Studios in Islington for a couple of weeks. No dawn drives back to Macc. Martin was still producing but without his Strawberry sidekick Chris Nagle engineering. We rented two flats off Baker Street, figuring it would be cheaper than a hotel. These were divided up along the usual party lines: nice flat – Ian, Annik and Martin. Across the landing- Not-so-nice flat: Bernard, Hooky, Rob and me.

The songs written when we went into Britannia Row were 'Twenty Four Hours', 'Colony', 'Atrocity Exhibition', 'Passover', 'Heart and Soul' , 'Isolation', 'A Means to an End', and 'Love Will Tear Us Apart' (started in Pennine Studios in January 1980, and continued at the Strawberry 'She's Lost Control' session in March; Tony turned up with a Frank Sinatra LP for vocal inspiration – I don't think Ian had been a particularly avid fan of Frank until then).

We also had rough versions of 'The Eternal', (a new idea), an instrumental called 'Cross of Iron' by some (later retitled 'Incubation') and a vague idea that would eventually become 'Decades'.

'Written' is perhaps not a completely accurate description. Let's say for the most part they were pretty well shaped up and most had been played live to a greater or lesser extent.

They needed arranging, a few words needed writing, ooh and of course titles. 'Decades' laboured under the descriptive name of 'Europop'; to me it was always 'The Cinzano One'. Why? I have no idea. Maybe I thought it would make a good soundtrack to an aperitif TV ad.

My one abiding memory is of sitting on the sofa at the back of the control room at Britannia Row listening to the tracks as we were recording them, thinking for the first time that these were songs that people might dance to. OK, not all of them and certainly not in the slow, slow, quick-quick, slow style of dancing.

As I closed my eyes, I could see rows of demented sparkly Tiller Girls high-kicking away. Our music was danceable? It had never crossed my mind before, certainly *Unknown Pleasures* had never struck me in that way. The 12-inch 'She's Lost Control' remix maybe slightly – but this was different.

A terrifying thought: we were getting groovy. Blimey, was I turning into the thing I swore I would never be? Was I becoming a swinging, groovy drummer? And if I was, was it really such a terrible thing?

Was I becoming a proper musician?

Noooo! Best put a stop to that right now! No way, José.

As an antidote I got the drum synths out, put them through a Shin-ei fuzz pedal that had been lying around because nobody was interested in it, and came up with some frightening noises. This was Martin's sort of thing! Together we made the sound even more sonically malevolent.

'It sounds like Hendrix jamming in a slaughterhouse,' I observed and we gleefully cackled together. This became the ambience of

'Atrocity Exhibition'. 'If it's sounds too musical, fuck it up with a bunch of effects' became another motto.

Martin came up with the idea that we needed a drum machine, particularly for the song that would be 'Decades'. The acoustic drums I'd recorded weren't working for Martin and my synthesised percussion parts were better but not that great.

'Can't really see it with a bossa nova beat myself, Martin,' I whinged.

'Nah, get Gretton to get us a Roland Compu-Rhythm. S'programmable . . .'

Inspired by Martin's confidence – he was a sort of boffin after all and never wrong when it came to opinions on cutting-edge technology – Rob got the studio to hire in a Roland CR-78 rhythm machine.

Was I upset or offended at the idea that I might get replaced by a machine? At this point it was just another experiment and Joy Division were nothing if not game for an experiment.

The CR-78 turned up and sounded exactly like a drum machine ought to: tsk, tsk, chugga-chugga-bong, ping, you know the thing. Think 'Heart of Glass' or even 'In the Air Tonight'.

Just like my childhood organ beatbox experience, it had all those slick Reg Dixon home organ beats: waltz, samba, etc. Great in its own whimsical way, but somehow a little too jolly for what I thought we were after.

'It's programmable, Steve. You've just got to go off and learn how to program it.'

Following Martin's instruction I took the wooden cuboid and the thin but impenetrable 'manual' off into the Britannia Row live room for an afternoon and took up the challenge.

If you have ever tried to decipher a 1970s Roland manual you will know that these things were not well-crafted pieces of literature. Most of the text was in Japanese and the English translation seemed to be more phonetic than accurate. It was a little like some of the assembly instructions I had so cavalierly ignored in my model-making youth.

I soon mastered getting the thing to play its various beats, variations of beats and tones, etc., but when I hit the chapter entitled 'The Operation of the Programmer Section' I was stumped. To accomplish this, I finally worked out, I needed the 'TS-1 accessory manual switch (sold separately)'. There's always a fucking catch! It's usually 'Batteries not included'. While I was waiting for this elusive marvel to turn up from the hire company, I set about seeing what else the box could do.

Just lying around in the studio, there happened to be a beige-coloured synthesiser, an Oberheim Two Voice. Some Pink Floyd cast-off, I guessed. I wasn't then and to be perfectly honest I'm still not much of a keyboard player. I understand how synthesisers work and I love the sounds they make. But I'm no expert. But being inquisitive I like playing around with them and seeing what happens.

No one was looking so I switched it on and started knob twiddling and noise making. Following a diagram from the manual, I connected the drum box to the synth and pushed stop/start . . .

Fucking hell, it sounded brilliant! You could press keys on the synth and they would bubble away rhythmically in time with the drum box. It sounded fabulous. Then open and close the filter for dramatic effect. It was a eureka moment. It was that 'Heart of Glass'/Giorgio Moroder-type sound. The sort of sound that makes you think, *This'd make a good song.*

'Hey, listen to this!'

Bernard, with his own interest in synths, was impressed, very impressed. It wasn't really what 'Europop/Decades' was crying out for but, all the same, it was something that had potential. Martin came in and cackled.

'Have you figured it out yet?'

I had to admit that in all honesty I hadn't. But the five magic beans I'd picked up were pretty handy ones.

Even with the black rubber stub of the TS1 accessory switch eventually connected, the CR-78 stuck resolutely to its samba, mambo, cha-cha-cha repertoire. It could not be persuaded to stray. It would not bend to my will or even Martin's gift for charming recalcitrant technology. It was a dead loss on the programmability front, but it had provided an unforeseen insight into something though, so I could forgive its foibles.

'There's a new model coming out, maybe you should get that one instead,' was the Hannett consolation.

I most certainly would and I wouldn't let its manual beat me.

By this time everyone had cleared off to the pub or the chippy. Watching stoned men wrestle with technology is pretty much guaranteed to do that. It's enough to make you cry with boredom.

Out came the big time-wasting guns – Martin got the ARP sequencer he'd brought down with him and had stashed behind the mixing desk, and we hooked it up to my SDS4 drum synth, stuck it through some delays and off we went, jamming away in the spirit of Kraftwerk. We knocked up the rambling electronic jam that became 'As You Said', almost universally acclaimed as 'the worst Joy Division song ever', an accolade indeed.

Synths were a much bigger part of *Closer* than *Unknown Pleasures*. I could go on about the joys of the ARP Omni-2 we'd bought around the time we recorded 'Atmosphere', but you would soon stop reading so I'll confine myself to this list. The Omni was:

- Polyphonic – you could play more than one note at a time, i.e. chords;
- A synth that made lovely ethereal string-type sounds;
- A cool bass synth;
- An OK polysynth – bit nerdy that, sorry;
- Used on *Low*, so was obviously magnificent even to Ian.

I hope that didn't hurt too much, because there's one more list for the geeks: in electronic terms, by now we still had Bernard's Transcendent, the Omni-2, Martin's ARP 2600 with its sequencer, my SDS4 and trusty/rusty Synare, the AMS DMX 15-80, Martin's new toy the Marshall Time Modulator, and a Lexicon Prime Time. The music biz term for this would be a 'synth arsenal'. And Hooky still thought he was in a rock band. Hooky though wasn't entirely missing out on the sonic exploration front. He'd got the Shergold six-string bass; this along with an Electro-Harmonix Clone chorus pedal would became a key part of his and Joy Division's distinctive sound.

Bernard did all the keyboard playing. The piano riff that he came up with for 'The Eternal' was hauntingly brilliant. 'Heart and Soul' came out of Bernard playing a synth bass riff on the Omni, and was my first stab at a proper disco beat.

Ian still persevered in his battle with the Vox Phantom. On *Closer*, he played more guitar – 'Incubation' springs to mind – but in the studio it was often quicker for Bernard to play the parts. With Bernard playing synth on 'Heart and Soul' and 'Love Will Tear Us Apart', the shy strummer would have to get his guitar out more often – however awkward.

By Martin's standard there wasn't THAT much drummer torture going on at Britannia Row. I was getting used to it by now anyway. Knowing what to expect and when always dulls the pain. But Martin could always surprise. Throw the unexpected curve ball.

'Love Will Tear Us Apart' was an exquisite example of that. It was always the singles that Martin fucked about with most, agonised over.

We'd had a couple of attempts at recording LWTUA and Martin still disliked the beat I played, he wanted something more . . . Well, he wouldn't say exactly what and the whole thing once again became a bit of a tug-of-war, a guessing game.

'Bit simpler, Steve.'

'Too simple, Steve.'

'Almost.'

'Not quite.'

'Again . . . but not as . . .'

Again and again and again. The culmination of this ordeal was, when knackered and confused after days of trying every possible permutation of beats, I'd knocked off at the studio at around three a.m., driven all the way back to Baker Street, crawled into bed and finally laid my head on the pillow, when the phone rang . . . Bernard.

'Hi Steve, can you come back? Martin wants you to redo the snare drum again.'

I was furious but, being the soft git that I am, I obeyed, got dressed and drove back up to Islington. There I angrily, very, very angrily, took out my rage on the drums. To this day I cannot listen to 'Love Will Tear Us Apart' without re-experiencing the fury I felt pounding that poor snare drum to within an inch of its life.

'Fuck you, Hannett, you fucking bastard' is all I can hear. To say there is some tension on that recording is a masterstroke of understatement.

'Thanks, Steve,' he whined sarcastically in my headphones. 'Just once more.'

'Fuck you, you cunt,' I whined back.

This it seemed was exactly what Martin had been after.

Oh, how we laughed.

At some point during one of our many late-night attempts at improving the drumming on 'Love Will Tear Us Apart', the door buzzer went and the control room was invaded by a small group of young Irishmen. They sat courteously at the back and listened to the playback of the last take.

'I'm not sure entirely what it is you're doing, but it is very effective,' said one of the recent arrivals. Turned out they were a band called U2. Whatever happened to them?

Britannia Row, with its Lignacite brick-lined control room, was described by one of its owners – Pink Floyd's Roger Waters – as looking like a fucking prison. It did have a certain brutalist air and the bricks were a bit oppressive. You could see where the idea for *The Wall* came from. The studio equipment was all state of the art, though, and the big studio monitors sounded fantastic at maximum volume. A big plus was the plate of fresh sandwiches that greeted us every morning. Much more than we got in Stockport. The free use of Roger Waters's full-sized snooker table in the huge recreation room made Strawberry's coin-eating pool table look puny. Rob professed himself an expert snooker player and began to lose a fortune in marathon double-or-quits tournaments.

I had been a big fan of early Pink Floyd (well, everything up to *Dark Side of the Moon*). I loved their record sleeves – Hipgnosis's designs were always great works of art. Very clever and a big influence on my ideas of what an album cover should be. In retrospect, there would be a lot of similarities in the Floyd's career and our own: we would even copy some of their greatest mistakes. But that was way off in the future. For now I was happy listening to the house engineer Mike Johnson telling tales of Nick Mason's car collection and the band's ongoing studio battles.

At some point we took a few hours off from Britannia Row and went to visit Peter Saville to discuss ideas for the sleeve. This was the first time we'd done this. I'd only met Peter briefly once before as I was trying to herd the band into the car for the drive back from the Nashville. Peter had a neat and tidy minimal artist's studio/office. He'd found some photographs of funereal stone statues that looked very interesting – black and white, moody and evocative. We all agreed they looked pretty impressive and record-sleeve-like and that was the main thing. We marked the ones we liked best and that was that – sleeve done. Easy as that.

What kept me going through this period, which in hindsight must have been a bit gruelling at times, was the anticipation of the next gig, writing the next song, making the next record, the trip to the USA that glittered tantalizingly on the horizon. As long as the momentum is pushing you ever onwards and upwards, the vigour of youth and optimism will take care of the rest.

This new album was going to be 'the big one'. The songs were better, we were smarter musically and technically, and 'Love Will Tear Us Apart' was a great 'pop' single. Whatever 'pop' is – maybe it was the inclusion of the word 'Love' that made it more pop?

Despite his at times unconventional approach, we all respected and trusted Martin. There were the inevitable disagreements, good-natured for the most part, with Rob playing devil's advocate. Bernard and Hooky would get increasingly peeved as they both became more technically proficient – they were keen; they knew what they wanted; they had put up with Martin fucking up their sound on *Unknown Pleasures*; they didn't want the same thing to happen again.

Of course, it did. Everyone hated what Martin did with his mix of *Closer*. Even before he'd finished mixing it, we wanted him to do nearly all of it again.

Ian was particularly disappointed this time. 'It sounds shit, fucking shit.'

'It sounds like Genesis,' was Annik's verdict

Martin, of course, refused point blank to even think about remixing anything. To him it was perfect.

Ian even wrote a letter to Rob expressing his misgivings about the sound of the record. It can be best summed up in three words:

Total.

Fucking.

Disaster.

Rob,

Judged purely on my own terms, and not to be interpreted as an opinion or reflection of mass media or public taste but a criticism of my own esoteric and elitist mind of which the mysteries of life are very few and beside which the grace of God has deemed to indicate in a vision the true nature of all things, plus the fact that everyone else are a sneaky, japing load of tossers, I decree that this LP is a disaster.

I K Curtis

What glum folk we were – but we were never happier than when we were moaning, like all the best musicians. We were becoming pros in many ways.

In light of what followed, it took me a long time – several years – before I could listen to *Closer* objectively. That had little to do with the songs, the recording or the mix; it was all down to the feelings that hearing the songs would bring back. The emotions that, unless you were there living them, are impossible to imagine.

To me, at that time, it felt like the future was opening up; but I got the feeling that for Ian it may been the other way around. That his options were narrowing.

At the Baker Street flat Ian and Annik continued their relationship, which had built up through the Buzzcocks and European tours.

It was an odd thing. They behaved like an old couple. A pair that had been married for years. It was very 'proper' and not in the least about sex – we did tease Ian about Annik a lot. Particularly Hooky and Rob with their 'Fucking Yoko' jibes. Annik was some sort of cultural muse, and to her Rob and the rest of us were naughty boys who should know better – savages. She sought to improve Ian by introducing him to vegetarianism, which was hilarious for us to watch for we knew how much he loved the baby lamb from the kebab shop around the corner from our flat.

It was a prime example of Ian's trying-to-please-everybody act. It seemed to me his relationship with Annik was sometimes less the artist and his mistress and more some kind of mirror image of his home life with Debbie. Keeping both separate was getting more and more difficult and complicated for him as time went on.

People do like to talk about the time when there was an R & R Wives and Girlfriends weekend trip down to London during the recording of *Closer*. The story keeps getting dug up and with each telling I become more and more tardy and unreliable. I was meant to pick them all up from Euston, and according to one well-publicised account it was gone midnight when I turned up at the station. I could have sworn it was still light. Admittedly, I may have been a couple of hours late; anyway my name, as far as Gillian, Hooky's girlfriend Iris and Rob's partner Lesley were concerned, was something worse than mud. You'd think being a drummer I'd have had a better understanding of time and being in the right place and all that – certainly to collect Gillian, you'd think – but no. Still, I never said I was a proper taxi driver – even though I wouldn't have minded becoming one. I bet you meet lots of interesting people that way.

The rest of the girlfriend invasion weekend was another awkward version of a bedroom farce. Debbie wasn't there, but we still may have asked Annik to hide in the wardrobe. I can't be certain, but I'm sure we thought it. It was inevitable that eventually something was going to give.

Shortly before Ian and Debbie split and Ian moved out of Barton Street, he called me and said he wanted to leave the band. He was going to move away to Holland with Debbie and Natalie and open a bookshop. Start a new life. He told me it was what he really wanted to do.

'Well, if that's really what you want,' I said, 'then you should do it.'

'Yeah, I think I will.'

Thinking about it later, I got the feeling that he wanted me to say something different, more along the lines of 'No, please don't go, Ian. What about the band? What will we do without you?' But if you really don't want to do something and doing it only makes you unhappy, then really it's better that you stop doing it, whatever it is. Unhappiness in bands is insidious and contagious. But it's easy to talk about leaving, much harder actually to do.

Ian never mentioned this plan to another soul, not even to Debbie. I wonder what else he kept from others, and what he kept from me.

With the useless benefit of hindsight (yet again), I felt he didn't really know what he wanted to do. One minute he was talking about this bookshop. The next he was thinking of leaving Debbie and Natalie and getting divorced. The next he was thinking of ending his relationship with Annik. I get the feeling he wanted to be told what to do but that was never going to happen – he wouldn't listen anyway. It was the old catch-22.

I had a much simpler life.

No longer an office-based shirker, I'd found myself in the enviable situation of occasionally having spare time during the hours of daylight. Most of this I spent with Gillian. I would pick her up from Stockport college with a bulging folder of artwork stuck under her arm. We'd loiter in Disco One, my friend Simon's record shop on Mill Street, listening to music and playing on the Space Invaders machine he'd stuck in the corner. Gillian would tut and roll her eyes as I

CLOSER

scrounged another 10p from her in my futile pursuit of the high score. Macclesfield, in case you hadn't noticed, is not a town noted for the wide range of glamourous rock-and-roll-type diversions. The daytime licencing hours were strictly observed and the place still ground to a complete halt on Wednesday afternoons. Once the ten pences ran out, Gillian would attempt to introduce me to the thrills of doing the family shopping. I found I was still a natural at sulking.

Straight after we finished *Closer*, Tony had arranged a series of nights (2, 3 and 4 April 1980) at the Moonlight Club as Factory showcase events. Three gigs in a row straight after recording an album might not have been the best of ideas as we were all a bit jaded and Ian was especially worn out. But troopers that we were, we didn't want to let anyone down. Then an extra show – a benefit for the Strangler's Hugh Cornwell, who had been given a prison sentence for possession – got shoehorned on to the final night. Two shows in one day was asking for trouble.

At the Rainbow gig coming over all cross and rock-star grumpy, I half-heartedly tried trashing my drums, so half-heartedly that to the untrained eye nothing untoward appeared to have happened at all. During the set, an exhausted Ian suffered a really bad seizure. The audience, for the most part, didn't notice that either, thinking it was all part of act.

'Don't ever do that again,' was Rob's rebuke to my childish petulance. Whether he was criticising my gear trashing or just the way I went about it was unclear.

If I'd been smart I would have replied, 'No, Rob, I'm fucking not doing this again – ever! It's fucking madness.'

But I wasn't smart, I was tired and emotional. Ian was shattered. I loaded the gear up for the trip up the road to West Hampstead via Euston station.

In an attempt to make up for my girlfriend's weekend in London debacle, I'd invited Gillian down for the last of the Moonlight gigs and a generally Joy Division-themed fun weekend. Never let it be said that I didn't know how to show a girl a good time.

The band's embargo on female friends at away shows had gone out of the window in the light of Annik's continued presence over the last few months. It was all getting too much. Ian's seizure at the Rainbow was followed by a much more serious one later at the Moonlight.

'Joy Division convince me I could spit in the face of God' was the *NME*'s verdict on our performance that night.

Thank goodness we didn't have another gig the following night.

Oh hang on . . .

The next day, with Gillian squeezed onto the Cortina's back seat, we headed north to Malvern.

Despite near complete exhaustion and Ian's poor health, the set was extended by a two-band jamboree drum-a-thon. This was theoretically based around Section 25's single 'Girls Don't Count', which Rob and Ian had recently produced. At the end I felt a sense of euphoria. Fill up the car. We were going home – for a couple of days.

I couldn't really blame Rob or anyone for what was a very heavy workload. It was self-inflicted. We'd all agreed to it willingly. No one put a gun to our heads and said you will do four gigs at the Moonlight Club or else.

Like so many things, it sounded like a good idea at the time. It might even be fun, so why not? We were young. The madness of youth.

While we had been in the studio recording *Closer*, the idea came up that as we had two more songs than would fit on the album (these would eventually end up being 'Komakino' and 'Incubation'), why not put them on a separate disc to go with it? Not a single, just an additional disc of the extra tracks. Eventually this Britannia Row control-room discussion between Rob, Tony, Martin and myself had moved on to a social experiment to see if it was possible to actually give something away for nothing. We even decided to throw in 'As You Said' (aka 'The Worst Song Joy Division Ever Wrote'). We would do a flexidisc and just hand it out at record shops.

'This Is a Free Record' and 'This record should not have cost you anything, wherever or however obtained' would be printed on it so people wouldn't get ripped off by profiteers. *Brilliant*, I thought.

Of course, the profiteers won. It currently goes for up to £20 – so much for idealism. This is an early example of Factory's wilful economic perversity. They definitely lost money on that marketing experiment. There was a lesson there that I failed to pick up on. Some things you just can't give away, no matter how hard you try.

Maybe we should have done a limited edition run of four copies and charged a million pounds each. But sooner or later someone always finds a way to sell something old as though it is something shiny and new – they'd do another limited release but include a free T-shirt as well.

Cunning bastards.

25

A DAY AT THE MUSEUM

In Macclesfield's West Park Museum they've got a panda. They keep it near the dead. Not exactly adjacent but near enough.

They've got a mummy that never knew King Tutankhamun in a corner and some earthy fragments of turquoise jewellery in a glass cabinet along the wall.

There used to be a scold's bridle, an ancient rusty black metal and leather contraption that was used to forcibly silence troublesome women. It was kept on public display as a deterrent (until the PC mob got in and said it was too scary and violent).

Not far from there is a huge rough ball of rock that may have fallen from the sky.

Or been dropped off by a passing glacier.

Or lorry.

Three monolithic black fingers of stone stand uneasily next to the children's playground. Pagan relics displaced from the fifth century, they seem to be waiting to be moved on by an angry parent.

There used to be a Victorian bandstand but that fell into disrepair (along with Victorian bands) and has now been replaced by a skateboard area. And there's a finely manicured bowling green.

They've got some weird ideas in this town. A triangular park hemmed in with hospitals on two sides and a cemetery on the other.

Putting a panda midway between the sick and the dead – a peculiar bit of planning.

When I was an energetic young boy I would run up and down a muddy patch of grass between two trees chasing a ball. I was not alone. I was in a pack of would-be Charltons and Moores shrieking, 'To me! To me! Centre it!' and very occasionally 'GOOOOAAAAALLL!'

When the rain got too much and the mud reached the top of our grey woollen socks, a whistle would blow and we would troop off to visit the panda on his plinth and the mummy in the corner until the sky cleared and we'd dried off.

It wasn't far, maybe 10 or 15 yards. Sometimes if the teacher (Mr Worthington) wasn't looking, one or two of us would sneak off for a piss in the bushes.

Once a year, when the sun shone, there would be a maypole and pairs of boys and girls would dance spirals around it to scratchy accordion tunes. Weaving the coloured ribbons in and out. Making patterns, folk dancing – the old ways, football and witchcraft – weird ideas.

A place where time seemed to misbehave or stop.

I think, *What better place to spend a few hours on a Sunday lunchtime?*

It's 18 May 1980. Another sunny day peeps beneath the orange window blind in my bedroom. Radio 1 for a wake-up call.

Coffee in the kitchen. Pick up the phone and call Gillian.

'Fancy a trip to the park? Just for a bit. Got to get back and get me packing finished. Or started. Those new trousers Rob got us are a bit on the long side. I got this tape stuff. I don't know what you're supposed to do with it though. Are you any good at turn-ups?'

Not the subtlest of hints.

'See you in a mo'.' Hang up the green telephone on the kitchen table, check coat pockets for cigarettes and matches and off into the sunshine to pick up Gillian.

Do they actually have No. 6 King Size in the States? I wonder. *Probably best to get a few extra packets and stock up just in case.*

Stop off at the newsagent's on the way

In New York, they're just going to bed after a Saturday night out. The listing for next week at Hurrah (the rock disco) is in the 'what's on' sections of the papers: 'Wed–Fri May 21–23 – Joy Division – Rough Trade recording artist from Manchester.'

That's where I'm heading to join the procession of UK new wave exports in what became known as the 'second British Invasion' as though someone was keeping some sort of a campaign tally.

I'm excited.

I wonder what the film will be on the plane. Will there even be a film?

How many people can you fit on a Pan-Am jumbo jet? Will we get to go in the upstairs bit? Wonder what's on American TV?

Rob went over to sort out the gigs a couple of weeks earlier. He's still complaining about the jet lag.

Wonder what that's like?

Should I take a bit of dope for when we get there or is that too risky? What's American dope like? How do you get it? Rob or Tony'll know.

Rob had taken us all spring shopping in Manchester on Friday. Buying us smart new clothes. I am shit at buying clothes. I never look any different, whatever I wear I always end up looking exactly the same. Plus I hate trying stuff on. I once tried on this second-hand black ex-Navy top in the underground market near the Arndale and couldn't get the bloody thing off again. God, that was embarrassing. Just paid for it.

'No, I'll keep it on, it's fine.'

It must have belonged to a tiny sailor, a midget submariner most likely. I wonder what became of him.

Rob thinks we're scruffy bastards and should take more care of our appearance.

Ian always does, he's good with clothes, Bernard's pretty good too. But me and Hooky – he despairs.

'S'not that bad for Steve, no fucker can see what he looks like anyway. But you should smarten yourself up a bit.'

Naturally Ian did best at the wardrobe shopping on Friday – carefully choosing, then getting indecisive over which items looked best on him, then talking Rob into getting him everything. I just grabbed a pair of baggy grey trousers as an afterthought so as not to be left out. They looked sort of all right but even I could tell they were too long. How do you fix that?

'Get Gillian to do it for you,' Rob advised.

'Good idea, fancy a pint?'

Then on Saturday – yesterday – back in Manchester again. Ian wanted to take stuff back from the shopping expedition, swap it for what he now thought he really wanted. He seemed a bit unsure generally. Not that this is unusual at the moment. In a bit of a quandary he is – a lot of one actually. Annik on one side, Debbie and

Natalie on the other. Us – the band – on one hand, being ill and tired on the other.

All those chickens coming home to roost all at the same time. What to do? Can it get any worse? Will it ever get any better? Weather the storm? We were often a bit comically depressed, you know, grim-up-north stoic young men.

It's all them other bastards' fault – if it wasn't for them ... That chip again – not fully paranoid but defensive in that little world of our own we shared together. A kind of glue you wouldn't understand and couldn't ever talk about or even mention. Trying to defeat the world and all the problems it gave us. If we just keep on playing, it'll all go away; do another gig. The hifalutin I'd taken to reading called it a 'belief system' or more aptly a 'reality tunnel', as if knowing what it's called helps.

So, indecisive Ian was in the Cortina on Oxford Road that Saturday, just in front of the BBC. Not gloomy though – never that gloomy to me.

'Drop us here, here's fine.'

Smiling as he got out of the car.

'Not going back to Macc then?'

'Might do later on.'

Since he and Debbie had split up, he'd been a bit 'no fixed abode'. He'd stayed with Tony and his wife, Lindsay, in Charlesworth and with Bernard for a bit. Then back to Debbie.

'OK, see you at the airport then,' I said. 'You want to try that Mexican over there on the corner. It's really good.'

'Oh yeah, might do that, bit peckish. See you tomorrow at the airport. Tara.'

And off he scampered across the road through the traffic.

I autopiloted the car back up the A34 in silence – radio's fucked again.

*   *   *

An ordinary run-of-the-mill, half-hearted Saturday night in Macc and I was back at home watching telly on my own. Waiting for the Herzog film on BBC2, 9 p.m. *Stroszek*, another weird movie from Werner Herzog – a favourite in the Joy Division Film Club. We like weird. That's what they called me at school, weirdo, so it's only natural that I should. The movie was about a German busker fleeing his home for a life in America and trying to understand and fit into an alien landscape. No big production numbers or bells and whistles. Just simple, witty, straight but weird and to the point. My eyes got a bit heavy halfway through but I managed to keep up with the subtitles. The ending was beautifully poetic, thought-provoking. My thoughts were definitely provoked.

So that was Saturday.

'Shit! Forgot to bring the trousers.'

'Never mind, you can always do it later. You've got loads of time.'

So off we trek, Gillian and me. I think of parking in the hospital car park but change my mind and cheekily park up right next to the museum with the clearly marked NO PARKING bays.

'It's Sunday, who's going to be bothered?'

We wander round the park. Watch old geezers rolling bowls on the green before dinner, try and find the plaque – I'm sure there used to be one – that explains how the giant boulder got there. We wonder what the three stone pillars are about and why they're positioned there.

'I used to play football here,' I say as we make our sunny way across the keep-off-the-grass verge back to the museum.

Ever had a song suddenly appear in your head for no reason? Well the Doors' 'The End' pops into my head and won't leave. It's had a whole new lease of life since *Apocalypse Now*, but there are no Huey helicopter gunships making their way across the valley from the cemetery. No burning trees. No grunts on patrol shout, 'Medic!' None of that.

I say to Gillian, 'Funny, "The End" just started playing in my head for no reason all. The intro and that and Jim singing "No safety or surprise."' (In the years to come, I'll find out that Debbie imagined hearing the same song earlier on the same day.)

'Mm, we're not going in the museum are we?'

'Why not? Go on, let's go and see the panda.'

And we do. First the mummy then the panda. It's as unaware as I am, but Jim keeps going on about friends and killers before dawn, over and over.

Just across the road from the museum is the mortuary, like it was planned alphabetically. Keep the Ms together.

I drop Gillian at hers and nip home for the troublesome trousers.

The green telephone on the kitchenette rings.

'Probably for me!'

It is for me. It's Hooky . . .

'It's Ian . . .' he says. 'He's done it again.'

From the way he says it, I can guess what 'it' is.

'No! He's not tried to top himself again has he?'

'No, he's done it . . .'

'What, he's had another go? An overdose or . . . where is he?'

'No, Steve, he's actually done it, he's gone . . . dead . . .'

'What? Are you sure? How do . . .'

'I've tried calling Rob. I don't know where he is.'

'Yes, best tell Rob.'

Numb shock. That feeling of no feeling of all, the feeling being sucked from you and being replaced by a fog of disbelief. Like getting punched in the face for no reason.

It must be a mistake. It has to be. What do we do now? It'll be a mistake. Only an attempt. Stupid, stupid bastard!

'I'll try and find him . . .' Hooky says.

I sit quietly blank for a while. There must be something I can do, something someone can do.

Rob'll ring up in a minute and say it's all been a mistake. He will, or Tony.

I put the phone down.

Pick it up again and call Gillian and try and recount what I've just heard, what may or may not have just happened.

She's shocked and confused and the chain letter of disbelief goes on.

I still think we'll be going to America, still think we'll be getting on that plane.

'But you can't, how can you?'

'Oh, it'll be all right.'

'No, it won't.'

Gillian is right, as usual.

This wasn't Ian's first attempt at meeting his maker. The previous one had been filed under the 'cry for help' heading. Highly strung, his illness and its heavy medication, his emotional predicament and exhaustion all likely suspects. Oh, and artistic temperament. With the lead singer CV comes the right to act the petulant child at a toy-hurling competition and take things to the extreme. Ian could at times get incandescent about minor things.

He'd taken an overdose at the start of April 1980. Just after the Rainbow, Moonlight endurance test. Maybe by accident, maybe not, the day before a gig at the Derby Hall, Bury. I remember a phone call from Rob saying Ian was in hospital getting checked over after trying to end his life.

'Well, I suppose the gig's off then,' I said logically enough, at the risk of stating the obvious.

'Oh no, I still think we should do it. I've got an idea . . .'

'What? He's just nearly killed himself and you think we should still do the gig? It's not that important – a gig in Bury. It's a fucking mad idea, Rob.'

'No, he wants to do it.'

It really was the maddest thing I'd ever heard. I know there was a sense of pride involved of the 'Joy Division don't cancel gigs even if the singer's dying' variety but, really, it was a recipe for disaster. It had BAD VIBES in block capitals all over it. Surely Rob or Tony or Alan would see that and postpone the gig for a bit.

No one likes letting people down, and going on and on about what a bad idea something is just gets you labelled as boring, negative or awkward. Usually getting a 'tut' accompanying the comment, 'Fucking musicians,' from Tony. No, nobody wants that, especially not when things are going a little bit (to put it mildly) 'off the rails'.

No, think positive, it'll be fine. So that's what we did – except I honestly reckon we all thought, *No, this is a really bad idea and sooner or later someone will actually say so but it's not going to be me.*

So you've got an emotional, frayed, ill, medicated, post-suicidal singer – what's going to make him feel better?

Why, doing a gig of course. What could possibly go wrong?

The good people of Bury had paid for a Joy Division gig. Most of the crowd would have seen us before and had a good idea what we looked like. There was no small print or announcement that the Joy Division that had come to watch might not be the full Joy Division. If there was, it was either very small or very quiet.

What they got was Bernard, Peter and myself doing Joy Division songs with Alan Hempsall from Crispy Ambulance doing the singing. A clearly not 100 per cent Ian came on for three songs. I think Section 25 did some too.

Now this was not what the audience wanted. They were upset and one or two cried deceit. This fire spread and turned to anger, to brawl and, with grim inevitability, to what we call a riot. There was damage to property and there was injury done to people – blood was spilt. No matter how Tony tried to dress it up in the aftermath as something that will go down well in Rock Folklore, like Lou Reed at the Free

Trade Hall – remember that? – there was no getting away from two
things. One, the entire thing had been a debacle/disaster, a fine example of the ill-conceived notion. Two, it went to show that the paying
customer was paying to see Ian first and foremost – the rest of us
now the support band and, though we didn't quite see it that way, I
suspect Ian did. He'd let the fans down. More responsibility. Another
thing to disturb the balance.

Debbie and Natalie – The Band

Annik – The Band

Epilepsy – The Band

Put it all together and he was trying to balance:

Life – The Band

And now it was him that the crowd wanted, not so much 'the band'.
It had been going that way for a bit, to be honest. It always does. The
band was no longer four people equally sharing the weight of expectation. Maybe he felt the responsibility for that side of the equation
was now resting on his shoulders.

Six weeks later he hanged himself. No 'cry for help' there then. No
accident. Part of me still thinks there was a bit of 'this'll show the
bastards' crazy petulance in there as well.

Within a week of his death the fables started. Singer found dead in
Manchester street, singer dies in heroin overdose. A variety of grisly
ends was sensationally reported in the column inches of the local
and national press. He was a singer – they got that right (not a genius
or poet yet) – and he was dead – also correct. As for the rest, you can't
libel the dead, so go to town.

I remember ranting down the pub about this media fest. 'I bet
some fucker's going to come and make a film about this – I'm not
having anything to do with that shit when it happens . . .' Well, I got
that bit wrong, didn't I? Sell-out that I am.

*   *   *

Later, we were near West Park in Macclesfield again, this time at the cemetery on the opposite side of the valley from the museum and its oddities. Rob and Tony had been to the undertakers to say their goodbyes the day before. I couldn't face it. I was still clinging on to the hope that this would all turn out to be a dream or a mistaken mix-up that would still somehow sort itself out and we would all have a laugh about it.

Ian was cremated less than a mile away from the panda. He was born, raised, educated and died in the town, so why wouldn't he be? He knew the stuffed bear well, everyone did. A memorial stone was laid in the cemetery. It said, 'Love Will Tear Us Apart'. Which was true.

But why did he do it? That's the riddle of suicide. Why choose death over life? Why throw it away? The dead feel no guilt – they don't feel at all, so maybe that's the attraction. An end to all ills, isn't that what they say? They leave the guilt for the living. The ones who have to live with the fact. Live with all the 'what ifs' and the 'if only I'd . . .' that would never leave, not truly. Always there in the dark, waiting to torture again, to lay the finger of blame.

I've had my share of black-dog days, weeks, months even, mostly when I was younger, in my teens or early twenties, buying in to that 'Hope I die before I get old . . .' and 'Five Years' and 'All the Young Dudes' and 'Rock and Roll Suicide'-ness, some sort of doomed glamour that's nice to wallow in for a bit – a comfy bed. But sooner or later you run out of others to lay the blame on and, in the end, it's just you on your very lonesome own and a choice that is starkly monochrome: this or that, black or blacker. Look enquiringly at sharp edges and little brown bottles and wonder.

Sometimes the black pit gets so deep there doesn't seem any way to claw out. To end the numbness. Feel something else.

Then get angry again – get angry with the world. The world can take it.

Suicide is generally a permanent solution to a temporary problem. It is overkill.

Over the years, as Joy Division grew from a reality to a myth and Ian became a legend, the cemetery near West Park became a Père Lachaise of the north-west, a place of pilgrimage. Fans would come and leave notes and cigs and lighters and other precious things as offerings like he was a latter-day saint. (He was a long way from that in reality but death works its magic.) He became a big draw, a reason to visit Macclesfield at last.

Then one day in the early twenty-first century, Ian's stone was stolen. Some people will stop at nothing. It no longer surprises me. The only surprise is that the police didn't think of pulling the panda in for questioning, for surely there was motive there. He was 'one of the largest ever killed'. He used to be the biggest thing in Macclesfield.

* * *

We went to the Factory office on Palatine Road, had a bit of a wake, watched *The Great Rock 'n' Roll Swindle* on VHS and said to each other, 'See you Monday?'

'Twelve o'clockish?'

'Yes, why not?'

What else were we going to do? The only thing we knew for sure was what we weren't going to do, and that was give up.

So I asked myself, what do we do now? Coming up with any sort of plan was a bit difficult, obviously. So it was easier to find a way through by saying what you were not.

Not Joy Division.

Not giving up being a band.

Not replacing Ian.

Not talking about the past.

I think of Joy Division as some sort of deep space rocket that escaped our gravitational pull with Ian's suicide.

I would think that such a catastrophic mechanical failure would be the end of the mission. That would be that and we could all go on to wherever the rest of our lives might lead. Death gets you like that: everything must stop. For that to happen, the past must stop too, but the recordings we made still remained, pressed on to inky black vinyl.

That's quite pretentious, but more pretentious would be 'You can kill the man, but you can't kill his work.' Which would make a tagline for something slouching out of Hollywood on a particularly off day.

So the space rocket Joy Division was off on its own, voyaging through the dark and lonely night, and we left it mostly to its own devices.

True, to tidy up – well, I thought we were tidying up – the end of Joy Division, we put a recording of our final gig at Birmingham and all the out-takes that we could find on a third LP, *Still*. We went in to Britannia

Row for a couple of days to fix up a couple of things, musically. *That*, I thought, *should be it. Close that door for there is no more to be had. No more extra tracks hidden away somewhere. No best-ofs, no special editions of* Closer *with extra tracks.* For me at that time, *Still* was a full stop. There was no more, and there never would be.

Finito.

Surely?

I spent the next few months going through the usual range of emotions – depression, anger, denial, resentment. Anger mostly. At one point, in a fit of petulance I started smashing up the furniture in my cupboard bedroom. Now I really was treating the place like a hotel – very rock and roll.

I got the old life-goes-on speech from my dad. You know, the one that begins, 'I'm very sorry about your friend, but . . .' I suspect he thought I'd be after my old job back in the none-too-distant future.

I told him to fuck off and went out on a drunken bender. The things we do.

I felt devastated. Yes, I felt sorry for what Ian must have been through, and I felt deeply sorry for what his family were still going through, but I felt sorry for me too. If I wasn't careful, I would end up wallowing and that wouldn't help anyone. Bands rarely survive the loss of their lead singer – that was something that I was reminded of on several occasions by Rob and Tony. But I'd spent all my time getting into a band. The thought never crossed my mind that it might one day come to an end.

Certainly not like this.

I listened to Suicide's second album and their single 'Dream Baby Dream', and went back to reading a lot of psycho-mystic books about conspiracies, anything to do with the occult, communicating with the dead, Colin Wilson's outsider stuff, Tarot cards, *I Ching* – the usual guff. This sounds like I was going through the seeking-enlightenment stage of rock stardom, which is a terrifying thought. Perhaps I was. If so, I never found it. But at the same time I began to get very interested in computers and how they might help the drummer. This would soon become an obsession with technology.

Everyone likes a doomed rock star and when it came out in June 'Love Will Tear Us Apart', a fittingly doom-sounding title, was what I believe they call a posthumous hit.

The video was scheduled to be on *Top of the Pops* and everything. But owing to a BBC technicians' strike, that particular edition of *TOTP* never got screened. Yet more evidence of our apparent curse and more fuel to the doom rep.

In fact, the video – our one and only attempt at a pop promo – was in itself a fiasco. We had filmed it back in April and had insisted that it should be a live recording of us playing the song in T. J.'s, our old rehearsal room. Owing to a disagreement with our regular PA company, the gear didn't turn up, so we had to rummage round Manchester to get a PA rig at short notice.

Then, of course, Ian took his exit from the world and shortly thereafter we realised that the vocals on the video were pretty badly recorded. In fact, the whole thing was. So Martin was co-opted into repairing this – a pretty difficult job even with today's digital equipment. Martin did his best, but it was not a great success. The overall effect was a bit like watching a badly dubbed spaghetti Western. I began to suspect that in a previous life I, or at least one of us, must have done some truly evil deeds. To compensate we developed an enhanced version of northern gallows humour. (We would take the piss out of ourselves and our situation by incorporating death into some of our future titles – 'Death Rattle', 'Little Dead'. The assumption that 'ICB' stood for 'Ian Curtis Burial', though, wasn't one I considered at the time; it stands for 'Int@@@@@ Co******* Ba9990112', obviously.)

Closer came out on 18 July 1980, two months after Ian's death, and was 'hotly anticipated' by the music press. It received great reviews.

Well, I was told they were great reviews. I could not make head nor tail of the ones I read. They seemed to be talking about a completely different band. They read like a eulogy for the most part and spoke with great reverence about something that to me was tragic, yes, but now just a fact of life. Something I had to live with.

The photograph we had picked for the sleeve seemed either like an eerie prophecy or some bad taste, cash-in joke. It'd been a good idea at the time but, after Ian died, became yet another of those awful coincidences. Who in their right mind would put a tomb on the front of an album by a band whose singer had just died?

Talk about unlucky curses.

I was getting used to them and numbly thought, *Oh fuck it, who cares?* There was nothing we could do except laugh bleakly. I did my best to avoid looking at the front cover, as if it would go away.

The way the press talked about Ian turned him into someone I didn't recognise. As time went on, I began to feel less and less sure that I had actually known him at all.

In the forty years that have passed since then, a mythology of Joy Division has only grown. A mythology fuelled by books, films and bands that have taken the music as a starting point for their own lives. I listen, watch and read them and with each passing year feel as though it all happened to someone else. The story becomes more and more dream-like. Less and less real. As though something has been altered over time, taken over and, a bit like a Burroughs cut-up, rearranged for dramatic effect. Leaving me curiously confused.

Ian has become a serious individual, his life a tragedy. There is some truth in this, of course. There always is some truth in every myth that ever was, that's why we like them, believe them, buy into them as talismans. But he wasn't only serious. His life wasn't just a tragedy.

Joy Division changed my life ... the songs we wrote together, the records we made in that all too brief span of time. That something we created has resonated with so many people over the years goes so far beyond anything I could ever have hoped to achieve.

Joy Division would turn into such a perfect story. It's perfect because Joy Division and Ian in particular would never age, would never go on to make all the mistakes that bands make eventually (we'd made all those earlier on anyway). We'd never make that so-so third or fourth album. Ian would never become a 'celebrity'. His words are there forever. He'll never let you down.

26

STARTING OVER

I bet you know what's coming next.

Yes, it's the bit where we become ... 'The band that raised itself from the ashes of Joy Division' ... as the overused cliché goes.

The only ashes I can honestly remember were the ones spilling out from the overflowing ashtray of my increasingly clapped-out, nicotine-stained, rotten-egg stinking and possibly haunted car.

I had this eerie feeling that Ian's spirit was still lingering in the back seat. An earthbound wraith refusing to accept the heavenly tobacconist's wares. I kept expecting a disembodied arm to reach round and offer me a phantom Marlboro, mostly when driving home alone, exhausted in the wee small hours.

A couple of red warning lights kept flickering on and off, which I took for further signs of possible communication from the other side, rather than the Cortina desperately trying to tell me that it needed urgent mechanical attention. I unwisely ignored its pleas. My mind was on other things, the future being the main one.

They say necessity is the mother of invention, or is that war or curiosity? Never sure about that one. Let's just say upheaval is the mother of invention then and move on.

A band losing its lead singer or frontman is certainly a fairly big upheaval, but nowhere near as tragic as losing a father or husband.

The three of us wanted to continue making music. There was

never any suggestion of giving up and returning to the day job. We all enjoyed making and playing music together too much to consider stopping now. On the other hand, solely playing instrumentals wasn't a secret ambition of ours.

Carrying on without Ian obviously meant something had to change. To continue as Joy Division Mk2 just felt wrong somehow. But to continue as what exactly? That was the question.

I and the rest of the world used to marvel at the way David Bowie 'reinvented' himself on each album and wondered how he managed to do it. How does anyone reinvent themselves?

'From today I will no longer play the drums, but will only play the sousaphone instead.'

Is that how it works?

Or

'You will henceforth refer to me only by my new name: Gregor Samsa the human cockroach.'

That all sounded a bit pretentious and contrived, if that's how you are supposed go about it. I am pretty sure it's not though.

You constantly change by small degrees, a little at a time. Different things interest you. And as time goes by, changes happen naturally. To stay the same is boring and boredom equals death.

There's that word again.

But here we were in a situation that required some sort of drastic change, sooner rather than later preferably.

Change is never enjoyable for me – for I love certainty and predictability – but sometimes it can't be helped. It's got to happen. If you're a little bit out of your depth and a tiny bit uncertain, sometimes – behind the fear and trepidation of getting it wrong – subconscious instinct kicks in. What's the worst that can happen? You fail. So what? And though it might not seem enjoyable at the time, something interesting usually happens, something that in the normal course of events would not have happened.

Technology, for me, was the catalyst for change. It helped me see the future beyond Joy Division. I began reading more magazines about home computers and homemade synths and sequencers. The articles might as well have had a byline of 'Written by nerds for nerds', but I read an article about Dave Simmons (the guy responsible for designing my SDS4) and found out that he was working on producing an entirely electronic drum kit. Now that sounded like something really interesting. That sounded like the future. Finally I would be able to fulfil my Kraftwerk drumming dreams.

But all this was shilly-shallying around. It was avoiding the huge elephant in the band. We had decided to keep the last two songs we had written with Ian as a kind of starter for ten, but there was a sense of awkwardness that plagued the early days of the band that wasn't Joy Division any longer but kind of was, a bit.

You know what's coming now, as well, don't you?

'What are we going to do about the singing?'

No, not that. Not yet. In the meantime, and more importantly, 'What the fuck are we going to call ourselves?'

We were back to writing band names on bits of paper and voting. I stuck 'The Witchdoctors of Zimbabwe' and 'The Sunshine Valley Dance Band' down for a bit of a laugh. Tony liked 'Stevie and the JDs', but it was Rob who'd clearly been thinking about this the most. He had a long list in his notebook: 'Black September', 'Mau Mau', 'The Immortals', 'Man Ray' . . .

We had a meeting in a pub (of course) and decided that we wanted something neutral-sounding for our new name. Something with no possible Nazi or political connections whatsoever.

Rob had been reading about murderous dictator Pol Pot. 'How about "Khmer Rouge" then?' he suggested. 'That's pretty neutral.'

'Fucking hell, Rob. No, it bloody isn't.'

We argued about that for a while, until, realising it was going nowhere, he said, 'All right, how about "The New Order of the Kampuchean Front" then?'

'Still a bit political.'

'Bit of a mouthful, isn't it?'

'All right, "The New Order" then?'

'"The New Order" is not bad.'

Somebody didn't like the 'The', so that got dropped and we ended up adopting the completely neutral-sounding name of 'New Order'. A name with absolutely no Nazi connotations whatsoever . . .

'Wasn't Pol Pot a Communist anyway?' asked Hooky.

I piped up with, 'Wasn't "The New Order" a MC5/Stooges splinter band?'

'Don't know, but Ian would've liked that anyway.'

That settled it.

We were now New Order.

27

NEW YORK NEW YORK

We kept the last two songs we'd written with Ian. 'Ceremony', which (in my opinion) had hit single pressed though it like Blackpool rock, was probably the only Joy Division song that I played repeatedly on cassette; I liked it that much. It was somehow uplifting and well ... up. And 'In a Lonely Place', the title of which came from a film poster pillaged from the Kant Kino gig in Berlin. It served as wallpaper at our rehearsal room. The large posters listed forthcoming attractions and became our main source of song titles ('Cries and Whispers' was another). 'In a Lonely Place' is an extremely dark song, as far from up as it's possible to get. Talk about chalk and cheese.

Still in summer of 1980 these emotionally polar opposite songs were our entire repertoire. They had the two essential ingredients – words and music.

We had problems with words.

We didn't have any.

We had none of Ian's lyric books. So in order to work out what exactly the words to 'Ceremony' and 'In a Lonely Place' were, we booked a day in a studio to try and decipher them from what tapes we had. It was grim. The closest thing I could imagine to a sonic autopsy. Listening to Ian's words so closely was like reading a suicide note over and over again. Rob wrote down our interpretations of the lyrics. We tried to laugh.

'Christ, he was a bit depressed, wasn't he?'

'No wonder he topped himself.'

There wasn't much to smile about really.

The first actual New Order song we wrote, if memory serves, was 'Dreams Never End', which Hooky wrote the lyrics for and sang. Shortly followed by 'Truth': an exercise in how to programme the newly acquired drum machine with me playing keyboards. I wasn't especially fazed or bothered by this. At the time it made sense. Someone had to play the keyboard and someone had to sing. None of us could do the two things simultaneously. If we were going to change and get anywhere there was little point in being precious about swapping instruments; something that had occasionally happened in Joy Division.

The main thing that changed was we began to write songs that worked as instrumentals, in the hope that if we stuck some lyrics over the top they'd sound even better. As opposed to the words and music happening simultaneously, which had usually been the case in Joy Division. Bernard would write and arrange the musical parts, then would come the hard part of writing words that would fit over the music. What the hell did you write a song about? I had no idea, so the bits that I came up with sounded a bit like something Ian might have written on a spectacularly off day. It would take quite a while before we realised that it might make things easier if we changed the music to accommodate the words.

Various bands that we'd played with in the past had used a reel-to-reel tape machine live. And on the basis that if it worked for them it'd work for us, we opted to use the tape machine instead of the shiny new drum machine as an extra pair of hands. We hired a 16-channel mixing desk that none of us knew how to operate and set about making backing tracks for a couple of songs as an experiment. (Working late into the night at Pinkie's, we disturbed the rodent population with our labours. Bernard was the first to jump up on a chair for safety.) We recorded the drum machine for 'Truth', thinking it would be more reliable than the drum machine itself and recorded the real drums for 'In a Lonely Place' for reasons that don't make any sense now. But it must have done then. Perhaps I had drawn the short straw and was supposed to be singing? Or most likely keyboard playing? This all worked fine and dandy in the rehearsal room. These things always do.

Then a last-minute gig presented itself. I could be wrong but there wasn't a lot of notice, perhaps a day or more likely an afternoon. Our first live outing would be at the Beach Club upstairs at Oozits behind the Arndale. That this would be a low-key affair was some sort of encouragement: we weren't billed and would be first on the bill supporting Action Holiday and our friends A Certain Ratio.

Bernard's intro patter was: 'Hello, we're the last surviving members of Crawling Chaos.'

Things were all right – for a first-ever gig in the nervous, jittery way that most debuts tend to be – until the tape machine was called for (a foretaste of what was to come in later years). I was in charge of the tape's operation, another short straw or more than likely I foolishly volunteered myself. So the thing was precariously balanced next to the drum kit.

'Truth' was fine but things went very wrong with the tape machine on 'In a Lonely Place', which meant wheeling out the tried-and-tested fall back of jamming 'Sister Ray' until things sorted themselves out. It could have been a lot worse.

Looking back at it now, besides the obvious vocal struggle, it was the drum machine's appearance (hidden by tape at the Beach Club) that passed unnoticed and uncommented on. Maybe it was a fad of the time and every band was starting to use one, but I doubt it. It had never been there with Ian (all Joy Division's synthetic rhythms were handmade, well live at least they were). But there it was at the very first New Order gigs, confidently chattering and pinging away, just quietly biding its time. The Doctor Rhythm was in.

My Favourite audience comment of the night was: 'This lot are just ripping off Joy Division.'

The reel-to-reel was retired from gigging and we went back to the drawing board for any future live appearances before the paying public. In retrospect it seems unbelievable that Ian had been dead for only eight weeks. Only two months. At the time it felt a great deal longer than that.

If you're going to make mistakes and learn on the job it's probably a good idea to do it somewhere where nobody knows you. Less embarrassing all round that way. Somewhere like the USA, for example. Another bit of symmetry or unfinished business perhaps. Why not start off in the place where Joy Division left off? Kind of . . .

Another whinging Morris postcard.

It was late when we arrived in New York. Tony, Martin and A Certain Ratio, who we were supporting, were there already. They'd come over a few days earlier to do some dates on their own and a bit of recording with Martin. ACR were staying in a loft somewhere downtown or was it up?

The Bronx is up and the Battery's down was how Sinatra explained it, though that meant nothing now. Three lads on shore leave. What was the Battery anyway?

The airline had lost my bag, it'd taken so long to get there that I didn't care. It'll sort itself out tomorrow. So luggage-less and basking in the novelty of jet lag I lay in the four-bed room I was sharing with Terry, Twinny and Dave at the Iroquois on W 44th St., listening to the sirens of the NYPD cops chasing bad guys down the city's steaming mean streets.

The Iroquois was described as a 'funky' hotel. Very popular with visiting British bands. Fixer of all things, Ruth Polsky, our American promoter and soon to be best friend and guide, assured us that it was the number one place in town in our price range. Being a local Ruth seemed to know what she was talking about, but I had to admit that the Algonquin next door looked much more refined.

The Algonquin, of course, was not our sort of place. A year or so later we would find out how much 'not our sort of place' it was, when we had to fight our way out of the Algonquin bar (favoured watering hole of celebrated critic and wit Dorothy Parker, who might have enjoyed the punch-up).

The bar at the Iroquois had the Algonquin beat hands down. The barman was not averse to tuning the TV to a local cable channel that specialised in showing topless shows when things got a bit quiet. NYC in the early 1980s was awash with sleaze of all varieties, Times Square being sleaze central. Street hustlers crowded the pavements, trying to lure the stupid into games of Find the Lady or Three-card Monte. The stores were almost entirely porn-based. From XXX live peep shows to nudge-nudge-wink-wink adult photographic supplies, there was everything you could think off and quite a lot you didn't think was even possible. It was all there. Definitely an eye-opener; it made London's Soho look like a village fête. On one corner Gene Palma, the slicked-back street drummer from Scorsese's *Taxi Driver*, was still demonstrating Gene Krupa's syncopated style on his snare drum. It was somewhere near Times Square that Twinny, on a wide-eyed-lads-sight-seeing tour, discovered 'poppers' (amyl nitrite), ready and cheaply available in every sex emporium. An instant hit with the band.

'Just smell this, Steve, it'll make your head turn red.'

He wasn't kidding. In seconds I felt myself turning into a living Belisha beacon. The aroma took me back to the dry-cleaning-fluid-sniffing sessions of my chemically experimental school days but the buzziness seemed less malevolent.

We'd come over for some gigs to support A Certain Ratio as well as to go into the studio with Martin to record 'Ceremony' and 'In a Lonely Place'. To be honest this didn't feel entirely like the start of something new. More like continuing a journey after you've fixed a puncture or a busted fan belt. There's still the sneaking feeling that the repairs you've made may not hold up. But no one admits to worrying about that.

Rob and I were more worried about where we were going to get some dope. (Martin and Tony had already sorted themselves out.) How do you go about scoring drugs when everyone has a gun?

New York in the '80s was a much more interesting place than it is today. It was statistically a dangerous place, although it didn't feel like it. I, typically, fretted about scoring dope more than how the gigs were going to go; more than who was doing the singing and what words we would be mumbling. Playing the gigs was a thing that'd sort itself out later after we'd got shit-faced. Dutch courage.

We went out to Hurrah, the club Ruth managed on W. 62nd St. Suicide were on that night. Joy Division had played with them at the Factory on one occasion. I remember Martin Rev being a bit bewildered with Manchester nightlife. This time it was my turn to feel alien. While waiting for Ruth to sort out getting us into the club, I watched a guy getting kicked (literally) out of the club by a couple of burly guys and booted halfway down the street like a human football. That didn't happen in Macclesfield. Well, not often.

Once in, Hurrah was nowhere near as heavy as I was expecting. A bank of TVs playing videos (cartoons mostly), a healthy queue around the Space Invaders machine (my kind of people), good music, beer that didn't get you pissed and a great atmosphere. It had an energy that many UK clubs didn't have. I felt comfortable and for me that's saying something. Almost at home. Ruth managed to fix me and Rob up with some grass, which we sampled in one of the back rooms. The locals couldn't understand why we wanted to roll up the stuff with tobacco; they preferred their marijuana unadulterated. We tried it their way. Before long we were laughing like giddy horses.

'Now how do we get home?'

'I don't think I can walk.'

Dazzled by the club and the discovery that the tickets Ruth had handed out could be exchanged for FREE DRINKS, we naturally overindulged. Finally weed blurry, jet-lagged and paranoid, we piled into a yellow cab that bounced us all the way home.

When I imagined America, I always had an image of wide-open spaces, a never-ending road trip in a massive streamlined Cadillac or Stutz. Something with plenty of chrome. The American car was king and we were all born to run. Driving bumper to bumper down 6th, overusing the horn was something to look forward to. An experience to savour like smoking a Camel while eating a hot dog. I thought with all the driving that I had done I would take to the roads of New York with some sort of relish or, failing that, competence. Sadly my motoring mojo seemed to have disappeared along with my suitcase.

Possibly impounded by US customs. Overexposure to American crime dramas was most likely to blame. The climax to these epic battles of kind-hearted cops verses cold-hearted, gun-toting villains invariably took the form of a dramatic high-speed car chase culminating in a blazing warehouse shootout. Death by firearm or dangerous driving were always key factors. Obviously the reality would be slightly different. I mean, come on, that's all made-up stuff. Things like that don't actually happen in real life, do they?

The reality of the place was not far removed from the idea I'd conjured up from watching too much TV and listening to *White Light/White Heat*.

We all hopped in a cab to collect a hire car from a garage somewhere uptown. The garage looked uncannily like the one in the TV show *Taxi*, only without the yellow cabs. I took the beige bit of cardboard that the man from the AA had assured me was an international driving licence essential for the visiting motorist and valid anywhere in the world. The proprietor of the garage had never seen one before. To him it looked very much like a piece of beige cardboard.

'What's this, buster?'

I'd paid good money for that cardboard.

A typical bit of New York negotiating later and the garage proprietor reluctantly agreed, on presentation of Bernard's provisional licence, to let us hire a car. A huge well-worn, duck-egg blue Ford station wagon. I'd never driven a car with automatic transmission before. That and the fact the steering wheel was in the wrong place added to my sense of disorientation.

Automatics were simple, I'd been told. No clutch, just two pedals (left one for stop and right one for go) just like a dodgem. This vehicle exhibited some very strange behaviour, especially when it came to stopping or more accurately not stopping. This, I guessed, was some quirk of the marque. I would press what appeared to be the brake pedal almost to the floor and the blue metal behemoth would show no signs of slowing or even thinking about coming to a halt. Maybe it was just me? When I pressed a bit harder, the thing juddered and eventually began to slow down. Still, I was convinced I was doing something wrong, but I'd no idea what it might be. Maybe there was some special knack to driving automatic cars that I didn't possess? This is when panic began to set in. It was as if the car had a mind of its own. I managed to get the wallowing leviathan down the ramp, out of the garage and around the corner without hitting anything. With an extended blast of horn, a loud screech and a crunch of metal, two cars now collided directly in front of me.

'Hey asshole, you blind or something?'

'You coulda killed someone.'

For me this was not going well. Shaken and not a little surprised that I had managed to stop the car at all, I become overwhelmed with a completely irrational but extremely intense anxiety. This came to its peak when I realised that we had just come to a stop outside the city morgue, just as a black-clad fresh cadaver was being wheeled out.

Talk about ill omens.

'Eeegh Steve, look at that, a stiff in a bag,' Bernard pointed out less than helpfully.

Maybe it was the aftereffects of last night's wacky-baccy indulgence combined with seeing my first ever dead American that did it, but that was enough for me. I suffered a death-traffic-related-mini-nervous-breakdown and fled the car shrieking.

My dreams of driving a speeding muscle car down the canyons of Manhattan came to an abrupt end, in a wimpy fizzle. A total distance of probably 100 yards covered and I had already thrown in the towel. I was of course tired and emotional. Of course my fellow passengers found this wildly amusing – the bastards – and it was thanks to some dodgy driving that we ever got back to the Iroquois at all.

The next day we went with Martin to EARS studio in colourfully named East Orange, New Jersey to see what American record making was all about. Martin was a bit shaken. Someone had tried to break into his Gramercy Park hotel room the previous night, while he was sleeping. Quite understandable really. British burglars tended to wait until the premises were vacant before starting work. Not in New York. Anything goes it seemed.

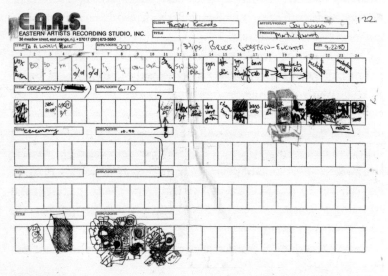

Tracklist for 'Ceremony' and 'IALP', decorated by Martin Hannett.

The engineer Bruce has us booked in as Joy Division. He'd never heard of New Order. Nobody had. He'd been in Vietnam (so he said) and drank coke with milk. Bruce was a bit of a space cadet. This predictably for Hannett made for a bit of an uneasy mix. When was it anything else with Martin and engineers? This was Bruce's first taste of it. Tony and Rob's thinking had been that we'd get that NY sound or at least a different sound by recording here. Somewhere different to Strawberry or Britannia Row. The studio had that seventies varnished wooden look (shades of beige and brown), complete with the impressively large monitors either side of the triple-glazed window that let the producer and engineer view the musicians toiling at their art.

In the studio I loved listening to the sound of tape rewinding. Waiting for another take (with Martin another take was never far away). Listening to the whup, whup, whup as the track played in reverse was to me a source of wonder and inspiration. Like Strawberry, EARS had the same chilly air-conditioning, the same fake leather sofa at the back and the same coffee machine that nobody ever bothered with.

'Where's the fucking tea?'

'Do you not have any instant?'

Our ice-breaking repartee. Or as in Bernard's case, his catch-phrase: 'Can you turn those lights off, they're getting in my eyes.' Lights have been causing Bernard's eyes distress since 1977. He can get very troubled by them.

Low light was essential for the recording of 'In a Lonely Place'. The brooding darkness came together pretty easily, aided by Martin's electronically manufactured ambience together with a pretty nasty white noise thunder impression from my drum synthesiser. I got the impression that this was not really the sort of music that Bruce was used to working on. The amped-up Omni strings sounded suitably malign. Eerie and frightening.

One of the objectives of this studio exercise was to bring to a conclusion the process of the New Order singer competition. 'Ceremony' was to be the song that would decide this. Bernard had always sung 'In a Lonely Place'.

On early live versions of 'Ceremony', the vocals were a bit of a free-for-all, each of us taking turns at delivering Ian's lyrics. Sometimes with no rhyme or reason. The contestants were all reluctant to win the poisoned chalice of the prize (look what happened to its previous owner). But we all did our best at singing and let Martin and Rob decide which one to use. I came last, which was both a blessing and a relief.

We still had to sing at the gigs though. This was something none of us looked forward to, but approached the task like the stoic, carefree men we hoped to be. I think Hooky was secretly the least indisposed to the idea and went at it with gusto. Bernard's approach of having a few drinks and keeping his eyes closed worked well in a don't-give-a-fuck kind of way. I went about it by not trying too hard to sing, more drunkenly shouting or failing that mumbling what lyrics I could remember (even the ones that I'd written myself). I did my best. But most of the time I couldn't hear myself, which was probably a good thing. The words were delivered in my excruciatingly bad pissed, pub-singer style, and that's being harsh to pub singers. I was truly awful. The only excuse I can think of is that my ambitions lay elsewhere. My mind certainly did.

'Whose turn is it to sing "Ceremony" tonight?'

Our repertoire at that time was comprised of eight songs, and if all else failed an emergency fallback cover of 'Sister Ray'. The songs were:

'Ceremony'

'In a Lonely Place' (Drum machine; I played the synth. Bernard sang and played Melodica.)

'Dreams Never End' (Hooky always sang that.)

'Homage' (Bernard always sang that one.)

'Procession' (Drum machine with me on keys and desperate wailing. Even though I wasn't drumming it didn't improve my singing.)

'Truth' (Drum machine, of course, with Bernard's voice and my ham-fisted keyboards.)

'Cries and Whispers' (Nobody was too sure who was singing this either. It changed a lot. Alternating between me and Hooky while Bernard played the keys.)

'Mesh' (Bernard playing guitar and synth while Hooky sang.)

As tradition demanded, there was a vague idea called 'The New One'. I think Rob called it 'Hour' on a set list, though it didn't last that long. Three minutes and then forgotten for good. God knows who did the singing on that one – Hooky I suspect.

Our first gig was at Maxwell's in Hoboken (birthplace of Francis Sinatra) and, despite the nervous vocalising, the gig wasn't too bad. Some people actually clapped. A few had turned up expecting to see Joy Division or at least to hear Joy Division songs that they might have heard of. 'Which one of them is the dead guy?' was the typical response. We were all nervously pissed. Bernard, particularly enamoured by the amyl nitrate, suspected its effects might be enhanced if he took to drinking it; much to Ruth's horror and Rob's amusement. Luckily nobody died that night; another trial-by-fire gig under our belts. I felt that things were getting better. Unfortunately Terry, Dave and Twinny had a bit of a roadie tiff and, as a result, had not been speaking to each other since they entered the Lincoln tunnel. This can happen with roadies. They need constant care and attention. Be good to them and they'll be good to you, as my father used to say.

The result of this breakdown of communication was that the U-Haul truck, containing all our gear, was not immobilised (by removal of the distributor rotor arm) and fell prey to NYC's musical equipment heisters.* They took the lot (it happened a lot). The van and all its contents. This was brought to my attention by Terry's wakeup call of 'You might as well have a lie-in, the gear's been nicked. I don't think we'll be going to Boston.' Which of course removed all possibility of further slumber.

'Shit, fuck, bastard fuck.'

'And Rob says we're not insured.'

'But he used to work for a fucking insurance company.'

'I know, ironic, isn't it?'

---

* The theft of touring bands' gear was a common occurrence in 1980, especially for groups from the UK. The thieves would go to the gig, follow the van back and help themselves to the gear (working under the assumption that the gear's guardians would either be too knackered or party crazy to notice what was going on).

Tony found this hilarious, presumably in a Situationist kind of way. We were supposed to drive up to Boston for the next gig, but with no gear even I found that unlikely.

'Are you sure that was where you parked the van?'

'Maybe it just got towed or something?'

But no, the van would turn up later, empty save for the huge transformer we had hired from Pink Floyd. That was too heavy for the villains to move easily. The luggage from the flight over had vanished and now the gear had gone too. It was almost like someone was trying to tell us something: like perhaps this was not the best of ideas; that maybe we really were cursed in some way. But we weren't going to let a little thing like this stop us, were we? We hadn't come all this way just to let some gang of New York crooks get the better of us. Hell no ... Hard men, true northern bastards that we were, we weren't going to take this lying down.

'Let's go back to bed and sort it out in a bit.'

And that's what we did, while Rob confirmed the intricacies of our (lack of) insurance policy.

As if Ian's death were not enough, this chain of misfortune only went to reinforce the 'whole world's against us' semi-jokey paranoia that infested our musical career since Warsaw. The seemingly supernatural curse continued to exert its malign influence on everything we did.

'We're all doomed,' we laughed.

Rob's long-distance calls to the insurance company only confirmed the fact that, owing to some unforeseen technicality, we weren't covered for the loss. The fact that the van wasn't alarmed and hadn't been immobilised by our temperamental road crew was the exact nature of the technicality. We now held a half-baked séance* in our

---

* When looking after me back in the sixties, my cousins Kath and Sue had scared me witless with tales of the Ouija board and the simplicity with which the spirits of the dead could be summoned. DO NOT try this at home.

hotel room in an attempt to contact Ian's spirit. The hope was that he would pass on information from the other side as to the whereabouts of our missing gear. It was a long shot but we were desperate. Needless to say the spirit of Ian Curtis was no help with the location of stolen goods. Shifting gear about had never been his forte and we got a stand-in instead.

The spirit we summoned via the traditional means of a glass and a hastily scribbled alphabet laid out on an Iroquois occasional table was definitely not Ian. This denizen of the nether regions was not exactly fluent in the English language either. It may have been speaking Polish, Russian, Navajo or ectoplasmic gibberish, who could tell? It was very good at moving the glass about though. I don't think anybody was cheating either.

We'd come all this way after losing Ian just to lose everything that remained of Joy Division in a fucking stupid robbery. The lack of insurance really was the icing on the cake though. The final straw, as in the one that broke the camel's back. It could not have got any worse. We were all that was left of Joy Division, and we were not going to give up and let the bastards win.

Whoever they were. We gathered together some hastily borrowed, bought and hired gear, and resumed our ill-starred tour. Just three more dates of my out-of-tune mumbling and ham-fisted keyboard prodding and we'd be home. At the Hurrah show Rob revived an idea he'd been pushing for a while.

'Err, Steve, why don't you set up the drums at the front? I think it'd look cool, y'know, different.'

It is one of the long-held traditions of music combos – from traditional jazz to heavy metal, wisdom that has been handed down the ages – that states stick the drummer at the back and put the guitars in the front. It's been tried and tested, and for various reasons that I'm not going to bore you with now, it works – it just does.

The trouble was nobody wanted to be at the front in the middle; it felt unnatural. Not the way things ought to be. So, at the very first New Order appearances there was a void at the centre of things. As we all took turns singing – Bernard and I alternating on keyboards – it must have looked a little weird from the audience's perspective. I could see Rob's point but hopping from the kit to the synth and back again on a tiny stage was difficult and stressful enough.

'What like Phil fucking Collins? Rob, that's a terrible idea,' chorused Hooky and Bernard in agreement.

Rob, thankfully, was outvoted but he would bring it up again and again, just to annoy me I think. I have to admit that the idea of singing drummers is generally not a good one. Singing and drumming always looks awkward and wrong, like simultaneously juggling bottles and spinning plates whilst swallowing nitroglycerine. Which is more or less what it felt like to me.

The Hurrah show was videoed. It is still an awkward thing for me to watch. My atonal 'singing' is a crime against music. God knows what I was thinking. We were trying though. We were doing our best – 100 per cent. I don't think we ever put in a performance that was ever half-hearted or without conviction. Whatever we did, we were passionate about the music. The show was more a recording of a rehearsal in front of an audience than anything else. Still it remains a moment in time captured forever, as Rob used to say; and I guess there's some merit in that, despite my cringing misgivings.

It was at Hurrah that we first met a young man from Baltimore, Michael Shamberg. Michael had been making a film with A Certain Ratio. Tony liked him a lot; he was Tony's kind of guy – a bit arty and well-connected.

He and his partner Miranda told us stories about the New York art and music scene. Michael would eventually become Factory's man in New York (Tony was thinking of opening a New York office) and ended up producing all New Order's videos.

ACR's funk sound really felt at home in New York; it naturally fitted right into the spirit of the place in a way that we didn't quite manage. I don't think we were even advertised at these gigs – just ACR plus support. We came away with a lot of ideas. We may not have had any gear but a bit of inspiration and some new friends kind of made up for that. The undriveable station wagon was returned. The car rental manager was a little anxious. The car should never have been hired out in the first place: it had a serious defect and was dangerous. They'd been trying to contact Bernard from the moment I had launched the thing on to the street.

See, I told you so.

The car's brakes were shot. It was unroadworthy; it wasn't safe; it wouldn't stop.

Neither would we . . .

PLAYLIST

At some point during the writing of this book, probably quite late in the night, the thought arose that it might be a good idea if it had a soundtrack of some sort. It was one of those things that seemed like a good idea at the time. Maybe a CD to go inside the front cover or something like that? Something that comprised the music that was the backdrop to my life. This turned out to be slightly more complicated than the initial idea suggested. So instead I opted for the simple and more up-to-date approach – the twenty-first-century equivalent of my teenage vinyl 'wants' list – the internet playlist.

It's okay, you don't have to listen to it all – 77 songs is a lot. I would have put a LOT more in but Spotify hadn't heard of some of my more esoteric '70s' listening material. Which was disappointing but not entirely surprising.

I am not convinced that internet music streaming is entirely a good thing for the future of music. But, hey, I'm an old vinyl-based bloke, so I would say that. The internet's not going away, though, is it?

There's always a choice.

You could always buy the records instead.

But, nonetheless, here it is:

https://lnk.to/StephenMorris-spotify

In no particular order and, yes, I know it's a bit drummy in places, but what did you expect?

In my experience it sounds best using the random-play function, but that's up to you.

Enjoy . . .

Can, 'Oh Yeah'
New York Dolls, 'Jet Boy'
Little Eva, 'The Locomotion'
Blondie, 'Heart of Glass'
David Bowie, 'Sound and Vision'
Popol Vuh, 'Brüder des Schattens'
Peter Hammill, 'German Overalls'
Sparks, 'The Number One Song in Heaven'
Wire, 'Outdoor Miner'
Joy Division, 'As You Said'
The Kinks, 'Lola'
Siouxsie and the Banshees, 'Helter Skelter'
The Doors, 'The End'
Dave and Ansel Collins, 'Double Barrel'
Doctor Feelgood, 'Going Back Home'
Todd Rundgren, 'I Saw the Light'
Sly and the Family Stone, 'Family Affair'
Harmonia, 'Dino'
The Damned, 'New Rose'
The Rolling Stones, 'Street Fighting Man'
Shirley Collins & The Albion Band, 'The Murder of Maria Marten'
Don Spencer, 'Fireball XL5'
Betty Davis, 'He Was A Big Freak'
Kraftwerk, 'Autobahn'
Faces, 'Debris'
Brian Eno, 'Back in Judy's Jungle'
Augustus Pablo, 'King Tubbys Meets Rockers Uptown'
Cluster, 'Sowiesoso'

The Velvet Underground, 'Foggy Notion'
Talking Heads, 'Love Building on Fire'
Parliament, 'Give Up the Funk'
ESG, 'Moody'
The Modern Lovers, 'Roadrunner'
Wild Man Fischer, 'Merry Go Round'
The Normal, 'Warm Leatherette'
The Tornados, 'Telstar'
Kenny Rogers & The First Edition, 'Ruby, Don't Take Your Love to
    Town'
Duke Ellington, 'Take the A Train'
Joni Mitchell, 'A Case of You'
Mott the Hoople, 'All the Young Dudes'
Elvis Costello, '(The Angels Wanna Wear My) Red Shoes'
Hawkwind, 'Silver Machine'
Thomas Leer, 'Private Plane'
Annette Peacock, 'Pony'
Nico, 'These Days'
Elvis Presley, 'Return to Sender'
Donna Summer, 'I Feel Love'
Syd Barrett, 'Late Night'
Faust, 'It's a Rainy Day, Sunshine Girl'
The New Christie Minstrels, 'Three Wheels on My Wagon'
Alice Cooper, 'Ballad of Dwight Fry'
The Mothers of Invention, 'Trouble Every Day'
The Stooges, '1969'
John Cale, 'Paris 1919'
Chris Spedding, 'Motor Bikin''
The Ramones, 'Blitzkrieg Bop'
Buzzcocks, 'Love You More'
The Flying Burrito Brothers, 'Christine's Tune'
10cc, 'I'm Not in Love'

Television, 'See No Evil'
Robert Calvert, 'Ejection'
Public Image Ltd, 'Flowers of Romance'
Silver Apples, 'Oscillations'
Eno, Moebius, Roedelius, 'Luftschloß'
Marianne Faithfull, 'The Ballad Of Lucy Jordan'
Amon Düül II, 'Archangel's Thunderbird'
Suicide, 'Ghost Rider'
The Who, 'Substitute'
Love, 'Alone again Or'
MC5, 'Shakin' Street'
The Slits, 'Typical Girls'
Throbbing Gristle, 'Hot on the Heels of Love'
Neu, 'Hallogallo'
Captain Beefheart, 'I'm Gonna Booglarize You Baby'
Roxy Music, 'Virginia Plain'
Timmy Thomas, 'Why Can't We Live Together'
Dee D. Jackson, 'Automatic Lover'

ACKNOWLEDGEMENTS

This wouldn't have happened without
Gillian, Tilly and Grace,
Mum, Dad, Amanda, Elsie and John,
Flo, Les, Julie and Kim

Rebecca Boulton, Andreas Campomar, Anton Corbijn, Kevin Cummins, Deborah Curtis, Ian Curtis, Jack Delaney, Will Edwards, Alan Erasmus, Lesley Gilbert, Rob Gretton, Jess Gulliver, Martin Hannett, Mary Harron, Peter Hook, Warren Jackson, Terry Mason, Bert McIntyre, Paul Morley, Tim Noakes, Susan Oldfield, John Peel, Dave Pils, Andy Robinson, Jon Savage, Peter Saville, Phil Sturgess, Bernard Sumner, Kath Tart, Becky Thomas, Richard Thomas, Twinny, Howard Watson, Malcolm Whitehead, Tony Wilson, Alan Wise, Michelle Worsdall.

ILLUSTRATION AND PHOTOGRAPH CREDITS

Page 42: Popperfoto/Getty Images
Page 64: © Lee Hawkins
Page 68: Chalkie Davies/Getty Images
Page 101: © Jon Smith
Pages 131, 138: © Steve Shy
Page 166: © Bernie Wilcox
Page 218: © Macclesfield Express
Page 269: © Manchester Digital Music Archive
Page 335: © Lex van Rossen/MAI/Redferns/Getty Images

All other illustrations and images: author's collection

Every effort has been made to obtain the necessary permissions
with reference to copyright material, both illustrative and
quoted. We apologise for any omissions in this respect and will
be pleased to make the appropriate acknowledgements in
any future edition.